# Better Get It In Your Soul

## What Liturgists Can Learn from Jazz

Reid Hamilton and Stephen Rush

**CHURCH PUBLISHING**
an imprint of
**Church Publishing Incorporated, New York**

Cover photo by Herb Gunn; *Quartex* musicians Michael Gould, Tim Flood, Mark Kirschenmann
Cover design by Brenda Klinger
Interior design by Linda Brooks

Library of Congress Cataloging-in-Publication Data

Hamilton, Reid.
Better get it in your soul: what liturgists can learn from jazz / Reid Hamilton and Stephen Rush.
p. cm.
Includes bibliographical references.
ISBN 978-0-89869-574-8 (pbk.)
1. Worship programs. 2. Liturgics. 3. Jazz–Religious aspects–Christianity. I. Rush, Stephen, 1958-
II. Title.

BV178.H35 2008
264--dc22

2008021903

Church Publishing Incorporated
445 Fifth Avenue
New York, NY 10016
www.churchpublishing.org
5 4 3 2 1

I would like to thank my Mother for having the brilliance, when I was only seven years old, to bribe me to play a short Mendelssohn piece in church. This was my first public performance and began my work as a church musician. Interestingly enough, my Mother inadvertently encouraged me to play something "secular" for the service. She sacrificed much for my early musical education, and I'm eternally grateful for her gentle, accepting, and unflagging support. Thanks, Mom.

I have had two amazing liturgical collaborators before Reid Hamilton, both of whom I count amongst a handful of my closest friends, both who have the ability to love, forgive, and challenge me: Don Postema and Matthew Lawrence. My experience with Don's book *Space for God: The Study and Practice of Prayer and Spirituality* is described in this volume, but what can't be expressed is the spiritual growth spurt that Don gave to me. With Don I became a spiritual adult and moved past the predispositions of my youth. I also learned that reverence and irreverence are completely inseparable. Matthew Lawrence had the quixotic notion of hiring me to work with him at Canterbury House at the University of Michigan. He had the openness to accept my faith for what it was, and my worship aesthetic for what it was becoming. This book contains many ideas that really grew out of our collaboration, and the first drafts of many sections of this book were written with his eye, at his urging, and with his inspiration. My indebtedness to both these fine and holy people is infinite, as is my love for them.

My co-author Reid Hamilton is a friend, a mentor, my collaborator, and my confessor. He is a veritable "forgiveness machine," and always brings an eyes-wide-open attitude to our work together that is unrivalled in my experience. He is someone I can tell anything to, and yet someone I can argue with without getting angry. I love him as well, and look forward to many more years of stewardship, honoring the gifts God has given both of us.

Finally, I want to thank my lovely bride of thirty years, Merilynne. She has seen me at my worst and has not left. She has also attended more Jazz Masses than anyone else on the planet (over 300 by my count). She has been a voice of criticism that has been harsh, gentle, subtle (or mute), attentive, and above all, intelligent. Without her perspective, the Jazz Mass would not have evolved into what it is today.

Stephen Rush

# Acknowledgments

Writing this book reminded me how dependent I am on the ideas of others. If I am limited to mentioning only a few, then I must acknowledge my debt to my professors, instructors, and mentors at the Candler School of Theology at Emory University. The director of the Episcopal Studies Program at Candler, now retired, was Ted Hackett, a priest with a fine liturgical and pastoral sensibility and presence, not to mention a wealth of historical and theological knowledge. Nancy Baxter, the Episcopal Chaplain at Emory, was the first to teach me an essential element of what I now call Jazz Preaching. She would give students their preaching assignment fifteen minutes before chapel and advise us, "Just tell them what you know!" Don Saliers, also now retired from the Candler faculty, was and continues to be a model of creativity and artistic expression (good music, especially) in liturgy. Bill Flynn, now lecturing in Medieval Latin at the University of Leeds, taught me how to analyze space, motion, light, sound, silence, and time in worship. Bill taught his students to chant "the way the medieval monks learned it—but without the beatings." Jim Farwell, at the time a doctoral student at Candler and now teaching Religious Studies at Bethany College, liked to say that everything we do in liturgy should have a theological reason, a pastoral reason, and a practical reason, and that if we could not articulate all three, we should rethink what we are doing. He tells me now that he is no longer sure he thinks this way; but I still do! Thanks to Jim also for connecting me to Church Publishing for this project.

I am grateful to Matt Lawrence, who was an inspiration to me in campus ministry long before I succeeded him as Chaplain of Canterbury House, and to Sam Portaro who, in addition to being a leader and role model in campus ministry, offered some very helpful advice and encouragement on how to get this book published. Thanks also to our editor, Marilyn Haskel, whose enthusiasm and support for this project has been an inspiration to both Steve and me.

The staff, board, and members of Canterbury House have been a constant inspiration and support, particularly our office manager Kathleen Peabody. Thanks also to our seminary intern Jeanne Hansknecht, who did a lot of work on the appendices.

I cannot say "thank you" enough to Steve Rush, who simply insisted that we write this book. We have spent countless hours thinking, writing, revising, reading back and forth, and mostly laughing. That's in addition to the joy of working with him week by week at Canterbury House. Steve has given me the gift of Jazz. I love it and him.

I dedicate this, my first published book, to my wife, Deb Garner. Without her support and encouragement, often despite her own inclination and best interests, I certainly would not be a priest today. She helped me find and respond to my true calling—the very definition of a gift from God.

Reid Hamilton

# Contents

# Introduction

If you come to Canterbury House a little before five o'clock on a Sunday evening, you'll catch our band *Quartex* rehearsing the prelude for the Jazz Mass. There will be a little bit of wood incense burning on the altar, as well as some competing sounds and scents from the kitchen. We'll give you a service leaflet and invite you to write or draw your own nametag. You'll likely be offered a cup of tea.

As people are taking their seats, the chaplain will welcome everyone and briefly introduce the service. Usually, we are observing the commemoration of a saint. What was notable about this particular saint's life and ministry? Was she an advocate for peace? Was her life an example of self-sacrificial devotion? Was she a teacher? A healer? What theme or themes are being expressed in the scripture lessons associated with this saint? The music director will also welcome everyone and will make explicit, again briefly, the connection between these themes and the music we will be playing, singing, and hearing.

You'll then hear a prelude performed by musicians who know what they are doing and who care about how they sound. The prelude will evoke the theme of the readings. Perhaps the band will play "Congeniality" by Ornette Coleman, or John Coltrane's "Compassion." They might play "Prophecy" by Albert Ayler, or sing Sun Ra's "Enlightenment." The musicians—who, like many in the congregation, might or might not identify themselves as Christians—are intimately aware that they are in the service of God. They have a sense of calling. There is a deep connection between God and the music they play.

After the prelude we'll spend a considerable time in silence. Silence is a key element in listening to the voice of the Holy Spirit. As Thomas Merton has said, "Certainly, in the pressures of modern urban life, many will face the need for a certain interior silence and discipline simply to keep themselves together, to maintain their human and Christian identity and their spiritual freedom."[1] By deliberately observing silence at significant points, we allow for the presence of God. A perusal of our sample services contained in Appendix A will show that, in effect, we have even replaced the traditional opening hymn with silence, requiring that the worshipper first come into the presence of God before making any sound at all.

Attention to sound is a key element of our worship, as expressed by the two-foot gong punctuating silences at intervals throughout the service, by prayers chanted or spoken, by readings, and by song. In planning our services, we are careful to consider when we choose to make a sound: What is the nature of that sound, and what does it imply about our theology?

Our service is generally based on the Holy Eucharist, Rite II, from the *Book of Common Prayer*. The

1 *Contemplative Prayer* (London: Darton, Longman & Todd Ltd., 2005), 19.

structure of the service is familiar to Episcopalians, and certainly adaptable to any mainstream Christian denomination, with collect, readings, prayers, and communion. There are notable differences, of course: readings for the service can come from a diversity of sources—the *New York Times,* the *Bhaghavad Gita,* or contemporary philosophers and writers, for example—in addition to the Bible. Prayers are more subject to improvisation than is common in strongly liturgical traditions. The Eucharistic Prayer may be from any number of sources, both historical and contemporary. In all cases, the focus of reading and prayer is to require the congregation to be mentally and emotionally engaged.

The chaplain preaches without notes, engaging the congregation directly, sometimes inviting dialogue. The congregation is seated in an arrangement that allows everyone to see each other. The chaplain is able to move about the room in order to see, connect with, and adjust to the response of the congregation.

And, of course, we sing. Singing involves our bodies, our breath, our voices, and our minds in praise. We may, at any point in the service, use one of at least four types of singing, all meant to help us worship in a more cohesive and meaningful way: Taizé singing or traditional chanting, pub-style or *Southern Harmony* singing, African-American or "gospel" singing, and traditional hymn singing in four parts. All of these types of singing, when done well, can produce deep emotional responses ranging from ecstasy to deep grief, joy, elation, community, or even rage. If singing doesn't evoke an emotion, why sing it all? At Canterbury House, the congregation is also encouraged to dance!

Here are some things that people say about their experience of the Jazz Mass:

A student, attending for the first time, said, "Jesus is here!"

Another student, in discernment for the priesthood, said, "The Jazz Mass is a perfect combination between music of the people and the mystical sense of Christ."

A Jamaican woman, after a Jazz Mass at Trinity Church, New York, said, "I never thought I would hear Bob Marley in church! Thank you so much!"

Desmond Tutu, after a Jazz Mass at a retreat in Houston, said, "Thank you for playing my tune!" ("Tutu" by Miles Davis).

Renowned theologian and mystic Tilden Edwards, after a Jazz Mass workshop, said, "Thank you for reminding me that our whole being, mind, body, and spirit, need to find a place in worship."

A student who had fallen away from the Church and is now in the ordination process said, "The style and content of the liturgy at Canterbury House allowed me to reconcile to Christianity."

Yet another student, a freshman, said, "I only know that I believe in God. I'm not sure of much else. But I can worship here."

Bishop Wendell Gibbs said, "If you want an experience of the Holy, go to Canterbury House!"

A music director visiting from another church said, "I get it! You are free to do *anything* here!"

In the spring of 1998, Matthew Lawrence was the new chaplain at Canterbury House, the Episcopal Student Center at the University of Michigan. When he first came here, community life at "Canterbury House" consisted of three or four students gathering on a Sunday night to share a meal and read Compline. Matthew asked Stephen to be the music director of Canterbury House, and together they decided to create a liturgy that might appeal to the intellect and aesthetics of the contemporary college student. Stephen decided to hire Jazz musicians—namely, musicians who could play more than one instrument, who knew more than one style of music, and who were capable of improvising.

Stephen reflects that in retrospect the choice to create a "Jazz Mass" was actually foolish, considering that most college students don't listen to Jazz, let alone really like it. Their decision was not an attempt to do something popular. They relied, instead, on the resources they had at hand: a worship space that lent itself to intimacy both in worship and in musical performance; musicians who could play well in many different idioms; and a diverse body of liturgical music that was creative, unusual, and resonant with college students, such as music from the African-American Gospel canon, John Bell and the Iona community, and Jacques Berthier and the Taizé community.

The "Jazz Mass" is not the only aesthetic decision for the contemporary church, but it certainly turned out to be the right decision for Canterbury House. *Your* community should do music and liturgy that resonates with *your* congregation and context. This may mean something like the "Folk Mass" that was developed in the 1960s. It may mean alternative services such as the "Hip-Hop Mass" or the "Rave Mass," which have been tried and are being developed in New York and California at the time of this writing. There is certainly a possibility for a "Country Music Mass." Stephen has seen, in the Upper Peninsula of Michigan, a "Polka Mass" beautifully celebrated by Finnish Lutherans, as well as Christian services in India celebrated with bhajans instead of Western hymns.

In this book we examine the theology of Jazz specifically because it is what we know (and, yes, what we believe in); but it is not to be considered exclusive of other musical styles by any means. *It can be a placeholder for whatever musical aesthetic might work best in the reader's community and church.* It is the "working best" that this book is about. The idea of making liturgy and music work as a cogent and coherent whole relies not so much on the style of the music selected as it does on the collaborative abilities of the worship planning team.

The spiritual and improvisational aesthetic of Jazz is our metaphor for the values of creativity, cooperation, and artistic quality that we believe are necessary to meaningful worship. Good liturgy is born out of a deep respect for structure and aesthetics. Its underpinnings are the love of God and a love of leading people into the presence of God. Beyond this fundamental core is an imaginative approach to structure and aesthetics that can lead the liturgy to a place that is colorful, emotional, and moving—that state mystically referred to as "worshipful." This book describes a creative process of linking scripture, music, prayer, and preaching to choices and outcomes that address the needs and challenges of contemporary culture, without discarding the wonderful structure and rubric of liturgy that tradition has provided.

Twenty-first-century liturgists are endlessly asking, "How can we make our services more creative and diverse?" The liturgy is discussed, the music and musicians are questioned, and the readings are pored over and rewritten, all in search of the magic answer for a "more creative and diverse" liturgy. Why do we keep asking this question? What do we really want out of progressive liturgy?

For years, we at Canterbury House have lived, worked, and wrestled with this question. Canterbury House is a liturgical laboratory. This book is based largely on our experience there as liturgists in the Episcopal campus ministry at the University of Michigan. We have been able to experiment at liberty. Because college is a brief experience (at least in most people's lives!), a large percentage of our congregation changes each year. Free from the constraints of a vestry or an entrenched congregation, and blessed with a bishop who encourages our work, we have the luxury of never hearing anyone say, "We've never done it that way before!" Our musicians include Jazz musicians as well as those who are classically trained, and we have collaborated with artists of all sorts—dancers, sculptors, painters, poets, and performance artists.

Most college students are much more concerned about grades, appearance, and "substances" than anything to do with God. Furthermore, they often perceive faith as intellectually weak, going to church as embarrassing, and having a prayer life as a social stigma. In truth, though, this is good news! College students are ideal "beta-testers" for a church. They question. They are reluctant. They are inquisitive. They are extremely diverse in their background, upbringing, and viewpoint. They are pluralistic. They doubt the existence of God. They doubt the "tenets of the faith." College students are aware that religions other than Christianity offer rich fruits as well as deep truths. They also have extremely diverse musical tastes.

The style of liturgy that has evolved at Canterbury House can be done in congregations large and small, young and old. We have taken the Jazz Mass to congregations of all sorts and can testify that they "get it" when they see it. Our object in writing this book is to assure planners of liturgy, priests, pastors, and musicians that it can be done. *You can do it.* It must be done with excellence and integrity, and you have to work at it! The result is worship that is a joy and an inspiration to plan, perform, and participate in.

To aid the reader, we have included a Glossary at the end of the book following Appendix D. The Glossary includes names (e.g. **Sun Ra** or **Bob Marley**), musical and liturgical terms (**bhajan** or **hagiography**), and concepts that may be unfamiliar to some readers (**harmolodics**) or are used in a particular way in this text (**singing**). Words that appear in the Glossary are indicated by bold type the first time they appear in the text.

The title of our book refers to the classic Jazz composition "Better Git Hit in Your Soul" by legendary bassist and composer **Charles Mingus**. It's found on his album *Three or Four Shades of Blue* (Atlantic Records, 1977), among others. The piece is set in a fast 12/8 shuffle **groove** with a complicated Bebop line, followed by a chorus in which Mingus shouts out to the band various miracles of Jesus: "He walked the water; he healed the sick; he raised the dead!" These shouts lead to an ecstatic reaction from the entire band: "We're talkin' 'bout Jesus!" The climactic ending is a very slow version of the opening melodic line, sung by the band: "Better git hit in your soul!" The piece is exuberant and comic, virtuosic and bluesy, full-throated, and enthusiastic. It draws from band and audience (or congregation) the kind of fully engaged reaction that we are always striving to achieve in performance and worship. We think that liturgists and musicians should be looking for the kind of musical, textual, theological, epistemological, and ontological response that this tune embodies.

# Chapter 1

## Jazz Liturgy 101

There is one consistent reaction we have seen to the **Jazz Mass** at **Canterbury House:** a feeling of inclusion. Worshippers, old and new, often comment that this **liturgy** was "fun," but just as often they tell us that it was meaningful, deep, or emotionally moving. Years of work developing a lively and cohesive liturgy has resulted in a service that engages the participants, as well as a community that is willing to open itself up to the many possibilities offered in what we call "Jazz Liturgy."

When a **Jazz** group performs a composition, they are likely to have something called a **chart**. A Jazz chart contains the tune, suggestions for chords based on a historical understanding of the composition, and guides for form or soloing. The musicians know the tune well. They know the tradition of performance associated with that composition. They are proficient players or singers. They will start to play along familiar lines, but very soon, they will relax into a collective feeling (usually called "**Swing**") and let their own mood, the mood of the whole band, and the response of the audience take them into "uncharted" territory. There, they will let the music do what it does so well—through its variations in melody, key, tone, rhythm, and dynamic, to challenge, comfort, teach, inspire, evoke, lull, or awaken. Most of all, they will be willing to extend themselves and take risks. If the **groove** is right, then musicians and hearers will begin to breathe and move together, and will become keenly aware of a common language that has arisen spontaneously among them.

The Jazz Mass at Canterbury House is an extension of this musical approach. Ideally, a worshipping congregation is much like the Jazz group we have described above. When they engage in a service, they are likely to have something called an Order of Service or a bulletin. It contains the scriptural passages for the day, suggested prayer forms, and guides for congregational response. The participants know the structure of the service well, and the traditions associated with their worship. As they open the service along familiar lines, they soon will relax into a collective attitude of praise and prayer, opening a space for the Spirit to do what she does so well. They, too, should be feeling invited to extend themselves and take risks. They will be moving and breathing together and be aware of their own common, spontaneous language.

We call our service at Canterbury House the "Jazz Mass," not because all of the music is Jazz. A typical service will also include folk, rock, country, electronic music, or even traditional hymns. **Silence** is a key "sound" in the Jazz Mass. It's called a Jazz Mass because the entire service is open to spontaneity and **improvisation**. The Jazz Mass is a principle of worship, not a style of music.

Most experienced priests can call to mind, without a prayer book, the typical elements of a Eucharistic service: from opening sentences through the Great Thanksgiving and its own attendant parts, to the blessing and dismissal. This, if you will, is your chart. Priests, musicians, and congregations have all memorized much material that is typical of these various parts. In addition, we have access to all manner of variations on them, drawing on a variety of liturgical resources and traditions (see Chapter Nine: Sources and Appendix B: Musical Resources for Liturgy for just a few of these resources).

Liturgists work creatively with music and words, with space, light, and shadow, and with acoustics, vestments, candles, and incense in a way that can be likened to instrumentalists playing a Jazz chart. If we are willing to trust our knowledge and experience, and rely also on our knowledge of our community, its gifts, and issues, then we can be "Jazz Liturgists."

Freedom of expression within a structure or form is the basis of most artistic ideas. Consider, for example, poetical forms such as the sonnet or the villanelle, visual forms such as the icon or the triptych, or musical forms such as the sonata or the symphony. Liturgy, any liturgy, is precisely that; it is a form or structure within which we express our worship. Our worship of God is a response both to God and to the circumstances of our world. We may be celebrating a birth, giving thanks for a harvest, or mourning a death. We may be in an attitude of joy, or praise, or fear, or loss, or ecstasy. How then, given the form, shall we express ourselves most completely in response to God and our situation? Further, how can we respond to God in such a way that we include the myriad expressions of our spirituality, giving the most clear and diverse voice to our hopes, fears, and prayers?

At Canterbury House our environment is academia. We have natural points of celebration in the academic year—the beginning of the semester, semester breaks, exam periods, graduation. We are working with a fairly narrow category of ages, so we can anticipate some specific issues, such as separation from home, experimentation with sex, drugs, or alcohol, freedom, limits, success and failure in academics and relationships, and a deep interest in politics and current events.

In the context of campus ministry, we have noticed that the traditional Episcopal **liturgical calendar** often works against us. Students come to school in the fall, deep in **ordinary time**. They disappear from campus just as Christmas comes around. **Holy Week** often falls during exam time. In order to respond better to the rhythm of our community, we have adapted the **sanctoral cycle**, the celebrations of **lesser feasts and fasts**, to the academic calendar. At Canterbury House our liturgical practice is to celebrate the lives of saints relevant to academic or social interests: for example, Aquinas, Hildegard, or Martin Luther King Jr. We do this without neglecting the seasonal liturgy. We observe **Advent** with anticipation and **Lent** with discipline. Readings for our services may include the lessons appropriate to the saints, together with news items, poetry, contemporary or historical literature, or scriptures from other religious traditions. We make a particular effort to compose our liturgies as a unified whole, thoroughly integrating music, readings, preaching, and prayer.

Any community can do this. The important questions are: What is our community? urban? suburban? rural? What is the rhythm of life here? Do people leave town in the summer? Do the children play soccer on Sunday morning? What are our resources, musical and otherwise? Do we have African drummers? Gospel musicians? a local Rock band? What are the demographics of the congregation? How do they differ from the demographics of our city or town? Why? The deeper the thinking and knowledge applied to these questions, the more relevant and engaging the liturgy will be.

Much of this book deals with the elements of liturgical style. We have a bias toward diverse or eclectic musical elements in the liturgy. We have assembled a database (see Appendix B: Musical Resources for Liturgy) that includes most of the music used at Canterbury House over the last decade. This music was chosen by means of diligent and prayerful study of the readings from *Lesser Feasts and Fasts* (New York: Church Publishing, 2006), as well as the **Revised Common Lectionary**. Using music from sources beyond the traditional hymnody found in standard church hymnals, we have listened to the voices of the many folk around the world who have expressed God's love through song. These songs have soul. They are full of worshipful intentionality, often have a rich national flavor, and are, at their core, excellent compositions. We routinely do music from Latin America, Africa, and the black Gospel tradition, as well as music from the **Taizé** community in France and the music of the modern master of hymnody, **John Bell**. We believe that diversity in music and liturgy opens up the structure and content of worship to include the downtrodden, the weak, the poor, and the disenfranchised. Diversity in worship music is an expression of an underlying ethic at Canterbury House of social justice and of God's love for all human beings.

Reid has been a church musician all his life and a priest for ten years. Stephen has been a liturgical musician (working exclusively with campus ministries) for sixteen years and has taught music as a university professor for twenty-three years. We are assuming in this book that liturgy is a collaborative process, planned jointly by the priest or pastor and the musician, as well as others, and executed by a willing, prayerful, and intelligent congregation. Indeed this is how willing, prayerful, and intelligent congregations are built. Our collaboration is based on respect and an acknowledged need for each other's input, spiritual perspective, and openness in the process of making liturgy that works. The word "liturgy" is derived from the Greek word *leitourgia,* meaning "work of the people." Priests and musicians seeking a meaningful liturgical experience for their congregations are encouraged to start first with their relationship to each other—nurturing respect, love, sharing, and a common language to discuss their faith.

# Chapter 2

## Planning and Celebrating Jazz Liturgy—Harmolodics and Homiletics

**harm-o-lod-ics** [hahrm-oh-**lod**-iks] *noun.* The art of music improvisation espoused and developed by saxophonist and composer **Ornette Coleman**.

**hom-i-let-ics** [hom-uh-**let**-iks] *noun.* The art of preaching.

So-called "**Traditional Jazz**" was usually structured in a simple and elegant way. The musicians in a small group used a chart. The chart contained a musical composition, usually written by one of the performers in the band. Just as often, the chart would be a variation on a pre-existent composition: the classic example perhaps is Charlie Parker's "Bird of Paradise," a stunning variation on Hammerstein and Kern's "All the Things You Are." The principle of playing from a chart is germane to thematic liturgical planning. The chart contains all the harmonic and melodic information for the improvisation, as well as the "**head**" or precomposed material for the composition. The chart also readily implies the rhythmic feel or groove of the composition. The chart is informed more by tradition than notation, however, as is the case with the relationship between rubrics in written liturgy and the local customary of actual worship in a community.

A community that gathers regularly for worship will inevitably develop a standard liturgical structure, intentionally or otherwise. In the Episcopal church, Holy Eucharist Rite II is one such liturgical structure. In the ***Book of Common Prayer*** one will find other structures, such as the Celebration of Baptism, Compline, Morning Prayer, and Evening Prayer. Every worshiping community, of whatever denomination or religion, has its own expected liturgy, whether written or according to custom. Liturgies are developed and informed by tradition, cultural preference, identity, and, of course, theological disposition.

Jazz musicians are intrigued as well by very basic but important musical structures. The **Blues**, for example, is one such structure. There are many others, of course. Song forms were often borrowed or interpolated from popular Tin Pan Alley tunes and Broadway songs (such as "All of Me" or "My Funny Valentine"). Another familiar structure is referred to as "Rhythm Changes," a standard progression of "blowing changes" for virtuosic improvisational work in a fixed structure (as in "The Theme" by **Miles Davis**, or "Oleo" by Sonny Rollins). The tiny and economical notation for these structures is the Jazz chart, from which the band can infer the entire composition. The Jazz chart is an innovative and convenient way to get everyone on the same page.

Worshiping communities, too, develop their own "tiny and economical notation," such as rubrics in prayer books or directions (sometimes very obscure or coded) in worship bulletins. No question, our service leaflets, bulletins, and prayer books provide exactly the same function as the Jazz chart.

Years of tradition, cultural tastes, identities, and local preferences bleed from these bound-paper icons every week in churches all over the world. Compare, for example, the clear stylistic differences between an evangelical church in Managua, Nicaragua, and, say, Riverside, California, or Dayton, Ohio. An even more stark difference might be found by comparing so-called "white" and "black" churches in the Detroit area. Many of the hymns are exactly the same, but given quite different treatments based on the congregation's cultural context. Nevertheless, the goal is the same: a way for people to encounter the holy and the sublime (not that different from the Jazz musician's goal), as well as a way for a group of people who have chosen to gather together to combine their energies into one collective expression of faith.

As we have said, Jazz liturgy does not depend exclusively on Jazz music. It *does*, however, depend on musical variety and especially diversity. One can do Jazz liturgy in any context, from synagogue to glass cathedral, using any idiom, from Gregorian **chant** to electronica. The difference between Jazz liturgy and "what we normally do" is the commitment of the whole congregation, and especially the liturgical planning team, to think *always* about "who is not there and why." Challenge, extend, experiment, *improvise.*

How is the liturgical chart conceived? How is it realized? Can/should it change from week to week? What can clergy, musicians, and congregation do with the basic structure of the service to vary it so that they add meaning, emotion, self-expression, local color, and, ultimately, beauty?

This is the **riff** portion of liturgical planning. A "riff," in Jazz terminology, is a phrase that extrapolates from the structure in an ornamental way. Duke Ellington and Count Basie, for example, rehearsed riffs on the tour bus as the band traveled around the country, giving the musicians material for improvisation as well as for compositional development. If Jazz were merely the reproduction of the basic structures (*e.g.*, blues, song forms, rhythm changes) discussed briefly above, Jazz would have died a quick and deserved death in the early 1920s. Instead, Jazz took these basic structures and intelligently extrapolated myriad possibilities for invention in melody, harmony, rhythm, and tone, crafting a distinctively American art form unparalleled in human history. The blending of diverse musical influences, technical and theoretical virtuosity, and traditional formal structures resulted in Jazz.

Jazz is a unique blend of diverse cultural heritages from Africa, Latin America, and, to a lesser extent, Europe. It is beyond the scope of this book to discuss the many cultural diasporas leading to the creation of Jazz, but interested readers may want to explore the topic on their own in greater depth (you can start with the discography included in Appendix B: Musical Resources for Liturgy). The tremendous diversity in the cultural/musical origins of Jazz underscores an important theme for liturgical innovation: that the church is the voice of the many, not the few.

At Canterbury House we attempt weekly to draw out the many voices of praise from around the world (see Chapter Seven: The Theology of Singing and an Exploration of Style). Central to our approach is that God is neither white nor black, male nor female, but rather both person and idea, beyond category. We present music from around the world and give voice to vital religious musical traditions from the entire planet. This takes research, study, musical technique, varied resources (books and musicians), and the enthusiasm of open-minded clergy and congregation.

Missing any one of these components leads to a disingenuous attempt to "perform a diverse church service" for its own sake. We often hear clergy and congregations say, "We need more diverse music." Merely adding a song from an African-American hymnal, or even putting an African-American hymnal in the pew racks, is not sufficient. Such an approach is insulting to people around the world who worship God with sincerity, deep faith, and musical virtuosity.

Finally, a look at contemporary Jazz improvisation techniques helps us to explore liturgy on an even deeper and more creative level. In the late 1950s, Ornette Coleman burst onto the Jazz scene with a principle of free Jazz that propelled Jazz into its modern age. Coleman felt that the musicians playing from a chart should be free to explore any and all of the (ultimately unlimited) tonal areas, rhythmic structures, and melodic possibilities therein, in an act of collective as well as solo improvisation. All of the harmonic and melodic material is *implied* by the chart—hence Coleman's term for the principle: "**Harmolodics**." But in Harmolodic music there is no strict or set notion of rhythm, melody, or even of musical key. Potentially, of course, this could result in chaos. With sophisticated Jazz musicians, however, it results, instead, in a completely different approach to improvisation, to wit, a sublime and complex web of ideas, personalities, and dialogue.

Harmolodics does not revel in the mere virtuosic display of interpretation from the chart, but explores the deep inner core of the chart, and in doing so, explores the human dynamism found in collective improvisation. This raises the questions: Is everything permissible? Does anything go? No. Harmolodics is just as rigorous, if not more so, as traditional or earlier Jazz, but implies a constant state of listening, care, and dialogue. Harmolodics, at its core, demands that every player be completely and totally aware of all of the musical elements, as well as the other musicians, at all times. No longer does one musician have an elevated position of importance. No longer does one musician have a prescribed function. Everyone is equally important to the articulation of the process and the success of the realized composition. How like this is liturgy! the celebration of each and every person in the congregation! the acknowledgement that every worshiper is loved by God! has a soul!

In a liturgy that employs the improvisational approach of Harmolodics, the worshipers feel a connection to God and to each other through collective engagement. This frankly African approach to liturgy (tribal music making is not a "leader-based" approach: everyone has a significant function) creates the feeling of inclusion, of acceptance and love. Each person is necessary to corporate worship in the church, and each person is acknowledged as a possessor of a soul, an identity, and a voice—literally as well as spiritually. In the end, these worshippers more readily feel that they are part of the larger community of God, that their access to God is direct, and that their contribution to the Kingdom of God is needed, expected, and celebrated.

Harmolodics, or collective improvisation, is our paradigm for a strong liturgical church. If every voice is heard, and every soul is engaged in the liturgy, just as the Harmolodic improviser is engaged in the music, church services are deeper and more intense, the quality of the service and the experience of the congregation are completely interdependent. People sing with more engagement. They sing louder, are more in tune, and are willing to risk singing in parts. People can pray with more depth of thought, knowing that each person's prayers are heard and necessary to combine in genuinely corporate prayer. Each person's bond to the community increases as well, because the shared vulnerability and ecstasy of such a service creates unity and joy.

Newcomers to the service, as well, respond to this theme-based approach with eagerness. There is a clear vision that they can see, and there is order to the service that is logical and carefully presented. The attitude is user-friendly because of this clarity, and the engagement of the welcoming congregation can help visitors to easily jump in. Newcomers to this style of worship feel more than welcome. They feel needed.

This is one of the main reasons we program harmolodic music frequently at Canterbury House. Not only is it music we love and that the musicians play well, it models the behavior of emotional and intellectual engagement for the congregation. If four musicians "from the street" can "get it in their soul," well, maybe so can they!

In Jazz terms, the service will swing.

*Stephen:*

Harmolodics demands that the musicians are engaged and committed, that they be perfect masters of the chart. Theme-based liturgical planning and celebration (and the conduct of the resultant service) is no different. In order to plan a Jazz Mass all the liturgical planners should be simultaneously attentive to the material (specifically the lectionary readings), their coplanners, and the unlimited resources of their own imagination and inspiration. Just as the Harmolodic improvisers are completely attuned to the chart and the other musicians around them, so must the liturgical planners be in an ever-constant awareness of the Spirit breathing through each one of them in a different way. They must plan the liturgy in an attitude of complete trust. The unlimited and collective expression of the planners' reaction to the lectionary will lead to the same beauty and cohesion found in harmolodic improvisation.

In the world of Ornette Coleman's Harmolodics, technical terms about listening and music take on an extraordinary and spiritual meaning. For example, "melody" is not only the most significant element of a chart in later Jazz, it is also the core and central spiritual idea for a composition. If all the musicians agree on the melody, or, more importantly, the greater idea behind the melody, how can they fail to play together well? Coleman calls this playing together well "Unison," a term that he capitalizes in his article "Prime Time for Harmolodics."[2] In traditional music theory, "unison" is defined as two musicians singing or playing the same note. You sing a C, I play a C, and we are in unison. There is a deeper unison in harmolodic theory. **Albert Ayler** called it a spiritual "unity." I like to think of it as a divine union. This kind of connection is what Harmolodics strives for, and what Harmolodic instrumentalists work at so rigorously. It is the sense that "we are all on the same page," or we agree about the larger idea of melody. In religious congregations, it could be thought of as a creed.

In Harmolodic theory, Unison can be understood to mean that the notes C and F# are equivalent. Jazz musicians, such as George Russell in particular, have been pointing this out for years, talking about the "Tritone substitution"—the relationship between C and F# is, indeed, called the interval of a Tritone. In harmolodic theory though, these notes are not substitutes for each other. They are the same. How is this possible, and what does this mean on a deeper level? It means that we can call notes by many names, but in the end they are all Sounds, and they are messengers of the Holy. In the same way, each of us has our own name, but God is present in us, trying to be revealed in each of us. Surely, we have, like the notes, our own names, our own identities. But in each essence, sonic or human or both, there is One Holiness. If we recognize this, we can be in unison. If we don't, we will be confused, lack inclusion, and defy diversity.

Harmolodics also addresses, on a deeply spiritual level, the assumed components of music such as emotion and intellect. Emotion, in this domain, is the receptor of the elusive and mystical elements in sound. Sound can be codified in terms of frequency or decibel level (amplitude). But can it be discussed in specific terms when it comes to the divine elements in sound itself? Ornette Coleman insists that intellect is the place where emotion (divinity) can be ascertained or sorted out and where one can truly listen to a sound or music. Intellect, then, is the refined skill of differentiation of the divine from the clamor of "non-Sound." In Harmolodics, the musicians are communicators of emotion.This is in contrast to many aesthetic predispositions of the twentieth century that deny the importance of emotion in music. Rather, musicians are to convey emotion through the divine vessel of sound, with an attempt to "hit the receptors," called "intellect" in Harmolodic theory. Your ears, in other words, are your heart.

Sound is Sacred. Musicians are meant to deliver the Sacred with care, honoring both the participant and the listener. The Holy is found not only in each listener and each musician, but also in each and every Sound. Playing with that level of intensity and care demands discipline, understanding, and a certain spiritual perceptiveness that is rarely discussed in western academies, and extremely

2 *Downbeat*, July 1983, 54–55.

hard to measure. Harmolodics shows us that music is a metaphor for the love of each human on the planet (every sound), and the honoring of the relationships between human beings (the intertwined relationship of notes, unison or transposed).

*Reid:*

It's helpful, therefore, to think of the Jazz Mass as one whole, single chart, composed by the liturgical team—whoever that may be, but at least the priest and the principal musician—and performed by *everyone* in the liturgy.

Seen in this light, preaching is an extended solo by the priest or pastor.

In **homiletics** class at divinity school, we learned how to write a sermon. Of course, there are at least as many ways of writing a sermon as there are homiletics professors, but they have a common goal of producing a written essay suitable for reading to a congregation. Delivering the composed essay, even from memory, is one way of preaching, just as playing the composed sonata is one way of playing; but it is not **Jazz preaching**.

Improvisation, in preaching as in music, is a means of creating an organic and developed whole, with an utterly different result from pre-written material. Jazz preaching is done without notes, but *not* without significant time and effort in preparation. It is a direct interaction with the congregation. It depends on feedback from the congregation and involves them in the end result: a dialogue that is open to the work of the Holy Spirit. We often see this done in African-American congregations but rarely in other churches on Sunday morning.

What is necessary in order to prepare for and accomplish a Jazz sermon? We can usefully think about how the Jazz musician prepares for a Jazz solo. The Jazz musician has a chart and an instrument. They have heard master musicians solo on this material before. So it is with the preacher.

Our chart is the passage or passages of scripture that will be the subject of the sermon. Just as the musician knows the chart very well, the preacher must know the scripture very well. This is precisely what we learned to do in seminary: to read the lesson, to understand it thoroughly both historically and theologically, to examine what comes before and after the section or sections under review, and to consult secondary materials where they might be helpful. If we are working with several readings from scripture (or plan to use other, additional sources for readings), it is important to think about how they do or do not relate to one another, or at least what common themes they might comprehend. As we think about and compose a sermon, we look for what these passages are saying to our congregation now.

In preparing for the Jazz Mass, both Stephen and I work with scripture in this way. Ideally, I will have some ideas about what music I would associate with the themes expressed in the scriptures, and he will have a notion of what he would preach about if called upon to do so. We are always paying enough attention to what is going on in the world and in our community to be able to discuss with one another how the selected scripture has spoken to each of us, and our discussion together helps us make these associations relevant to our congregation. When we are preparing a Jazz Mass, discussing the scriptures and the themes together prevents me from jamming out a solo on "Higher Ground" when the band is playing "Deep River."

The theme of the Jazz Mass having been identified and the music having been selected early in the week, I then spend the rest of the week praying and thinking about the sermon. I will try out passages in my head or out loud. I will talk to myself while doing the dishes. I will think about how my sermon is going to begin and end, and consider and organize the principal points I wish to make. I will try out ideas and phrases with sympathetic listeners, and I will listen and respond to their suggestions, adopting or rejecting phrases and riffs that might help to get the point across. A single melodic idea is always best.

The first time a preacher preaches without notes is understandably a nerve-wracking experience. Any musician can tell you that improvising for the first time is just as difficult. It takes practice, and one gains confidence from the experience of doing it many times. Experience and confidence do not prevent you from forgetting things or from making mistakes. Rather, they help you continue to make the music—to stay in communication with the congregation and to drive your sermon forward to its conclusion without becoming stymied or lame. Ideally, one can turn an unintended notion into a useful theme or incorporate a new idea when the Spirit suggests one.

The Jazz musician has an instrument that is well-tuned and familiar by dint of hours of practice. So does the preacher.

The preacher's instrument is the voice, body, and mind. Our tuning and our familiarity with our instrument comes from practice and experience in public speaking. The way we play it is our style. Like the Jazz musician, we must be true to our own style, developed over time. As the character based on Dexter Gordon says in Bernard Tavernier's movie, *'Round Midnight:* "You can't just pick a style off from a tree, it has to grow from within." It does no good for a preacher to suddenly adopt a style that is strange or unfamiliar to him or her. The congregation will know immediately that we have done so, and will be jarred and distracted.

Jazz preaching works best in an intimate setting. Intimacy is not a function of numbers of people. A surprisingly large number of people can fit in a space where everyone can see and hear one another. Rather, it is a function of space. It is difficult to preach a Jazz sermon in a space where one is distant from the nearest listeners, or the listeners are distant from one another, or the acoustics or sound technology do not permit modulation of pitch, tone, and volume. It is difficult, if not impossible, to preach a Jazz sermon from the confines of a pulpit.

The dynamic of the Jazz Mass is one of collective consciousness. This is not a metaphysical proposition. Many practical considerations are involved. When preaching at a Jazz Mass, I am watching the body language of the whole congregation. Are the listeners engaged? Are they awake? Are they watching what I am doing (which suggests that they are listening to what I am saying)? Even more specifically, have I struck a chord with someone in particular? Is someone nodding his head in assent? Is someone beginning to cry? These clues may suggest to me that I am headed in a right (or wrong) direction, and I must be prepared to adjust my approach accordingly.

There are many preachers who combine words and music in their Jazz Preaching. We know of a few excellent examples: Vernard Johnson of Fort Worth, Texas, actually preaches while playing the saxophone, accenting his music with text and vice versa. Incidentally, his playing sounds very much like Albert Ayler's. Another case is McCullough Sounds of Thunder, a trombone shout choir in Harlem, New York, which includes Ayler alumnus Henry Grimes. The trombone choir's liturgical role includes responding musically to preaching during the sermon itself.

In sum, Jazz preaching, like Jazz playing, begins with thorough knowledge of the material and competence based on practice and experience. It then continues with the willingness and ability to listen to others, to take risks, and to establish communication with the listeners. As is the case with the Jazz ensemble, where the audience contributes to the music by their active and vocal response, the congregation likewise contributes to the Jazz liturgy. By giving *their* response—vigorously singing, contributing audibly to the prayers of the people, reading with feeling, and dancing—they become emotionally and spiritually connected and engaged with God and with one another.

# Chapter 3

## A Jazz Mass—Constance and Her Companions

As an illustration of the Harmolodic and homiletic principles adduced in Chapter Two, let's take a look at the service we celebrated on September 12, 2004, at Canterbury House, commemorating Constance and Her Companions, commonly called "The Martyrs of Memphis." An outline of the service is found on pages 82–84

The hagiography of Constance and her Companions found in the *Lesser Feasts and Fasts* is as follows:

> In August, 1878, Yellow Fever invaded the city of Memphis for the third time in ten years. By the month's end the disease had become epidemic and a quarantine was ordered. While 30,000 citizens had fled in terror, 20,000 more remained to face the pestilence. As cases multiplied, death tolls averaged 200 daily. When the worst was over ninety percent of the population had contracted the Fever; more than 5,000 people had died.
>
> In that time of panic and flight, many brave men and women, both lay and cleric, remained at their posts of duty or came as volunteers to assist despite the terrible risk. Notable among these heroes were Constance, Superior of the work of the Sisters of St. Mary in Memphis, and her Companions. The Sisters had come to Memphis in 1873, at Bishop Quintard's request, to found a Girls School adjacent to St. Mary's Cathedral. When the 1878 epidemic began, George C. Harris, the Cathedral Dean, and Sister Constance immediately organized relief work among the stricken. Helping were six of Constance's fellow Sisters of St. Mary; Sister Clare from St. Margaret's House, Boston; the Reverend Charles C. Parsons, Rector of Grace and St. Lazarus Church, Memphis; and the Reverend Louis S. Schuyler, assistant at Holy Innocents, Hoboken. The Cathedral group also included three physicians, two of whom were ordained Episcopal priests, the Sisters' two matrons, and several volunteer nurses from New York. They have ever since been known as "The Martyrs of Memphis," as have those of other Communions who ministered in Christ's name during this time of desolation.
>
> The Cathedral buildings were located in the most infected region of Memphis. Here, amid sweltering heat and scenes of indescribable horror, these men and women of God gave relief to the sick, comfort to the dying, and homes to the many orphaned children. Only two of the workers escaped the Fever. Among those who died were Constance, Thecla, Ruth and Frances, the Reverend Charles Parsons and the Reverend Louis Schuyler. The six martyred Sisters and priests are buried at Elmwood Cemetery. The monument marking the joint grave of Fathers Parsons and Schuyler bears the inscription: "Greater Love Hath No Man." The beautiful High Altar in St. Mary's Cathedral, Memphis, is a memorial to the four Sisters.

Our service in commemoration of these powerful saints was structured along the lines of the Holy Eucharist, Rite II from the 1979 *Book of Common Prayer*. As discussed in Chapter One, other outlines are, of course, possible. Rite II is a familiar service at Canterbury House. This liturgy has a long development in history and a sound basis in liturgical scholarship. Rite II is a good chart for our context.

The *Lesser Feasts and Fasts* gives us our starting material: a collect, two readings (one from the gospels), and a psalm. We began our planning of this service by looking at the readings associated with Constance: 2 Corinthians 1:3–5, Psalm 116, John 12:24–28. The Reverend Nancy Baxter, Episcopal chaplain at Emory University, used to encourage her students to ask, "Why are these lessons, why is this gospel, associated with this saint?" In this case the question does not seem difficult to answer.

"I will fulfill my vows to the Lord in the presence of all his people. Precious in the sight of the Lord is the death of his servants," reads Psalm 116:14–15. God "consoles us in all our affliction, so that we may be able to console those who are in any affliction with the consolation with which we ourselves are consoled by God," writes Paul in 2 Corinthians 1:4.

The Gospel reading assigned in *Lesser Feasts and Fasts* is John 12:24–28, which begins with the saying of Jesus: "Very truly, I tell you, unless a grain of wheat falls into the earth and dies, it remains just a single grain; but if it dies, it bears much fruit." We found, however, as we often do, that looking at what comes before and after the assigned reading reveals contextual material that is important and should be included. In this case, starting at verse 20 includes the request of the Greeks to Philip: "Sir, we wish to see Jesus." We concluded that this was an important illustration of the meaning of Constance's life and ministry, so our Gospel reading for the service included this introductory story beginning at verse 20.

Canterbury House is a community of college students. They are young. They are by definition exploring their several callings. Truly, the overarching theme each semester is "What is God calling you to do?" Self-sacrificial devotion is, of course, a possible theme for the commemoration of any martyr. The challenge for us was to make it real to these young people, without irony on the one hand, and without any tinge of fanaticism on the other. Under what circumstances, truly and realistically, might we be called to place our own lives at risk for the benefit of others? Why would we ever do this? What would be the necessity to do so, and what would be the value? It requires college students ages eighteen to twenty-two or so to stretch their imaginations in order to consider these things.

This service is based on the story of Constance and the scripture readings, and was already percolating in our minds when we met together to plan the liturgy.

*Stephen:*

Someone asked me at a workshop what principal tool I used for planning liturgy. I replied quite simply, "MEMORY." I read the selections ahead of time and stir around recollections of visceral experiences with the topics I find in the readings. One could object to this approach, saying it is myopic, self-centered, and even anti-scholastic. However, I have found it to be authentic and honest, and a way to explore scripture and relate it to human experience, leading to open-ended outcomes in making the musical choices for services.

Upon reading about Constance and Her Companions (I admit that I had never heard of her before we began to plan this service), I was struck by the two most basic and obvious facts: she worked in Memphis, Tennessee; she stuck it out and died. The story is graphic in its detail, but not actually a statistical anomaly in light of the scourge of AIDS outbreaks in Africa and India, and the malarial devastation in those regions as well as South America. In fact, my encounter with Constance led me to consider contemporary medical horrors, and the people who work to combat them. One of those people is my wife, who works with campesinas and farm workers in a prenatal clinic to lower the mother/

infant death rate in Nicaragua. I have seen this clinic, as well as other clinics of this sort in India. I have a view of suffering and compassion in the malarial regions that is down-to-earth, real, and informed by my prayer life and commitment to justice on the earth.

That Constance worked in Memphis was a helpful musical cue. Truly, Memphis is one of the great centers of music in the United States, rivaled perhaps only by the Mississippi Delta and New Orleans. So much great music was recorded in Memphis that I decided to search there for our liturgical music. I started with Elvis, Johnny Cash, and the many Blues tunes we frequently do at Canterbury House. It was important to the process that I listen to many recordings and continue my research of Memphis music until I came to a result that really felt right. This time I was lucky. I popped in my Johnny Cash boxed set and soon came to "I Walk the Line." The lyrics immediately drew me to tears. Yes, Johnny Cash is saying to his betrothed, "because you're mine, I walk the line." It's a statement of commitment. What follows that first chorus is a quote from a hymn that our students probably would not connect with (and many highbrow churches wouldn't either): "I keep the end out for the tie that binds." The old hymn "Blessed be the tie that binds" was a perfect companion piece to "I Walk the Line" for our offertory hymn. However, we had the congregation *read* the text for the age-old hymn while the band played the memorable tune. From that blessed introduction we kicked off "I Walk the Line."

To review briefly the process so far, each of us prepared for planning the service by reading the story and the related scripture readings and reflecting deeply upon them. Then we let our feelings about the story and the readings, together with our own memories or experiences, flood over us in an honest and contemporary way, and we played freely with ideas for music and preaching. This led me to nothing other than a very popular Country tune and an old Baptist warhorse, neither of which would be standard fare at most Episcopal churches. In this context, however, the music completely expresses our reaction to the text in the most direct and heartfelt manner.

Now let's delve into the rest of the service, to see other approaches and revelations. Given Constance and her *constancy*, and her ability to love and serve the people of Memphis at her own peril, I consulted my database (Appendix B: Musical Resources for Liturgy) and looked up music listed for *Love* and *Hope* (on the basis that love leads to hope), *Obedience* (love, for Constance, was an act of obedience), and, finally, *Trust/Faith* (for how else could she and her companions risk their lives?).

For the prelude, I found a wonderful contemporary nugget by surreal guitarist **Sonny Sharrock**. Sonny Sharrock died in 1994 after a substantial career as a soloist and a sideman for greats such as Miles Davis and Pharoah Sanders. Just before his death, he released a magical album with Pharoah Sanders, Elvin Jones, and Charnette Moffett called *Ask the Ages* (Axiom Records). On this wonderful disc is found a composition called "Who Does She Hope to Be?," a tune that is reflective and calm, swings beautifully, and is a nice opener for this service.

An idea for the postlude came out of the blue when my bassist at the time, Tim Flood, emailed me a PDF of a W.C. Handy tune called "Memphis Blues." W.C. Handy, a Memphis musician, is often called "The Father of the Blues" although he was, strictly speaking, more of a Ragtime composer. The Blues is often used at Canterbury House as a liturgical "signal" or evocation of the idea that Christ suffers with us. The Blues is such an important idiom that I wrote an entire Blues Mass specifically for Canterbury House (see Appendix D: Blues Mass). Often during Lent, for example, we turn to the Blues as a healing musical form to salve the difficult times. "Memphis Blues" was therefore a perfect choice for the service at hand.

As for hymns, we already had one, and an old one: "Blessed Be the Tie That Binds." As described above, however, we read it rather than singing it; so I felt that we could add another older hymn to connect with the theme of constancy. "Abide with Me" seemed lovely. The musicians at Canterbury House are especially fond of this tune, as it was recorded by John Coltrane, one of the true heroes of 1960s free Jazz. Coltrane is often at the musical heart and soul of our liturgy, with music from his classic suite, *Love Supreme*, as well as the sequel suite, *Meditations*. These two suites include tunes with titles such as "Compassion," "Love," "Psalm," and "Father, Son, and Holy Ghost." Thus, we used "Abide with Me" as the opening hymn, and did it in a gentle bluesy rocking style.

When approaching dark themes such as *Death*, *Lent*, *Trouble*, or *Doubt,* I tend to interpret the music in an affirmational way, as opposed to a funereal style. After all, God is there, calling us to love and serve others even when it isn't easy. We are called to work, not merely to weep. We attempt to balance the opening hymn—its mood and connotation—with the closing hymn, to give an overall dramatic arc to the service. My old friend Don Postema once pointed out to me that a worship service is a kind of opera: with its stories, subplots, and themes, we shape the overall emotional arc of the service, clearly and dramatically. Certainly, the standard form of the "ordinaries" of the mass (Kyrie/Gloria/Credo/ Sanctus/Agnus Dei) has a dramatic and emotive structure. So do the various services in the *Book of Common Prayer.* So do the many other liturgical structures used by various denominations. Why not play with this structure, and reinforce it with musical interpretation? With this in mind, we chose "There Is a Balm in Gilead" as a closing hymn. Yes, we are called to work, often to suffer, but God is there to comfort us every time. The service seemed replete with "old-timey" hymns—hardly the first conception one forms on hearing the term "Jazz Mass"—but each one was selected because it fit the topic well.

Psalms used in the Jazz Mass at Canterbury House are sung to tones that I have composed. These are found in Appendix C: **Psalm Tones**. Reviewing and reflecting on all 150 psalms, I identified and categorized eleven specific themes. For each of these, I have written a psalm tone appropriate to the mood and spirit of the particular theme. My hope is to give emotion and meaning to the reciting of the psalms, rather than merely to provide a harmonic formula over which to sing the psalms. Myriad traditions exist for psalm chanting. Early Christian practice included chanting of psalm texts over simple melodic formulas. Examples of this can be found in the *Liber Usualis.* Through the popularity of the album *Chant* by the Monks of Santo Domingo de Silos (Angel, 1994), Gregorian chant, yet another method, is now familiar to all. What is intended in my settings is to reinforce the deep emotional content of the texts with contemporary musical syntax.

For Constance and Her Companions, we concluded that "Compassion" was the theme of Psalm 116: "Gracious is the Lord and righteous; our God is full of compassion." In fact, I wrote the tone "Compassion" specifically for this service. Sometimes the only way to have the appropriate music is to write it yourself. Consider the example of church musicians discussed in Chapter 10: Church Musician, Gig or Calling?

One of the great examples of a church musician who writes music as a response to contemporary issues is John Bell, hymnodist and preacher for the Wild Goose Worship Group of the Iona community. We deeply appreciate Bell's contribution to contemporary hymnody, and frequently use a composition from one of his several volumes in our weekly services. His ability to speak in a specific way about topics often unaddressed or overgeneralized in traditional hymns is an important contribution to contemporary worship. No less significant, his music is eminently singable. There are so many variables in hymn selection, but for us, one variable is simply non-negotiable: singability. Anyone who has met John Bell or attended one of his workshops has heard this expressed more enthusiastically and eloquently than I am able to do.

Our gospel hymn selection, therefore, was "A Woman's Care" by John Bell.[3] I had long wanted to do this lovely hymn, set to the old English folk tune, "Died for Love." This title itself reinforces

3 *Heaven Shall Not Wait* (Chicago, IL: GIA Publications, 1989), 24.

the reference to Constance and the theme of sacrificial devotion. I am particularly fond of the lines, "Has God turned his back on us forsaking those he loved and made?" (v. 2) and "My weary folk in ev'ry land, Your souls are cradled in my heart" (v. 3). My own theology tends toward the existential and the mystical. Thus, I find Bell's lyrics resonate with the cosmology found in Dostoyevsky, for example, whose characters struggle with redemption in an existential paradigm. Bell's lyrics allow the congregation to go to that space of despair where they can identify with Constance by feeling both her desperate situation and her radical commitment. This seems to me a much deeper and more authentic response than the dogmatic sentimentalism of a traditional hymn such as the nineteenth-century "How Firm a Foundation." Bell's plaint ends in this positive claim: "Then praise the Lord through faith and fear, In holy and in hopeless place; For height and depth and heav'n and hell can't keep us from God's embrace" (v. 5).

To follow the prayers of the people, we sang a **Taizé chant**, "In Manus Tuas Pater" ("Into your hands, Father, I commend my Spirit"), a dark and sad reference to Jesus' moaning on the cross, and a prayer that Constance and her Companions may well have uttered as they died in Memphis. This was a stark piece to use, but somehow, as we sang it over and over as a meditation, it became an indicator of both peace and solace, which is not an uncommon experience with some of the more bleak Taizé texts.

There are liturgical moments when it is impractical or undesirable for worshipers to hold service leaflets in their hands. For these, Taizé music is especially helpful. We use the music of Taizé to provide meditative content for intervals such as communion and the prayers of the people, when our eyes and hands are otherwise necessarily occupied. For more about Taizé music, see Chapter Seven: The Theology of Singing and an Exploration of Style.

The Sanctus we chose for this service is "Halle, Halle, Halle," which we played in an almost frenzied Calypso style (probably how it was originally performed in the Caribbean Islands) using steel drums, and accompanied by dancing. This explosive dance, by being placed in the middle of the Eucharist, broke us out of the dark place the service sank to after the sad lament of the Bell hymn and the chant "In Manus Tuas Pater." Too often, communion has the feel of a kind of depressing "mini-Lent" in the middle of what should be an ecstatic service. With respect to those who interpret communion as a solemn time, I nevertheless wanted deliberately to reverse that feel. An exciting and ecstatic Sanctus reminds us that there is nothing mystically *sad* about communion. It is the ultimate expression of God's love.

After the Sanctus (musically) followed the chant "Ubi caritas." At communion we chant all through the taking of the bread and wine. "Ubi caritas" is a popular Taizé piece with an ancient text translated: "Where there is charity and love, God also is there." In the context of this service, the text reinforced the point: where there is love, there needs to be a commitment. This chant continues in the service as an affirmational statement of commitment, obedience, and even bliss.

In summary, the service commemorating Constance and Her Companions was a blended offering of traditional hymnody, one very familiar Taizé tune, a Calypso Sanctus, one very *unfamiliar* Taizé tune, and a singable but not overly familiar John Bell tune. In addition to these were two works by American classic (but not classical) composers, W. C. Handy and Johnny Cash. The prelude was a lovely Jazz tune that referred, both in mood and title, to the ultimate question: "Who, indeed, do we all hope to be?"

*Reid:*

After our planning meeting in which we identified the theme of the service, worked together to select appropriate music, and thought together about possible directions for the sermon, I had the task to select an alternative reading and prepare to preach.

The outline of the Rite II Eucharist suggests up to three readings and a psalm. The *Lesser Feasts and Fasts* provides two readings for each saint. This is an opportunity to bring in a reading from alternative sources by using scriptures of other traditions such as the *Baghavad Gita* or the *Qur'an,* literature, or to use contemporary sources such as newspaper articles.

In this case, as I was contemplating these scriptures and the story of Constance and wondering about yellow fever, I happened upon an account of a death from yellow fever from *Morbidity and Mortality Weekly Report* that I found on the internet. It was very helpful in *a*) describing the excruciating symptoms of yellow fever, and *b*) making the point that the disease has been eradicated in the industrialized world, but remains endemic in developing countries.

Of course, plagues of all sorts are both a biblical and a contemporary phenomenon. There seemed, therefore, an opportunity to make a clear connection for our students between the yellow fever epidemic of the 1880s and the AIDS epidemic of the 1980s. Plagues are without question always a challenge to our compassion.

For this service I preached a sermon, without notes, on compassion. Of course, a Jazz sermon is not subject to being reproduced in writing; but I can tell you about the experience of preaching it.

I recalled for my congregation, composed primarily of students born after 1980, my experience of living in Atlanta during the early 1980s when AIDS first became a plague among homosexual men in that city. Many of these men were my friends and colleagues, in my law practice and in the choir of St. Philip's Cathedral where I sang at the time. When the AIDS epidemic first struck, little was known about the disease. Gay men in general were subject to discrimination and often treated with hostility. Those who had developed AIDS especially were viewed with fear. I drew a parallel between the yellow fever plague in Memphis in 1889, when those who were able to do so fled the city for the higher ground and healthier "air," and the AIDS plague in Atlanta, when even their friends would refuse to touch gay men, and medical personnel feared to treat them.

One of my friends, a tenor in the Cathedral Choir of St. Philip, had developed AIDS. He kept the matter secret and, when he became ill, withdrew from the choir. I fell out of touch with him. It happened one day that we passed one another on the long escalator at the Peachtree Street MARTA station in Atlanta—I going up, he going down. Our eyes met. He surely recognized me, but I nearly did not recognize him. He had dramatically lost weight, and was drawn and emaciated. I was too stunned at his appearance to move, much less to wave in greeting or to acknowledge him. I could not guess his mind, but both of us simply stared at one another as we passed. I never saw him again although all of us in the choir learned of his death a short time later.

In preaching about this incident, I did not anticipate the strength of my own feelings in recollecting the event, my subsequent shame over my reaction of shock and fear, and my grief at losing this and so many other friends to this terrible disease. Pausing in the sermon to gain control over my own tears made a powerful connection with the congregation, as it illustrated more clearly than mere words ever could the strength of the emotions and the depth of the challenge that Constance herself must have faced and overcome in order to devote herself to the care of the suffering citizens of Memphis.

One could argue about the stylistic cohesion of a service that included readings from scripture and contemporary scientific literature, with music that included Jazz, an Irish folk tune, traditional hymns, Country music, and early Blues. However, one could not argue about the distinct American-ness of the liturgical choices. For this American saint, we did music almost exclusively of the United States, honoring our own traditions of Jazz, **gospel singing**, Country, and Ragtime. Somehow, the playing of Bach and Howells for a service about Constance would present its own aesthetic contradiction, without the virtue of thematic coherence. In the end we felt that Constance was honored and that the Gospel (John 12:20–28, with its culmination, "If it dies, it bears much fruit") was conveyed cogently and consistently through the whole service, in readings, prayer, preaching, and music, to a congregation prepared, engaged, and receptive to a challenging message.

# Chapter 4

## Collaboration Between Musician and Priest/Pastor

**col·lab·o·rate** (kə-ˈla-bə-ˌrāt) *intr.v.* **-rat·ed, -rat·ing, -rates.** 1. To work together, especially in a joint intellectual effort. 2. To cooperate treasonably, as with an enemy occupation force. (*The American Heritage Dictionary of the English Language*).

We have heard priests and pastors who say, "I don't know anything about music." We have also heard musicians who say, "I'm spiritual, but I'm not religious." Needless to say, these two categories of persons are going to have a hard time working together to plan liturgy unless they are prepared to develop a common language.

If, as a priest, you seriously think that you do not know anything about music, start by checking your assumption. Do you have a CD collection? Do you sing in the shower? When you hear music, do you know whether or not you like what you are hearing? Do you ever attend concerts or musical theatre? Have you read about J. S. Bach or seen a movie about Ray Charles? If so, then it is not the case that you "do not know anything" about music. There is a saying from Zimbabwe: "If you can walk, you can dance; if you can talk, you can sing." We take the theology of this statement very seriously.

What the priest or pastor who feels insecure about her knowledge of music needs to do is increase her literacy. How to do this? Well, you just have to start. One way to start is by developing a relationship with your musician. Ask him what he likes. Ask for suggestions for listening. Better still, get together over drinks and snacks and listen to some music together. Talk about what you do and do not like and why, in as much detail as you are able. Then go browse the record store or an online music source.

You can go even deeper than this. Join a Gospel choir—the good ones do not require any prior musical training! They learn the music by rote, and you can learn in this way to listen for parts and to breathe properly (which, by the way, is important for prayer). You can even learn to move your body while singing. You will also develop literacy in a distinctly American musical tradition.

Similarly, you might join a **Southern Harmony** or shape-note singing group, attend a Taizé workshop, or try out for a chorus part in your local theatre's musical production of *Camelot.*

For the truly brave, buy a guitar or a keyboard and get some lessons in Blues or Jazz. Don't begin with the assumption that you "can't" do it, or you are, in fact, defeated before you start.

If you are a musician who feels out of your depth discussing theology, a nice place to start is to ask your priest for suggestions for books that have deep and transformative meaning for her. Most likely she will not suggest that you start right off with Karl Barth; but even if she does, it will help you develop some literacy in theological thinking, as well as earn you some respect and credibility from your collaborator.

Ask for books that are written from within the tradition you are working in. If as a musician you are working in an Episcopal church and have never read C.S. Lewis, go do it now! If you are a Lutheran, read some Luther. He's very entertaining!

Stephen admits that he has been lucky in his choice of pastors to work with. In his first long-term gig with a minister, he worked with Don Postema in Ann Arbor, Michigan. Stephen had read and taught Don's book *Space for God: The Study and Practice of Prayer and Spirituality* about eight years before moving to Ann Arbor and was so taken with Don's approach to prayer, art, and God that he read the entire (and extensive) bibliography. Stephen recollects: "One wintry day in Michigan, I happened past Campus Chapel, saw his name on the sign, and thought, 'Is this even possible that this is the same Don Postema?'

"We met, bonded, and developed a long relationship that is vital even today. Of course, the fact that I had read twenty or so books that were near and dear to him made it extremely likely that I could understand and value his perspective on life, liturgy, and theology. Naturally, this investment into his work spawned a deep investment on his part in my own creative work.

"Out of this close relationship came liturgies that pushed the boundaries of our church community, as well as our own comfort levels, and even the traditional boundaries of worship—we experimented with clown services, services with Ghanaian musicians, radical prayers, conversational services with improvised interludes, and service leaflets that had nothing inside them at all. Much of the foundation for my understanding of creative liturgy was born out of the nine years working with Don or the many discussions we've had since. Furthermore, we made an audio book out of *Space for God: The Study and Practice of Prayer and Spirituality* to celebrate our relationship and the role the book had in instigating it."

The musician who wants to develop a deeper spiritual life should get a spiritual director. You will learn more about theology if you learn to talk about what God might be doing in your life—a frequent subject in spiritual direction as well as liturgy. Developing some comfort in talking about the presence of God in your life will *certainly* deepen your conversation with your collaborators, and it will help you connect your musical knowledge with your life experience.

We suspect that readers of this book, both pastors and musicians, will find that they already have more personal resources than they might at first appreciate. We imagine that the musically illiterate priest is every bit as unusual as the "soulless" musician. It is the common knowledge or language between the pastor and the musician that establishes the basis for collaboration that should and can grow and develop.

For over twenty years, Stephen has taught collaboration at the University of Michigan in two very similar courses: Digital Music Ensemble and Dance and Related Arts. In each class, students from varied disciplines including dance, theater, music, and engineering gather to learn the art of collaboration. They are required to have extensive dialogue, usually based on a theme culled from the spiritual or mythological world, like "Garden," "Labyrinth," or "Chaos." This paradigm leads to an open and honest sharing of viewpoints, and gives students a chance to talk and listen, give and take, creating an atmosphere of trust as well as intellectual pursuit. The readings, once completed and discussed, lead to art making that is honest, interesting, and usually excellent. This is collaboration.

What is *not* collaboration is a musician saying to a dancer, "I wrote this great string quartet! Dance to it!" Or a dancer saying to a musician, "I need 400 bars of 6/8 time while I dance. Will you write something?" Such an approach assumes the superiority of one person over the other. It doesn't honor art that is about something other than self, or take into account, simply speaking, that two heads are better than one. Merce Cunningham and **John Cage** formed a brilliant collaboration, spending countless hours whittling away on the dance (Cunningham) or the music (Cage) and trusting each other so much that they would combine the music and the dance literally on the night of the performance. The results were magical, and at the core of the process was *trust.*

Liturgical planners who are unprepared with at least some knowledge and appreciation of *both* music and theology, as well as a commitment born of trust, will find mutual frustration in their leadership of impoverished, inchoate liturgy. The priest or pastor must trust the musician's abilities, truly. Equally important and necessary is the minister's trust of the musician's theological perspective and spiritual life, assets that the church musician must, of course, possess (see Chapter Ten: Church Musician—Gig or Calling?).

## The Planning Meeting

Collaborative liturgical planning is a process of developing a relationship with God and with scripture. Readings for the service should be studied and digested in advance. Time in the planning meetings should be allotted for the decompression of each person's views and feelings about the readings, followed by an open and freewheeling discussion of possible liturgical outcomes.

The two of us meet once a week during the academic year for about one hour to ninety minutes per session. Often we will invite others such as our student intern or other students who are interested in liturgy. If there are to be guest preachers on given Sundays their presence is necessary and helpful. Here is our own outline. Yours might be different, of course.

Greetings and the Making of Tea (10–15 minutes)
Discussion of the Lectionary—Train Wreck! (30–45 minutes)
Constructing the Service—Trusting One Another! (20–30 minutes)

## Greetings and the Making of Tea

The "greeting" is essential to the work of building trust and collaboration *and* to the work of planning liturgy that grows out of the context of the community. In our case, it involves the sharing of tea and the asking of questions. I certainly know that the other planners care about my opinions concerning liturgy if they care about the mole problem in my back yard or the fact that my grandchild just learned to roll over. This is relationship building through caring, loving, and respecting each other. During the greeting portion, we take time to discuss our personal lives and our spiritual lives. Are we elated? angry? tired? in love? worried?

During this time we also discover whether there are issues or feelings about the ministry or the congregation that need to be discussed. It is important both to engage in appropriate discussion of the genuine issues facing the congregation individually and collectively, *and* also to remember that the purpose of the meeting is planning liturgy, not solving all of the community's pastoral problems. Nevertheless, through this discussion, we often find that it is appropriate and necessary to plan a liturgy that specifically addresses community pastoral issues.

For example, at the beginning or end of an academic year, we are likely to make "purpose" or "calling" a theme of the service in order to provide a frame and an inspiration for our students. Another frequent example in our context is the need to address the anxiety of students near the end of the semester, which is a good opportunity to emphasize themes of healing and self-care.

In a parish or congregational context, it might be necessary to respond to the community's economic concerns. Nowadays in Michigan, for example, two deeply interrelated issues are the household budgets of church members and the stewardship of the church. As another example, it might take several services to address the death of a child in the community, starting from the aspect of grief and loss of meaning through a long process of understanding, recovery, and healing.

Note that this kind of responsive, contextual planning calls upon the musician to be pastorally involved with the community. Trust and confidence between pastor and musician is thus not merely helpful in planning liturgy, but of vital importance to the spiritual health and safety of the community. As professionals, both priest and musician should be schooled in matters of confidentiality, principles of pastoral care, and appropriate sexual conduct. Both must be sensitive to the possible confidential nature of pastoral issues within the community and they must be even more sensitive if others are present in the liturgical planning meeting.

That said, consider that the church musician works closely with the folks who may be the most involved group in the church, to wit, the choir or choirs. If you have a youth choir, the musician is a youth worker. Think about it! The members of the choir meet every week for hours at a time. They are more involved in the church than the vestry or the governing board who meet with you only once a month. If as a pastor you are not asking your music director how folks are doing—or worse yet, if your music director is not telling you about pastoral issues arising in the choir—you are missing some truly essential information!

## Discussion of the Lectionary

At Canterbury House before the beginning of each semester, Reid prepares a list of saints and associated readings for the whole term, that is, for about fifteen Sunday services. This too, by the way, is a collaborative process: Stephen often suggests favorite saints. Stephen also has a big bag of music that he really, really likes. You can find a list of all of this music organized by themes in Appendix B: Musical Resources for Liturgy. When we get together for a weekly meeting, both of us will have read at least the biography of the saint in question from *Lesser Feasts and Fasts (LFF)*, as well as any additional material that we might have at hand, together with the associated scripture readings.

The discussion of the lectionary will take different forms for different people. In our Episcopal congregation, our scripture selections are guided by the *LFF* for the reasons discussed in Chapter One, or, less often, by the Revised Common Lectionary. Whatever structure or method the liturgical planners are using to select scripture for a given service, it is important to come to the planning meeting well prepared.

After greetings and tea, either despite or because of any advance preparation we have done, we tend to blindly leap into a kind of "I loved *X!*" or "I can't stand it when Paul says *Y!*" or "Why in the world is *Z* a saint?!" dialogue. We jump into the stuff of scripture that we resonate with, or that triggers memories or stories. We don't spend the initial moments searching for a theme or a cohesive relationship between the readings—often we can't find one! Rather, we let the spirit, the Holy Spirit, guide us in our reactions to the text.

Your own preparation and discussion might be more or less formal, of course, depending on your own context, planning cycle, and mutual personal style. If a community's liturgy is more "formal" because its context is a large parish or cathedral, for example, then the planning cycle may need to be longer. Responsive, contextual liturgy is possible even in a very large church, but only if the planning team, large or small, commits to working together.

We realize that most music directors in parish churches must plan choral music far in advance of the service. We know from experience that priests tend to be reluctant or even incapable of deciding on sermon topics four to six weeks in advance. The necessity of a long planning cycle can contribute to a disconnect between musician and clergy, as well as between the lectionary readings and the other content of the service.

One approach to the longer planning cycle might be for a musician to read the lectionary, develop her own perspective on the reading, and choose an anthem that jibes with her interpretation. In this, the minister must support the musician by providing the readings in advance, or living with the lectionary they are consulting! The musician is invited in this process to imagine herself as a preacher: What would the essence of *your* sermon be? What story from life would *you* tell? How would you express that story in choral music? This assumes that the minister is comfortable with you expressing your theological and spiritual observations in the liturgy. It also requires, of course, that you are willing to be prayerful and reflective. This creates a kind of mutual vulnerability and responsibility between priest and musician.

It behooves the priest to develop a genuine appreciation for how truly difficult it is to prepare and perform choral music well. Visiting a rehearsal or two (and sitting in the back or singing) will dissipate the illusion that it is easy to simply "dial in" an appropriate anthem based on a theological whim.

If the priest and the musician have both looked some weeks ahead at themes and ideas for a given service, they will find, in the planning meeting, that they have differences of interpretation (text, pastoral necessity, music, and so on). Our assumption is that an honest mutual investigation and discussion of the texts for a given service will nevertheless result in a cogent and comprehensible liturgy.

## The Train Wreck!

We often find that much time and creative energy is helpfully expended on what we have come to refer to as "the train wreck." We once met to discuss a mid-January service for the commemoration of St. Hilary of Poitiers. In preparation, Reid had noted mainly that Hilary was a didactic, orthodox, Trinitarian theologian. Stephen was excited about Hilary's work to fight slavery—in the fourth century no less. Reid came to the planning meeting in some dread at having to preach a sermon on the Trinity, which is not a topic of deep interest to college-age students. Stephen came to the meeting with a passel of exciting music about liberation, including barn-burning spirituals such as "O Freedom!," "Down by the Riverside," and "Didn' My Lord Deliver Daniel." Realizing the huge divide between our respective interpretations, Stephen was crestfallen at the prospect of having to discard his careful and heartfelt planning for this meeting as well as the awareness that the service was going to be quite different than he had anticipated. Equally difficult for both of us was the realization that we were moving away from music that we both really liked; therefore, we had to work through some considerable discouragement, frustration, and confusion.

Out of this train wreck, however, came a beautiful and surprising result. In the tea and gathering time at the beginning of the meeting, we had discussed our mutual surprise at the unusual level of anxiety among the students so early in the semester. In our lectionary discussion, after a lot of heady theological conversation about the Trinity and the dynamic relationship within the Trinity as necessary to and symbolic of human healing, we returned to the topic of the students' anxiety, and began to cobble a coherent liturgy from these disparate elements. What we ended up with was a service that brought together the Trinity, liberation, and healing. Ironically, much of the music that Stephen had initially chosen was perfectly appropriate for the theme as it evolved. Reid was also inspired to preach about the Trinity in a fresh and dynamic way that was as pastoral as it was theologically compelling. In other words, the resulting service did not feel to either of us like a compromise. Rather, it felt like a newly conceived interpretation, fostered by our collaboration.

We find that our planning includes this "train wreck" phase more often than not. This is perhaps to be expected when everyone comes to the liturgy planning session fully prepared with a conception of how the liturgy might look. We suspect that this is one of the reasons that priests and musicians *avoid* planning collaboratively in just this way. Our commitment to the mutuality of the process, however, has taught us to like and respect each other a good deal, and to trust the Spirit to guide the end result. Both of us invariably wind up being happier with the result than we had any right to expect. The result of collaborative effort is better music, better sermons, better liturgy!

Our planning meetings might be considered a less reverent version of the practice of *lectio divina*, the Benedictine method of reading the text three times, listening to the words out loud and in silence, and letting each reading take us deeper into the truth contained therein. The result of *lectio divina* is often deeply transformational, and gathers the listeners/readers around scripture like equal spokes on a wheel, all supporting and depending on the hub. Notice, too, that each person is being heard in this process and that only the Holy Spirit is really in charge of the meeting. No one works for anyone else, and no one is "hired/employed" or, in a certain sense, even "working."

We should say that often our discussions are noisy, disorganized, and bawdy, filled with rants, guffaws, and raucous stories of saints, dogs, and miscreants! In no way should there be a specified tone to the lectionary discussion. It would ruin the spontaneity of the process and lead to an expected and predictable result. Many times we will weep with resonance over scripture or an especially appropriate musical selection. Just as often we will rail against the historical misuse of one passage or another to alienate others, take lives, steal from the poor, or imprison the weak.

## Constructing the Service—Trusting One Another!

Constructing the service can come smoothly out of the lectionary discussion. Often, specific musical choices, readings, or prayers will occur to the planners during the lectionary discussion. Say them, and move on. It's crucial to keep the parts of the meeting separate. Getting sidetracked too soon with a discussion of specific musical choices can bog the process down. What is needed here is a real sharing of deep spiritual inquiry. Once a clear theme is established jointly, the music, prayers, and supplemental readings will follow, usually with great ease. It is only at this point that the pragmatic necessity of the meeting should take over. Now someone should take notes, and the actual writing of the liturgy should occur.

This is the part in the relationship between liturgical planners that requires the most trust. When a musician spouts off three hymns that "must be done" this Sunday, the priest or pastor is left twisting in the wind, being robbed of their agency in the process. Equally, the musician could be told, at this point, that the service will be about "reconciliation," or "social justice," and that the music must bend to this agenda. Such rigid approaches disassociate the collaborators and break the bond of trust.

Take turns. Voice ideas for the elements of the liturgy that must be decided upon, and see how the planners feel about them. What is the litmus test? Simply this: do these elements jibe with the discussion of the lectionary that the group just had? This clearly is no time to insist "our choir has been rehearsing the Haydn for three weeks, and we're ready this Sunday!" This is equally no time for a priest to say, "I simply hate that tune." While that might be an honest admission, the spirit of collaboration is to trust that two or more heads (plus one Spirit, at least) are better than one.

Trust means that all the planners have a voice that is heard in the attitude of respect. Trust also means that sometimes someone has to let the other person "be right." If the musician picks every piece of music, and the priest guides every sermon topic, the process is skewed, over-entrenched, and defensive. Collaboration means that everyone shares in the work of the people (again, the literal definition of liturgy), and that the Spirit guides them all. Collaboration assumes that all members of the liturgical team truly believe that the Spirit of God is in each and every member of the team. If we fail to honor these basic tenets, we are falling short of the potential God is calling us toward.

Ultimately, this process can lead to a deep spiritual relationship between and among the liturgy planning team. For years Stephen has been asked by church musicians, "What do you do if you just don't get along with your priest/pastor?" He always says the same things: "How much time do you spend with them? Have you gone bowling or canoeing with them? Have you read the books they find interesting? Have they read yours?" Liturgical planning lives and dies based on the relationships between the members of the planning team. The planning meeting itself should not be the only interaction between the planners. Make time for social engagement, fun, and decompression. In the end, make time.

We do not insist that you become intimate friends with everyone on your worship team. It does sometimes happen that liturgical planners can develop a relationship of inappropriate intensity. In such a case, it is helpful to recall the wisdom of Kurt Vonnegut: "Perhaps we need a little more respect and a little less love."

# Chapter 5

## Diversity and Context

### Why do we want or need diverse, contextually sensitive liturgies?

Liturgical custom in the United States is every bit as varied as the congregations who engage in it. Certainly, it is subject to and driven by those cultural forces and theological controversies that have roiled (or energized) every mainline protestant denomination in the country; and, of course, the Roman Catholic Church and the various orthodox denominations have not been unaffected. A comprehensive examination of contemporary liturgical practices is well beyond the scope of this book. Suffice it to say that in every denomination, indeed in every congregation, there exists some tension among competing values of order in worship, respect for tradition, responsiveness to the pastoral concerns of the community, and connectedness to God and to one another.

Many liturgical planners from the baby boomer generation and younger have grown up in a culture that has moved strongly in the direction of human and civil rights, and are reacting to sexist, racist, and homophobic language in liturgies, such as the exclusive use of the words "He/Him," "Lord," and "Father" for God, the exclusive characterization of the relationship between God and Christ as "Father" and "Son," the imperialism and triumphalism implicit in such phrases as "put all things in subjection under your Christ," and the sexism and homophobia that taints most marriage liturgies.

Patricia Lynn Reilly expresses the disjunction our generation experienced in its religious and liturgical education: "Rather than employ a variety of names to more effectively illustrate the mystery of God, the teachers and preachers of our childhood always used the male pronoun. Their words contradicted the lessons they taught us. Religion had given God a man's name while claiming that God was beyond naming, that 'he' was a mystery."[4]

The civil rights movement has seen much development in the past fifty years; feminism has wrought considerable changes in our language and thinking in the past thirty-five years or so. Liturgists and church musicians are responding to these changes. In denominations with a strong liturgical heritage, such as the Episcopalians, the Lutherans, and the Methodists, many changes in language and music have begun to appear. These traditions have made considerable progress in revising gender specific references to God, offering alternative descriptions of sin and redemption, and responding to contemporary pastoral issues. Priests, pastors, liturgists, musicians, and the congregations they lead are experimenting with liturgy at the local level.

Similarly, musicians and liturgists have recognized not only that the language of our hymns can be very off-putting, but also that the way a given hymn is received, written, transcribed, edited, and performed can be highly problematic. The need for greater diversity and sensitivity (as well as the

4 *A God Who Looks Like Me* (New York: Ballantine, 1995), 53.

inclusion of more up-to-date music) has brought many new resources, such as *The Faith We Sing* from the Methodist Church, the Christian Reformed *Psalter Hymnal*, and *Lead Me, Guide Me: The African American Catholic Hymnal*. The hymnal portion of the newest *Evangelical Lutheran Worship* book, popularly called "the cranberry book," is a particularly good effort. Among Episcopal sources, we especially like *Wonder, Love, and Praise.*

## The Aesthetics of Zacchaeus

Zacchaeus (Luke 19:1–10) was an unheard, unwanted, barely tall enough seeker. If his "song" were to be heard, it would be in a key foreign to our own, strange to our ears, accompanied by an unfamiliar instrument. Christ's approach to ministry was to place a particular emphasis on the Zacchaeus types, and to spend an inordinate amount of time alienating the administration. If our liturgies were filled with music of the Zacchaeus aesthetic, what would they sound like? What would Zacchaeus's poetry be like? Surely, hymns for the desperate, music for the seekers. If we believe that the poor and the meek are blessed, let's listen to *their* song. Music from India, El Salvador, and Ethiopia can shed light on the Christian ministry in a direct way, pointing us quickly to places in our lives and in our world culture where the work of Christ can be heard and expressed through music. This is an aesthetic that should, perhaps must, be pursued even if every single person within a hundred miles of your church building is white and middle-aged. At a certain level, our context is America—the whole hemisphere. It's all *terra nova* all the time: our mission field is filled with indigenous people, with Africans, Irish and Polish immigrants and their descendants, Meung and Afghan refugees, and "saints from every tribe and language and people and nation" (Revelation 5:9). Our obligation to this context is to respond.

## Radical Messages, Traditional Music—Defusing the Battle

The core of what we perceive as the traditional Christian message has remained the same through time: "You shall love the Lord your God with all your heart, and with all your soul, and with all your mind. . . . You shall love your neighbor as yourself" (Matthew 22:37, 39). It's the second great commandment, by the way, that *necessitates* constant liturgical change and revision. With the advent of the airplane, television, and the internet, we live on a much smaller planet, are more in contact with the entire world, and are less likely to simply overlook entire cultures based on a lack of a personal encounter. Our grandparents and even our parents lived in a culture where it was possible never to encounter or befriend people outside their own religious or personal ethnic tradition. In our time, however, it is likely that we will encounter Hindus, Muslims, and Buddhists on a regular basis, and may count these people as close friends. Some of them may even belong to our congregations. We cannot expect our liturgies to continue using the same content in this newly hued present. This new personal encounter with the entirety of the world's population requires a retooling of the Gospel message. Old messages of missionary or "great commission" colonialism are inappropriate. Sin-dominated or patriarchal hymnody causes us to shudder.

We recently had an experience of singing "Faith of Our Fathers" at a church we visited. We're sorry to have to say that it was quite painful. It is not without reason that hymnal editors frequently alter the words of this text. The title of the hymn is suffused with patriarchal ownership; the text, with the forcible dissemination of the faith. To the modern ear the text implies that women should listen to men for their faith-shaping, meekly accepting men as their intellectual and spiritual betters. Worse still is the blatant colonialism of the hymn, so contrary to Christ's message of love. We are frankly suspicious of the sort of faith and prayer that "shall win all nations unto thee." We doubt that we are the exclusive possessors of "the truth that comes from God." We candidly fear the imperialist and patriarchal sentiment of this hymn that lies behind its culminating line: "Faith of our fathers, holy faith! We will be true to thee till death." This feels to us like a song to be sung going into war, going into battle, going into a dangerous foreign territory where "victory through Christ" means both land ownership and some kind of coerced confession of faith. How can we, in good conscience, sing songs like this in light of imperialistic and colonialist adventurism in Iraq, Honduras, and Somalia? The two of us can perhaps imagine a context in which we might be willing to use "Faith of Our Fathers" in a liturgy at Canterbury House; but as a practical matter, unless we wanted to spend a long time in a sermon critiquing or contradicting what had been said in this hymn, we'd consider it better to simply leave it behind.

It is worth the time needed to scour our hymnbooks for hymns that still tell the Good News, without pummeling conscience or intelligence into the dust. Of course, they exist, and are even plentiful. "Amazing Grace" will always be there. "Rock of Ages" is a very good hymn that stands the test of time, with its affirmation of an eternal God who is, as the psalms often tell us, a shelter within our own existential hells. We are not calling to throw the baby out with the bathwater, but for a heightened sensitivity: a new, updated habit of care and awareness to replace the practice of selecting hymns haphazardly. A hymn's presence in the hymnal is no guarantee of its decency, appropriateness, or musical quality. Our argument is simply that liturgical planners should not use *any* hymn or music in a worship service without thinking about it. The same is true of the texts of prayers and sermons.

The same is true also of readings, both from scripture and other sources. Our scripture readings are often taken from lectionaries that may present us with significant challenges: how *does* one talk about the parable of the talents? (Matthew 25:14–29). With scripture, for the most part, we contend with what we are given. The responsibility of the preacher especially, but also of all of the liturgists, is to think through what the scripture is saying to our community, in this time, in this place, in this context. Remember that often the most important thing to consider in a lectionary is *what is left out.* In the Episcopal lectionary, the story of the slaughter of the innocents (Matthew 2:16–18) was never read at a principal Sunday service, but the Episcopal Church has corrected this omission by adopting the Revised Common Lectionary. Even the RCL omits Psalm 109 (admittedly a dreadful little hymn to revenge) from the cycle altogether. Challenging sermons can be constructed around the discussion of what has been expunged and why.

As we have said previously, at Canterbury House we have the advantage of working in a community that has a diverse population in the first place (though we always wish it were yet more so), and is not resistant to change and experimentation in the second. We do know, however, that we could easily drive away any given segment of our congregation by employing liturgical language and music of a specific cast. The converse is true. Any liturgist *can* make the liturgy of the community more welcoming. For example, Richard Fabian and Donald Schell, founders of St. Gregory's of Nyssa in San Francisco, have made clear that their first ethic in constructing liturgy is to make it as welcoming as possible. We, too, consider this the primary and continuing work of the liturgy planning team.

## Building Diversity in Your Congregation—Liturgical Change

A useful way for any practitioner of liturgy to think about the need for liturgical revision is to think about who is *not* in your congregation. Your denomination may or may not be debating its liturgical language and practices on the macro level; but at the local level you may find that your congregation is monochromatic, or missing young people, Spanish-speaking people, women under the age of fifty, gay or lesbian people, or college students. Then you *and your congregation* have to ask yourselves whether you actually *want* them there? Be honest! It may well be that resistance to liturgical change in a congregation is representing a resistance to diversity and inclusiveness in general.

If your congregation lacks diversity and you wish to build it, then radical changes in your approach to liturgy may be needed. Who in your congregation as it is presently configured will not like this? Why not? What teaching may need to take place in order to overcome their fear and discomfort? Are you willing to lose them altogether?

If you conclude that making your liturgy more contemporary, more inclusive, and more responsive is desirable, then it's useful to visit other congregations. We would recommend that you go to different church services. Get out of your own tradition. If you have never done so, go to a variety of churches, temples, synagogues, and mosques. See who is there. See who is *not* there. Think about why.

Finally, accept that not every liturgy is going to appeal to every seeker. This is an inherent, perhaps ironic tension that you will encounter in the endeavor to make your liturgy welcoming. After all, the purpose of attracting people to your congregation is to teach them difficult, challenging, counterintuitive things. We've had to get used to this at Canterbury House as well. Our space, small and intimate, demands a liturgy that is "in-your-face." All of the members of the congregation, new visitors included, must participate because there is simply no place to hide. We are sure we've lost prospective congregants because of this. The point is, know who you are, know who your congregation is, know your mission field, and know what type of worship you are working toward. Especially, get as much knowledge as you can about what the alternatives might be.

If you do not think you have gifts for writing liturgy, or if you are not in a place where actual experimental liturgy is encouraged, there are still very many resources for contextual liturgy that you do not have to invent whole cloth. They have been tried in community, examined by committees and commissions on liturgy and music, and approved by bishops. The Episcopal Church, for example, has recently published *Lesser Feasts and Fasts 2006,* the *Enriching Our Worship* series, and *Changes: Prayers and Services Honoring Rites of Passage* (available from www.churchpublishing.org). Consider the resources available to you from your own denomination and from others. If you need the permission of ecclesiastical superiors to broaden your liturgical scope, ask for it. In any event, you and your congregation will benefit from your broadest possible knowledge of contemporary liturgies and practices from many communities and cultures.

# Chapter 6

## Liturgical Space Is Part of Your Context

Each year Canterbury House observes the Eve of All Saints, using the "Service for All Hallows' Eve" from the *Book of Occasional Services.* We do this in a particularly gloomy graveyard located close to the University of Michigan. Each year I check on the internet to see what time sunset is going to be on that day, and set the time for the service accordingly. Why do this? At sunset the large flock of crows that lives near this cemetery takes wing to the west almost directly overhead. You can't *buy* the effect of having crows fly across a darkening sky at the very moment you are preaching about death and resurrection!

Whenever I am planning a liturgy that is at all out of the ordinary, either because it is for a special occasion such as Easter or the bishop's visitation, or because it requires the congregation to move from place to place such as Palm Sunday, or because it will be in a different space, as when the Jazz Mass goes on the road, I try to go stand in the space where the liturgy is to happen and imagine to myself every movement, every word, and every sound.

The location—the space—in which you are doing a given service is part of your context. It is useful and necessary to think systematically about your space. Is it large or small? Is the ceiling low or high? Does the congregation sit close together, or are they spread apart? Is the seating fixed or moveable? Are there places where visitors will be tempted (or invited) to hide? Are the participants able to see one another, or are they oriented in a single direction? Are the acoustics "live" or muffled? All of these things will certainly affect the singing of the congregation. It isn't only about singing though; it's also about light and mood and color and movement within the space. Is the lighting bright or subdued? Might the lighting and the sound be altered artificially, and if so, is this desirable for a specific liturgical effect? What do the windows look like? What is on the walls? What are the sight lines?

The worship space at Canterbury House is a 14 x 40–foot room with large clear windows and white walls that can be left blank or decorated in a gallery style. The eight-foot ceiling is quite low for a worship space. The room is bisected by support pillars that block the sight lines from almost any perspective. Fortunately, the seating and the altar are moveable. Though the space is small, the acoustics are lively and the reverberation time is very short. When the space is filled up with people (this is not hard to do!), the acoustics become somewhat muffled, but it remains a "live" room. This is neither desirable nor undesirable. It just *is*.

In this space we do Jazz Masses and Taizé services, as well as Solemn Evensong complete with incense and bells. The seating, the placement of musicians, the lighting, and the mood are different for each of these types of service. Generally, worship at Canterbury House is demanding because there is simply no place to hide, sonically or physically. In this space it is best to move about while preaching so that everyone can see the preacher at some point. Under these circumstances the preaching is necessarily very intimate. The music has a great range of dynamic variation because loud playing at all times, even on acoustic instruments, would be simply overwhelming. Even though the space can be cramped, we encourage the congregation to move, to clap while singing, and to dance.

Is it impossible to do a Jazz Mass in a large, open cathedral? By no means! But several things might need to be adjusted. There are things we can do at Canterbury House that we would not attempt in a cathedral space. I would not stand on the floor of a cathedral full of people and attempt to preach. No one would be able to hear me, few would be able to see me (I am nearly as short as Zacchaeus), and the whole thing would be lost. Since I would have to preach from the pulpit in that situation it means, probably, that I would preach from a prepared text, even though I might prefer otherwise. A large cathedral space might (*might!*) be a difficult place to try to get the congregation to dance if, say, the pews are narrowly spaced and fixed to the floor. If, however, there are chairs that can be moved, then we'll certainly create some space to get people up and moving around.

Cathedral space does lend itself to rites of welcoming and of going forth that can and should be long, decorative, interesting, exuberant, dancelike. There *is* a difference between "reverence to the patriarch" in a procession, on the one hand, and welcoming everyone into the presence of God on the other. If the center aisle is the only place where there is enough room to dance, then the entrance and exit rites are good liturgical moments to do so. Go ahead and use the twenty-verse hymn with lots of improvised interludes. This is also the place for colorful flags and banners and balloons and streamers, and for an opportunity to get the kids involved. Of course, a cathedral space also lends itself very naturally to a solemn service, and offers much opportunity for choral and antiphonal music. No one loves candles and incense more than I. The point, again, is to plan the service around the occasion, the liturgical season, and the readings, to consider the theme and the mood you wish to convey, and to conduct the liturgy with coherence and integrity.

What about worship outdoors? Many churches avoid this. It is inconvenient and difficult to plan for the weather. People complain about their allergies, the sun, the insects, the grass stains. Nevertheless, if you have an outdoor space properly prepared with shade and with comfortable (natural) seating and a bit of shelter for musicians and their instruments, then a "spontaneous" decision to do a service outside can be amazing. Such spontaneity requires careful planning! At Canterbury House we plan particularly for the services of St. Francis's Day, All Hallows' Eve, and Palm Sunday to be outdoors.

On Palm Sunday, weather permitting of course, we have a long parade across the "diag" at the university. Clearly, we have to think about what instruments we can carry outdoors, and what music we can sing that does not require us to carry any paper. Last year we had a trombone, saxophone, fiddle, **djembe**, **dumbek**, and **agogo bells**. We sang in procession a "Klezmer Gloria" written by Stephen. Arriving in place, we sang "Ride on, King Jesus" *a cappella* in a Gospel shout style with an improvised harmony. Instruments for the All Hallows' Eve service can include an acoustic bass and some heavier drums, since the musicians can be in place ahead of time and the instruments do not have to be carried in a procession. Again, we select music that is familiar or uses short phrases that can be picked up quickly. We often encourage our congregation to sing *a cappella.* We refuse, however, to believe that we have better singers in our congregation than any other congregation. We *do* have good (by that we mean passionate) musical leaders. So do you.

Perhaps you are looking at a space that is "impossible." Stephen says that could be Canterbury House! Every liturgical space has advantages and disadvantages. It is necessary to know the space, think about it, and respond to it by appropriate planning. Here are some suggestions for responding to specific problems.

Cramped space: The advantage of a small space is that it encourages intimacy in worship. The disadvantage is, you would like a thousand people to enjoy this intimacy! Our solution to having a small space at Canterbury House has been to add more services. A small space is the setting to use the daily offices. There is much community to be had among ten people saying (or singing!) psalms together.

By the way, "singing" in this context can mean a lot of things. It might mean chanting on a monotone and breathing in unison. Monastic communities have done this from the earliest days of the Church, as an aid to memorization and as a way of praying together. For a wonderful discussion on singing Gregorian chant in liturgy, see Rembert Herbert's *Entrances: Gregorian Chant in Daily Life* (New York: Church Publishing, 1999).

Seating in a small space should be arranged so that everyone can see each other. Using simple music and lots of silence is helpful. It is good to build the musical repertory over time. Liturgical movement should be measured, avoiding a lot of popping up and down for prayers and readings. A conversational style of liturgy and preaching lends itself to small spaces.

Music in a small space can be particularly challenging if the space limits the number of people who can be present. Stephen insists that good congregational singing requires not less than thirty people. Scaling down from this may mean using a single instrumentalist (guitar, autoharp, fiddle, or flute) and using a lot of Taizé music, well-known hymns, and Southern Harmony tunes.

Bad sight lines: At Canterbury House, we deal with the problem of bad sight lines by shifting the focus of the liturgy often, particularly by moving the altar and the band from semester to semester so that reading, preaching, and making music occurs in several different positions in the room. In a larger space, it's good to try to take advantage of bad sight lines. They can create good places to hide—very welcoming to introverted newcomers. If you have immovable surfaces or objects that obstruct the view, use them to display icons, banners, and liturgical art.

Poor lighting: Poor lighting and bad acoustics both can be remedied technologically. Failing that, a dark space is a good place to start with a quiet and down mood, and then move into more exciting (familiar or easy) music: sing an African chant and move around. Challenge the darkness! Then get some light! Conversely, lighting that is too bright may discourage contemplation. In a sense, bright lighting is "too loud." Natural sunlight will seldom be too much. Artificial lighting can and should be adjusted as necessary. Full spectrum lighting with adjustable dimmers will certainly resolve most of your lighting problems.

Too much space: This can, in fact, be a considerable problem. When people walk into an open space they will either arrange themselves in isolation, if they do not know anyone, or into small groups of people who do know one another that psychologically exclude or discourage others from joining them. The result is a scattering of people in a large open space that operates against a sense of community and especially discourages singing. Stephen remembers a story that John Bell told in a workshop, of the time he came to lead worship at a church with a large space occupied by a small and scattered congregation. His solution was to rope off all of the seating except for a small section close to the musicians. By thus gently encouraging everyone to sit together, he strengthened all aspects of the worship—music, preaching, and corporate prayer—and found that as his congregation grew, it was necessary to open more of the seating each week.

An old theatre impresario trick with moveable seating is to set up slightly fewer chairs than the number of people expected, and to have ushers bring out extra seating as more people come. In this way, whether you have a few people or many, it appears that you have drawn a crowd. Use this idea sparingly and only for special services!

Seating in rows facing one direction should be avoided or reorganized wherever possible. Row seating, long used in churches, suggests that the congregation is to be the passive recipient of information, or to interact with a small group of "performers" rather than with one another. It is perhaps appropriate if you are presenting liturgy that is frankly a performance or a museum piece; but even a Palestrina motet is going to be more interesting if people are seeing and hearing it from many differing perspectives.

Give some thought about arranging the space and the seating for liturgy. Remember that your seating also sends a message. The message it sends implies a theology, and it may or may not be a theology that you intend. Look at the space carefully, and think about the liturgy you intend to conduct. Who will be standing where? What are their various roles in the service? How will people move through the space? What will latecomers see when they walk in?

We recently attended a service where the priest led most of the service from within the congregation. Perhaps the intention was to convey that all participants in the worship are equal before God—certainly a true principle. Unfortunately, the seating was arranged in a semicircle with an obvious center, occupied, only briefly and with obvious discomfort, by lay readers in turn for various readings and prayers, and by the priest herself for the Eucharistic Prayer. The effect was to create a focal point with an implied message that it was "not okay" to be in it! The liturgy was clunky and uncomfortable as a result of this poorly thought out arrangement and use of the space.

Liturgists must be prepared to lead, comfortably and confidently. Of course, one way for them to do so is by occupying a focal point in the space. Thinking ahead about whether there can or should be more than one such focal point, whether they should shift from time to time, whether they can be discovered in unexpected places or created in unexpected ways, or, if appropriate, whether they can be deconstructed altogether, will help your liturgy be coherent.

As for music in large, reverberating spaces, simply imagine that every note is like playing a piano with the sustain pedal duct-taped to the floor. Decay times are extended and the space fills with sound from the preceding several measures. Renaissance music, such as that of Josquin and Lassus, was written with this notion in mind: a kind of accumulation of sound that leads to a cosmic experience with a mystical text. Contemporary musicians such as Arvo Pärt and John Tavener have also used this approach in some of their music. Certainly, some of traditional hymnody and much of the medieval music found in hymnbooks is written specifically for such a space. Here is a place where context will dictate a good deal of your selection of music. Some Taizé music is adaptable to this principle. Drums, sadly, will just become muddied in a space such as this.

While modal music can be employed in a large space, chromatic music creates a problem. Chromaticism denies the presumed modality of the previous measures and allows the composer to move into new key areas. St. Thomas Church, Leipzig, where Bach played, is not a large space, and even Bach does not always translate well into a large cathedral setting. The English notion of cathedral was complemented by Gregorian chant or Elizabethan motet, decidedly modal and not usually chromatic. African chant is designed for outdoors, where decay times are essentially zero, rather than for large enclosed "lively" spaces.

The tradition of seating singers opposite one another in a choir evolved from the monastic practice of singing the offices together. Certainly, choir seating encouraged good singing among the monks! In the present, however, placing the choir up and away from the congregation encourages an objective and observation-based liturgy, rather than a participatory liturgy. Placing the good singers down with the congregation, or within it, encourages a solidarity and inclusiveness that will result in better corporate singing and more of a sense of community. If your church is having a problem getting people to sing, you may want to consider the ill effect of separating the best singers from the others, Sunday after Sunday.

In many older churches, the organ is situated away in the back, in an organ loft. The acoustic purpose for this is to allow sound to flow through the church, placing the organist close to the source of the sound so as not to have to adjust timing according to the reverberation of the organ's sound. However, the hidden musician creates a liturgical problem: If the congregation cannot see the musician(s), they must guess at the musical cues. Contrast this with an orchestra concert of the Classical period, where the pianist (Haydn or Mozart, for example) played the continuo part in front of the orchestra, keeping the band in sync and leading through difficult passages. Having musicians hidden off in a balcony away from the congregation is the equivalent of having an orchestra with no conductor. Chaos, or disenfranchisement, will ensue.

A few solutions come to mind. At Saint-Trinité, Messiaen played preludes, voluntaries, offertories, and postludes from the balcony, letting that gorgeous instrument pour forth all its glory. For congregational singing, there was another organ up front—smaller, so as not to drown out the congregation—along with a conductor to lead the singing.

The musicians at Taizé are hidden, but the musical forms are completely different, and one could even say static. There is no need for dramatic cues between verses, or tricky antiphon/verse problems to solve. The music flows evenly. The only cues needed at Taizé are when to start and when to stop. The congregation joins in singing when they feel comfortable after hearing several bars, and they stop when the musicians slow the accompaniment, just a couple of bars from the end.

Many contemporary churches situate the musicians up front, and the choir is facing the congregation. This is the same way any professional choir gives a concert. We were laughing together recently about the notion of a professional choir lining up in two huge lines, singing while facing each other instead of the audience! Having the choir face the congregation has the advantage of allowing the congregation to see and hear everything very clearly. The choir and congregation can easily sing together. The emotion and the performance of the music are inclusive rather than exclusive or worse, private. The disadvantage to this approach is that it can encourage a "TV aesthetic" complete with a roaming minister with wireless mic, a band up on a podium, and perhaps even jiving and joking between the music director and the minister. This should, of course, be discouraged. Again, the tendency with placing all of the liturgical leaders at the front, facing a congregation seated in rows, is to turn the liturgy (the work of the people) into a performance (the work of certain, more talented people).

We are of the opinion that a U-shaped arrangement of seating, with musicians at the base and the altar at the open end, generally provides the best flow for a Eucharistic service. Sermon and Eucharist can come from the open area, with the musicians situated at the other end as a kind of energy-complement. This also places the musicians as part of the congregation. In general, we use this arrangement at Canterbury House. Readers and leaders of corporate prayer are appointed from the congregation, and read or pray "in place." In this way, the liturgy flows coherently: The focus of the liturgy shifts through the room without losing energy, leadership roles are shared without confusion, and everyone can hear each other sing.

# Chapter 7

## The Theology of Singing and an Exploration of Style

We have argued in favor of diversity and excellence in liturgy. Diversity and excellence in liturgical music takes training for the musicians and for the congregation as well. Diversity should come from an appreciation of scripture, a deep understanding of the lectionary readings, and a wide breadth of musical knowledge. Only with this combination can a musician, priest, or liturgy planning committee select the most appropriate music to accompany, complement, and enhance the liturgy.

It is too often assumed that we have to dumb down the music because the congregation "can't sing." In fact, however, the more limited a congregation's musical vocabulary, the more limited the expression of the glory of God—and this is not the fault of the congregation! The music director's responsibility is to call forth excellence not only from herself but from the congregation as well. We are teaching the congregation not only about God's grace and glory; we are teaching them also to articulate God's grace and glory through musical expression.

Even more basic than this, the church musician may have to teach a congregation that they *do* want to sing. This is done by letting them enjoy singing in the first place. Many people have never had the opportunity to *enjoy* singing either in church or in the home. What a pity! In the opinion of these writers *every* human being is created by God to be an artist, a musician, and a dancer.

I have found four basic styles of singing to be useful in what I do as a music director in a church: Gospel singing, Pub singing, Taizé chant, and Traditional Hymn singing. Each is based on a highly specific style of music, as well as a style of singing. In every case I have found that congregations need to be trained in order to sing these styles well, and that the process of training them honors their inner artist. It is certainly worth spending the time at the beginning of a service to rehearse new music and to help the congregation gain familiarity with and excellence in singing these styles.

### Gospel Singing

This is music from the United States, deeply rooted in African singing. It is usually quite physical, and demands volume combined with dancing and clapping. It is a fully visceral music. To separate music and dance in African music is to misunderstand the aesthetic of the culture entirely. The rhythm of the music is usually a combination of 12/8 and 4/4, resulting in a kind of "three-against-two" time feel. Harmonies that avoid chord extensions or chord substitutions deflate the beauty and color in this music. Musicians should take great care to investigate these issues before imposing their way of playing and singing on a novice congregation (the same could be said of all the styles discussed here). In other words, in order to teach a congregation how to sing in this style, you have to know something about it yourself. Check out a good Gospel choir. If you are close to any big city in the United States, you are near at least one and probably several.

The four-part harmony settings found in most hymnals are a reflection of a Scandinavian or Germanic style of singing, but not necessarily of an African-American style of singing. It is certainly not the style of instrumental playing found in most black churches or even in the white Baptist churches of my own childhood. Consequently, the task of the accompanist is to improvise a free texture around the harmonies implied by the four-voice notation in the hymnbook. In a word, most hymn arrangements are in vocal notation rather than keyboard notation.

Broken chords, thickening of texture, and inclusion of passing tones (either triplet or eighth note) are all part of the improviser's arsenal in accompanying this style. All of this is in service of a broad dynamic range.

Consider the hymn "Spirit of God, descend upon my heart."

Words: George Croly (1780-1860)
Music: Frederick C. Atkinson (1841-1897)

"Spirit of God" is not a particularly "black" Gospel hymn. The tune "Morecambe" was written in 1870 by Frederick C. Atkinson, an English church organist. Nevertheless, it has enjoyed such popularity in black churches that now it particularly grates on the ear if played "square," that is, precisely according to hymnbook notation. Here is a different way of thinking about this wonderful hymn:

I improvised this version of the piece, recorded it, and then transcribed it. There is no attempt to "compose an improvisation" on this piece. It is an honest improvisation with (I think) characteristics of good gospel improvisation.

As discussed above, the music found in hymnals are templates; these templates assume the reader has an understanding and familiarity with the tradition out of which the hymn evolves. Remember, there are no tempo markings, pedal indications, dynamics, articulations, or passing tones/nonharmonic tones. This certainly doesn't imply that one should avoid fundamental aspects of musical interpretation. Still less does it give the musician permission to play the music verbatim, hoping that it will be "good enough." What is written, usually, is a vocal part. There are some exceptions to this in contemporary hymnals. Usually, hymns are published with an SATB choir sound in mind, and this hymn is no exception.

Now, then, how do we interpret this pearl? First, notice the tempo and the dynamics. Quarter = 80 is slow, right? Wrong. The harmonic rhythm of this piece starts at the half note, giving the impression of a slow piece. By measure three, though, the harmonic rhythm speeds to the quarter note. What's the message? Waiting, listening for the Holy Spirit, then experiencing Her arrival (this quickening is underscored with the great phrase, "descend upon my heart"). Start *piano* since quietness is usually our attitude in prayer. Would we start a prayer, pleading for the Spirit of God, by shouting at God in full voice, "HEY, ARE YOU UP THERE?" That is really not what this song is about. So we are fast enough and at the right dynamic range. Notice that the first two bars are exactly the same as the hymnal version, except that they are specific in terms of tempo and dynamic.

We now turn to the somewhat tricky issue of voicing. The original, remember, is a vocal setting so it doesn't reinforce the bass by using the lower octave. My m.3-4 leaps down an octave. That also increases the dynamic, along with the thickening of the texture in the right hand. Measure four introduces a subdivision for the first time in the improvisation: a triplet. Why a triplet? Because the rhythmic basis for all African music is 12/8, or 4 against 3. Get a CD of Ghanaian chant, and you will hear it almost immediately—a 6/8 groove that sounds like 3/4, then 6/8, and back again, or all at the same time. Notice, too, that the next bar (m.4) uses constant eighth notes. Using triplets against eighths would be too complex for this simple hymn, but the implication of that flux should always be there. (I say flux rather than conflict because conflict implies a problem; there is nothing "wrong" or "exotic" about 3 against 2. It's simply African.)

Now notice the increased density, mostly through arpeggiation, in m.3 and m.4. The chords are thicker, and every eighth-note value is articulated with the exception of the triplet figure in bar 5 (again, 2 against 3 in a linear way). The syncopated stasis in the left hand (m.7–8) increases tension and dynamic, introduces a subtle almost boogie-woogie or blueslike rhythm, and predicts the great pedal point in this hymn in m.9–12. Jumping down yet another octave in m.9 further increases the tension and dynamic, as does the static right hand part. Measures 11–12 use every right-hand finger possible to increase the dynamic to maximum range, while the left hand continues the blues like throbbing in the lowest bass possible. I use a chromatic passing tone on beat 4 of m.12. Note that this will conflict with anyone singing the soprano voice (most of the congregation). That's okay! Dissonance demands resolution, and there is nothing more resolute than the arrival of the Holy Spirit into our hearts. The whole piece is about pleading for some peace. Not a "prophet ecstasy" or "ecstatic vision"—just a little peace. This is why the last line of the piece should be a cathartic triple-forte, *quickly* melting down to *piano* (or *pianissimo*, why not exaggerate!) at the end of the piece. Notice that the loudest chord of the piece also uses the highest note in this setting, a trick seen in most mid-nineteenth-century Romantic piano music (see Chopin's *Nocturne in E♭*, for instance).

The warm and low setting of the ending of the piece implies the presence of the Holy Spirit ("burning flame"), and simplifies the rhythm, taking it back to the half-note harmonic rhythm of the beginning. Don't "sit on" the last bar, though. There are three more verses to come!

About the harmony, there is no question that there could be an entire book about chord extensions in Gospel music. I will just point out a few instances in my improvisation above that may help the reader to explore harmonic possibilities a bit more. Notice in m.3 the use of the sevenths on beats 3 and 4. Just as important is the voicing in the right hand—open voicing, not clunky parallel sevenths. This is not Debussy! See m.7, beat 3, where the passing tone in the alto voice is a ninth. Often we can use ninths, elevenths, and thirteenths without really thinking about it, as passing tones. If Bach chorales were taught in such a way as to identify passing tones or nonharmonic tones as chord extensions, we wouldn't think of these chords as quite so exotic. It is too bad that these things intimidate us. We need not be afraid!

Measure 10 uses the most "Jazzy" harmony in this improvisation, a quartal voicing of the G7 chord. Some would choose to analyze this as a Gsus4 chord. It makes no difference, the C and F anchor in the alto voice helps to increase tension and dynamic here. They also predict the tension, using the same chord, in m.12, leading to the climax of the piece. Notice the dangerous D# in m.12. This is an augmented chord. A perusal of Stevie Wonder's music, as well as the *Passions* of Bach, will reveal a lot of augmented and diminished chords. These chords contain the most potency in terms of dissonance, and yet provide the most relief when resolved. Why do we avoid these things in church? Isn't the whole point of liturgy to resolve the greatest tensions of humankind?

In playing fast Gospel music, the principles are generally the same. The main problem arises when this music is played too slowly. It is a mistake to play "Jesu, Jesu" on the organ at quarter = 60. Aside from the fact that it should not be played on the organ at all, it is much better done in a strongly syncopated rhythm—a three-against-two feel. Try tapping your right hand at quarter = 120 and your left hand at dotted quarter = 80. "Halle, Halle," a Calypso tune, should be done at roughly quarter = 120. Notice how most of these metronome markings are close to quarter = 120, or march time. Ghanaian master drummer Torgbui Gideon Foli Alorwoyie says that all Ghanaian music is derived essentially from the march. If this music does not at least approach march tempo, it is drained of its authenticity, vitality, and exuberance. Consider "Siyahamba" ("We are *marching* in the light of God").

"This Little Light of Mine" should not be played slower than a fast boogie rhythm (quarter = 112). "I'll Fly Away," or "Every Time I Feel the Spirit," should be played in a fast swing tempo (half note = 126). For guidance on how to play a Blues boogie, listen to Otis Spann or Meade Lux Lewis. For a good example of swing rhythm, listen to late-1950s Thelonius Monk or Miles Davis.

We'll leave this technical discussion of improvisational syntax by saying that we have only dipped into the topic. The subject of improvisation is truly endless, and can only really be explored by listening to hundreds of recordings and performances by the masters. We have provided some of these titles in Appendix B: Musical Resources for Liturgy. Enjoy the journey, and be brave with your exploration as well as your performance!

## "Pub Singing"

It is often said that some of our best hymns come from traditional pub songs. We note that this assertion is not without controversy. Some of our Lutheran brothers and sisters bristle when it is suggested that Luther adapted drinking songs as hymns; likewise, our Methodist colleagues deny that Charles Wesley ever darkened the door of a pub. True or not, the style of singing certain hymns is at least potentially the same as that of drinking songs. In the view of these authors, who regularly play contemporary popular music in worship, the use of music from the "secular world" is fully consonant with the message of Christ. He himself was accused of being a wine bibber, and was criticized for associating with drunkards and prostitutes. Pub singing is the music of the people—often the most depressed or cast-aside people. This music should be sung with gusto, full-breathed, and with a sense of abandon.

Popular or folk tunes endure because they are fun and easy to sing. Pub singing is organized around a melody suitable for a high male voice, developed by men singing around tankards of ale, celebrating patriotism and *machismo*. All of this is presented through the vessel of a high male voice with antecedent/consequent or periodic phrasing, such as in the tune *Hyfrydol*. Similarly, work songs, military songs, and sea chanties have a strong rhythm to establish moving and breathing in unison. The problem with a seemingly bawdy musical style as it is translated into liturgical music is that the musical intentionality is often lost in the translation. The same thing happens with challenging scripture readings. They lose potency and meaning when they are edited, polished, or tamed for church use.

For these songs or for this style, it's good to recover some of the raw edge of the music, to sing with gusto, to sway back and forth, and to sing from the belly and not from the neck. How does the musician encourage people to do that? Try singing "What Wondrous Love Is This?" at a *forte* dynamic, rather than *piano*. Encourage the congregation to sing loud and with volition. To use a ballet term, sing in an "open second" position: feet shoulder width, legs slightly bent, and shoulders over the hips. Sing with a firm stomach, supporting the voice (often pub singers use a tight throat as well, though this is not a healthy vocal technique).

For us, there is no question whether or not "bar music" is appropriate in church. We're looking for music of a style that encourages people to sing with passion and meaning, with gusto and verve and panache. As it happens, we are already singing these songs in our churches, and we should sing them correctly: with an aggressive and committed approach to the rhythm, with appropriate ornamentation like the fiddle tunes they are, and at correct tempos. Consider "What Wondrous Love Is This?,"a Southern Harmony tune that is often accompanied on the pipe organ at quarter = 64, a dismally slow tempo, more suited to Gregorian chant than to the kind of singing we are advocating here. Rather, the tune should be sung *a cappella* or accompanied by drum and fiddle at quarter = 76. This will set your congregation dancing!

## Taizé Chant

The music of the Taizé community, written and adapted by Brother Jacques Berthier, is fairly simple to learn for most congregations. This music reflects perhaps the oldest form of prayer, the style of prayer that includes constant repetition of a small element, over and over. Of course, in contrast to the other styles we are discussing, Taizé music is generally quieter and more reflective. In fact, we use it to vary the dynamics of our liturgy at Canterbury House, especially to slow the service down for the prayers of the people or for communion. One of the advantages of this music is that it is quickly learned. The congregation does not need to hold on to a service leaflet or a hymnal, leaving their hands free for communion, for example, or for moving about the room.

The experience of singing Taizé music is radically different from the other three styles discussed here. Taizé music reflects an experience of God that can be cosmic or direct or ecstatic. This quiet, repetitive music leaves space for the Holy Spirit to speak to the singer in a deeply individual or personal way. Taizé music evokes a mystical experience of the divine in contradistinction to the more visceral approaches of gospel music or pub singing.

The Lord's Prayer, the Jesus Prayer, as well as many other traditional prayers from Buddhism, Hinduism, Hassidism, and Sufism rely on the vast power of constant and lengthy repetition to create a kind of deep spiritual place in the person who prays. This can result in a deeply mystical, trancelike state. The problem many churches encounter in using this music is that like all meditation it requires considerable attentiveness. Dynamic fluctuations are important, and a natural part of the music. It is not new age Muzak that is dull, lifeless, and flat in tone; nor is it Praise Music, with vacant theological premises and weak harmonic and melodic integrity. The music of Taizé has harmonic tension that must be accompanied by dynamic fluctuation. It also runs the risk of slowing down or going flat, both tendencies openly admitted by Brother Roger of Taizé. He warns against such problems, and acknowledges that they usually arise out of a lack of spiritual engagement on the part of the singers.

Just mentioning these issues to most congregations usually solves the problem. The role of the accompanists can be helpful in keeping the tempo moving and supporting changes in dynamics through changes in density and range, and in supporting the tone or pitch. A properly attuned congregation can sing several phrases *a cappella* as long as the accompanists return before the singing goes flat or slows down. A flute or recorder can suffice as well to keep tempo and pitch in place.

An important consideration in studying Taizé music is that most of the compositions of Jacques Berthier are traditional dance forms. For instance, "Jesus Remember Me" is a sarabande. "De Noche" is in the style of a tango. "Bless the Lord" has more than hints of an allemande. Accompanying Taizé music can challenge all of one's skill in improvising Baroque music.

"Stay with Me" is a Taizé staple for those already familiar with this work, and serves as a moderately complex piece, with some simple harmonic shifts, characterizing most of the works from the Taizé community, especially their primary composer, Jacques Berthier.

A few words about improvisation in Taizé style are in order here, and are demonstrated in the example below. Again the improvisation is provided as an honest improvisation. I played it, recorded it, and then transcribed it. This was not "composed" according to any agenda, in other words.

## Stay with Me

The use of the constant eighth note (which can be divided into left and right hands) is of importance. This style of writing is completely Baroque in its approach, and a perusal of any of the *Goldberg Variations* by Bach will demonstrate this amply. The idea of the constant eighth (or whatever subdivision) is to provide constant momentum, leading the singer through the composition without disengagement or ennui. Brother Roger Schutz, in his introduction "How Can We Keep on Praying Together" (printed in eight languages in *Taizé 2006–2007*, or what we call the "little orange book") says this: "The person who begins the songs should make sure the tempo does not slow down too much, as this tends to happen when singing goes on for some time." Slowing down in music has a function, but it is rarely desirable in liturgical music, as the message behind slowing down could be unbelief, boredom, or lack of concern.

The improvisation provided above features a little motive in measure one. Most improvisation is rife with motives (as in Miles Davis's classic solo in "So What" on the *Kind of Blue* album). The motive is repeated in retrograde in m.4 (transposed) and used as a transition in the last bar. This is simply a tool to create subtle counterpoint against the singers, as well as to provide material for improvisation beyond the chord structure or the given (and slower) melody.

Using antecedent/consequent phrasing helps the improviser as well. If one can create a statement, it is much easier to conjure a complementary statement (if *A*, then what? *B!*). Notice m.1–2, answered higher in m.3–4. The same motive is found in diminution, then m.5 is answered by m.6. The turnaround (last two bars) is usually cathartic. The departure from this "*A*, then *B*" phrasing signals to the listener that the end of the form is coming, and prepares them for the return. Taizé music is actually a lot like Blues, with a short form (sixteen bars or less, usually) and continual repetition. In Blues, the turnaround is usually cathartic, and the loudest part of the form. This doesn't have to be the case in Taizé music, but it does help people to continue the structure of constant repetition, as opposed to resenting each repetition of the form. Such resentment will, indeed, happen if you slow down at the ending of each repetition.

Having said this, is there a subtle way to indicate that you are coming to the end of the form, but not the end of the sung piece? What I did in m.5–6 is a possible solution. Stopping the constant eighths for almost two bars shows that I am aware that the repeat sign is looming. On the other hand, the increased density in the last bar or so gives the singers the cue that they are to keep singing, to inhale, and to scan the eye to the beginning (if they have not already memorized this short piece).

The left hand part of this improvisation is extremely simple, but illustrates a few worthwhile subtleties. Notice the tango rhythm of the first measure. It would probably be in poor taste to continue this throughout the entire piece, even though we at Canterbury House have been known to do such things. Many of the pieces from Taizé were derived from Renaissance dances (like most of the works of J. S. Bach, for that matter), so why not highlight these derivations a bit more? Either way, it's a fun little rhythmic thing well worth investigating. Notice too the left hand part here: open fifths, or root/fifth dyads followed by a tenth above on beat two (m.4, for instance).

More important is the use of range in the left hand to reinforce the dynamics. The roll in m.3 creates the loudest left hand gesture in the piece, and underscores the quite predictable crescendo in the middle. Notice that the text here is under the word "watch," which gets three beats—way more emphasis than any other word in the piece. Why is this? We can speculate that Berthier is saying to us that watching is an important aspect of praying. Watching is a deep part of mystical prayer, and that is what gets the emphasis in this piece. As such, we should reinforce this "watching" with a dynamic underpinning—not tastelessly indiscrete, but noticing the setting of the text enough to let the dynamics flow in accordance with the meaning. Of course, this is true for every hymn one plays or sings.

How does one let the congregation know when to stop the piece (a legitimate concern)? Simply ritard, but *only* on the very last verse. Make the ritard long enough to alert the congregation but not too long. Only twice in about five hundred services have we heard a congregation miss this obvious musical cue.

Numerous examples of excellent accompaniment from the Taizé community can be heard on the Taizé website and on domradio.com. See Appendix A: Service Outlines for a sample Taizé service structure.

## Traditional Hymn Singing

The problem with traditional hymns is quite simply that we already know them. The tendency is to reinvent them completely (unnecessary) or to ignore their inherent subtlety (wrongheaded). It does help to explain again the text of the hymn to the congregation, or point out why this hymn was chosen to accompany this particular lectionary reading or season. Explaining music or liturgical themes to a congregation is not an interruption in the liturgy, especially if you take a few minutes at the beginning to do so. Rather, it is *part of* the liturgy. The congregation will gain from this a deeper appreciation of their own prayer. Remember: "who sings, prays twice."

The poetry in many hymns is often more important and more beautiful than the music itself, so congregations could be encouraged to read the words, perhaps during an improvisation on the hymn. Due to the dominance of the organ, many congregations are comfortable barely singing at all, while the organ provides the hymn. This poses a troublesome theology, one that elevates the organist to the role of mediator of the congregation's words, sounds, and soul—the "drowning out" effect, in other words. One way to deal with this problem is simply to play the organ (or piano) more quietly, or observe radical dynamic shifts based on the text. For example, I always have a congregation sing verse three of "Spirit of God" *a cappella*. This is an extremely personal text, and everyone should be able to hear their own voice.

Congregations can reacquaint themselves with the beautiful harmonies of these hymns by brief rehearsals, dividing the congregation into a four-voiced choir. It is a great tradition of church musicianship to reharmonize familiar hymns. Consider the Renaissance motet that uses Gregorian chant as a *cantus firmus* for polyphonic work, as in "Pange Lingua Sacramentum" or the many versions of "Salve, Regina." Consider also Bach's many cantatas reharmonizing familiar tunes from the psalters of his day, as in "Sleepers Wake" or "Break Forth, O Beauteous Heavenly Light." It is not, in fact, necessary to lead the congregation methodically through the first three verses of a familiar hymn before concluding with an alternate harmonization. Reharmonizing in accordance with a musician's personal, theological response to the text is a classical tradition that is centuries old.

Again, by conducting a mini-rehearsal, you are reminding the congregation that their participation is paramount in the conduct of the liturgy: it is not an option not to sing! Remember in the process of doing this to reward the congregation for their participation. At Canterbury House, we will at times thank the congregation during the service for particularly beautiful singing. Another approach is to allow the congregation to enjoy singing a well-done hymn twice.

As the study of hymnody will remind us, most hymns were sung *a cappella* for centuries. Thus, we might remember that the accompanist's role is not primary but optional. If your church can sing traditional hymns *a cappella,* you have taught them well!

We do lots of *a cappella* singing at Canterbury House, in all four of the styles we have discussed: Gospel, pub singing, Taizé, and traditional hymn singing. We do this, we should add, with students who have compunction about singing in public, and many or even most of whom do not consider themselves musicians *at all.* They are able to do this because *a*) we expect them to, *b*) they are rewarded for it—not the least by some really beautiful sound, *c*) we teach them how to do it gently but with high standards, and *d*) because they have *got it in their soul.*

Music comes from God. We can talk endlessly about acoustics, harmony, music theory, and even technique; but ultimately music is Spirit. I once interviewed the famous composer and founder of minimalism LaMonte Young, and asked him, somewhat impertinently, "Are you a vessel of God?" He replied, "Yes. I'm a musician." When I asked Ravi Shankar the same question, he gave me the exact same answer!

# Chapter 8

## Where Can We Find the Musicians?

### Where *Can* We Find the Musicians?

Perhaps the best liturgical musician we know came to Canterbury House as a nineteen-year-old Jewish Jazz saxophone player. Obviously, he is too young; obviously, he is the wrong religion; obviously, he plays in the wrong idiom; obviously, he plays the wrong instrument. What makes him so good? Well, he cares. He has a spiritual life. He is a very fine, very competent musician. He is musically literate. He knows a broad range of music that is specifically related to the expression of faith and the interior life. And where did we find this young phenom? He is originally from Los Angeles and has a band there. He and his friends play all kinds of music, all the time. They can be found in bars, Jazz clubs, block parties, house concerts, and at the University of Michigan School of Music, as well as at other colleges and universities.

When we present our ideas at church conferences and seminars, we are invariably told something like: "Well, you are lucky. You have a great big music school to draw from." We have heard this from people who live in places like Nashville and Kansas City, places with vital and thriving music scenes.

The problem is not that there are no musicians, nor even that we don't know where to find them. The truth is, there are musicians everywhere—really good ones! The key is to ask around, look around, and spend a lot of time listening. We found Joey Dosik at the University of Michigan; but the presence of a lot of music students in your area, by itself, is not enough. If your community has a music school, look for the students who have the energy, the courage, and the talent to play music for audiences. Check the bars and the music clubs! Look for musicians who play for dances and weddings. In rural communities, look for musicians who play for contra dances and barn dances. Check out every folk music festival, Bluegrass festival, highland festival, and Jazz festival in your area. Look for musicians who can connect with people on a spiritual level and who know how to make people want to move, in body and soul.

We've already said and will say again that Jazz musicians are particularly helpful to find because you get a lot of bang for your buck. They are skilled in many different musical idioms, and usually are excellent sight readers. They know how to improvise. They are steeped in a tradition that has evolved in the United States from African drumming and singing, from Caribbean and Latin American dance forms and European contemporary harmonic practices. In other words, *diversity* is in their musical nature. They often have great recordings of hymns in their collection, regardless of their personal faith. Louis Armstrong, Duke Ellington, Thelonius Monk, John Coltrane, and Albert Ayler all recorded hymns and as such provided a model of inclusiveness and excellence for this kind of music.

Ask everyone in your congregation if they play an instrument, and what kind of music they play. Find out where they go to hear the music they like. Go there yourself. In developing musical resources for your congregation, you must be careful about the notion of "musical expertise." Many very specialized performers in classical music or especially organ music have a particular focus that might preclude much or most of the kind of music we are advocating for. Folk music *v.* classical music, or secular music *v.* sacred music are false dichotomies. We are arguing that all music can have a place in liturgy. It is rare that an education in classical music performance will include an education in ethnomusicology. Contemporary ethnomusicology recognizes the relationships among all kinds of music. A young music student recently asked Stephen what class she could take to study Stevie Wonder. Sad to say that at a major university forty-five minutes from the city of Detroit, there is currently no such class. Her education in music performance will, alas, not include an important American musician. It should be clear from this example that a classical music education is not a complete education for the would-be church musician.

When you are looking for musicians, have a budget. There is no use looking for volunteer musicians and paying them nothing. This is true even of musicians whom you select from within your own congregation. If they are worth listening to, they are worth paying. If they want to contribute what you pay them back to the church, that's one thing; but make the offer. If you do not feel comfortable with paying them (for whatever reason), you should not ask them to play. If they are not worth paying, they are not worth listening to. This is the economics of your local bar: if your tavern keeper would not hire your musicians, why should you?

Instead of paying one musician a lot of money to do all of the music, pay several musicians. For contemporary liturgy, having a band is usually better than having an organist. Remember that the organ evolved and was brought into churches for the purpose of allowing one musician to fill up a space with sound. Why not pay several musicians on a "per gig" basis, and fill up your space with a band? Here's an analogy: If the rector of a church has a staff of assisting priests, why shouldn't the music director have a "staff" of musicians? Of course, this is done in some large churches or cathedrals in the form of staff singers and choir directors. Smaller churches can certainly do the same on a smaller scale. The music director is the bandleader, selecting music, planning liturgy (along with the other liturgists, of course), and conducting rehearsals. The point is to think of creative ways to divide *and expand* the music budget. The result should be an expansion of the participation of the community and the congregation in the musical and liturgical life of the church.

Build a roster of musicians who are capable of fulfilling the creative vision of the liturgical team. Keep a Rolodex or directory complete with phone numbers and appropriate compensation. Whenever and wherever you hear a musician you like, get their card, get their phone number. Ask if they would be interested in playing *that kind of music* for your church. Let them know that you are willing to pay them. Believe us when we tell you that they are often asked to play in churches for free and may turn you down if you do not make yourself clear on this point. If asked to play a paying gig, they will usually say yes. Then it is your job to match the kind of music they play with the kind of music you are going to use in liturgy. The whole point of this book is that you *can* use the music that these musicians play in your liturgy. You and your congregation will be enriched spiritually by the effort.

The process of looking for and listening to and finding musicians, of having these conversations with them, and carrying out this kind of vision can be difficult and a lot of work. Don't think of it as work. Instead, think of it as *evangelism*. Musicians talk to one another. Word will get around in a whole new community and subculture that your church is cool. The people who like these musicians will show up in your church to hear them play.

Another good place to look for musicians is among teenagers. A very popular form of entertainment for young people is to play drum circles. Many teens that you already know have djembe and dumbeks. Some of them are in your youth group. Get them together, and teach them some African chants that you can then use as an offertory or presentation hymn. Don't do it just once. After the third consecutive week of doing a new African chant, the congregation will have learned the music. Having found their favorite SATB part to sing, they will look forward to it, and even dare to dance to it. They will realize that this is not a one time thing, that the church is serious about wanting their participation in the music. It is not "special music," it is *ordinary,* in the medieval sense of the term!

Musicians, you are not expected to know anything about world music. No one knows everything about everything, but you can learn. There are trained ethnomusicologists at most major universities. In addition, a search on the web will guide you toward resources of music of almost any culture—sound files, music, books, and CDs. Most missionaries have spent significant amounts of time singing with indigenous people, usually songs from that culture. Musical diversity can be a project for an outreach committee in your church. For example, if your church is engaging in work with the Latino community, find Latin music to use in your worship. Look for music from cultures where your money is already being put to use. If you are sending money to India, consider using bhajans in your liturgy.

Let's say that you have no taverns or music clubs in your county. There are no guitarists or saxophone players in your congregation. Your teens play video games instead of drums. You have not yet exhausted your possibilities. Untrained musicians can play Taizé music. See our Taizé performance notes in Chapter Seven. Any young person that has played for two or three years in high school band or orchestra can manage playing along with Taizé music in your church. Invite them to do so. Paying them modestly will encourage them to become better musicians. Do not, however, play Taizé music in your church without first listening to Taizé services. You can find these at the Taizé community website or podcast on www.domradio.de. Again, there is no reason or excuse to play inauthentic music from France (or Niger or Mississippi) when you can listen to and learn from authentic performances so readily available in recorded form.

A word to the wise: why aren't we asking, "Where are the priests or pastors who are willing to implement innovative and exciting liturgy in their churches?" Inquiring musicians want to know! We imagine that some musicians have picked up this book, saying to themselves, "The priest at my church knows nothing about music and doesn't care. How can I make the liturgy and the music better?" Priests and pastors, be warned: your musician might be looking for a more interesting, more spiritually fulfilling gig! No less a musician than Johann Sebastian Bach did exactly that, moving from St. Boniface in Arnstadt to St. Blasius in Mühlhausen in 1706 to work with a more sympathetic collaborator.

## How To Hire a Music Director

For churches that have sufficient financial resources, the task of bringing the deep musical background to liturgical planning and of finding the musicians we have described above will fall to the music director. Thus, it is a sensitive and important position. A music director who is capable, broad-minded, spiritual, and dedicated is perhaps the single greatest asset a church can have.

Have a search committee that includes, in addition to the clergy, someone who is very young, and someone who is very old, someone who really loves the adult choir, and someone who has young children and who loves children's choir. The committee should be comfortable singing together.

Committee meetings should begin with singing together. The committee should meet before any interviews take place, perusing resumés for evidence of scholarship, diversity (musical and otherwise), and open-mindedness. Remember that virtuosity has many forms, and that a DMA or PhD or an AGO membership does not necessarily prepare anyone for worshiping or having a spiritual life. The musician who evidences faith or prayerfulness in whatever form is most likely to be the musician who will be able to pray with, worship with, and lead your congregation.

Open up the search as wide as you can, including notices at area music shops and universities/colleges/community colleges, as well as the American Guild of Organists and Chronicle of Higher Education. Consider that the organ may not be the best instrument for accompanying liturgy at your church. If it is, that's fine. If it isn't, then ask whether a piano player, drummer, or guitar player might be the best music director for your congregation. In the end you are looking for a very talented musician who loves God, loves people (People + God = Liturgy), can get people to sing with great volition, tone, and excitement, and can improvise.

After thus reviewing possible musicians on paper, you will have narrowed your field to candidates whom you wish to interview and audition. Be sure to allow at least ninety minutes for your interview. Ask the applicant to discuss their religious life. If they are not able or willing to discuss this with you, then how can they relate the meaning of the text to a children's choir, or to a priest while planning liturgy? This is perfectly legal since you are hiring a musician for a church, not a public school. Remember, however, that one need not be a member of your denomination, nor even a Christian, to have a profound religious life. It is the depth of their spirit that matters, not its flavor.

In the audition, have your candidate select and teach two hymns in differing styles to the search committee. Then, ask for accompaniment to two familiar hymns (again, differing styles) while the search committee sings. If the musician drowns the committee out, you may have to ask difficult questions about dynamic sensitivity. If the applicant balks at these questions, beware! You have been warned. Their dynamic is the right dynamic, and listening is not part of their musical aptitude.

Ask for improvisation. Possible approaches could be a free improvisation on a spiritual like "O Freedom!" or a long (five minutes) improvisation on a Taizé piece such as "Jesus Remember Me" or "Wait for the Lord." Listen carefully! Does the music slow down? Does it keep your interest? Does it sound inspired? Remember, improvisation is not merely playing "Lift High the Cross" with an alternate harmony on verse three.

Have your candidate conduct a short rehearsal with the choir. Ask for three differing styles, with ten minutes (maximum) per piece. If the styles are Bach, William Byrd, and Poulenc, you can ask whether your candidate is aware of other choral traditions such as Scandinavian, South African, or Shape-Note Singing.

Let the musician pick all the repertory, including the hymns referred to above, but let it all be based on a lectionary reading (for example, Lent 3, Year C). You can quickly learn about their creativity in programming through this process.

Notice that in contradistinction to the process of most search committees, the performance of a concert work is not on this audition list. Giving a concert is neither necessary nor desirable in a liturgical situation. The prelude and postlude are there to shape the liturgy, and give musical commentary on the Eucharist, prayers, and readings. The offertory is in the liturgy to raise one's awareness of gratitude to God, not to feature an "amazing choir" or an impressive organist. *Liturgical music is not an end unto itself.* Do not by your interview and audition process encourage a church musician to become a "concert musician who plays at your church." The church musician is a liturgist, first and foremost.

Realize that you will not get everything you want. Remember that your musician can develop over time. I know from my position in the university that asking for skills on a job description often leads candidates to develop those skills—sometimes in advance of applying for the job. Knowing that improvisation is required for your church music position, for instance, may inspire a young organist to take Jazz lessons, or begin for the first time experimenting with improvisation in a Baroque or Blues style. I wasn't aware that I could improvise a minuet in the style of Bach until I was asked to do so by a modern dance instructor while playing for an audition. We were both pleasantly surprised!

## Improvisation in Church Music

We should expect improvisation from our church musicians. The best writers of hymns, musicians such as Charles Wesley, Isaac Watts, and Ludwig van Beethoven were all, among other things, good improvisers. Bach, Buxtehude, and Messiaen were known for their improvisational technique as well as their compositions. Former Canterbury House musician Mark Kirschenmann wrote his doctoral dissertation on improvisation related to composition, specifically in the Western European tradition. Dr. Kirschenmann maintains that improvisation is essential to the process of composition, as well as being part and parcel of a composer's identity. Music is not written without improvising. Why then should it be performed without improvisation?

Hymnals are generally printed with no phrasing marks and no indications of tempo or dynamics; but, of course, this does not mean that hymns should be played without phrasing, or slow and ponderously, or in a loud, stoic manner without dynamic fluctuation. The lack of these indications suggests that the musician is to make the music her own. Church music should be played in response to the personality of a worshiping congregation. See examples of notated *v.* performed music in Chapter Seven.

Where do we find musicians who can improvise? The fact is, all musicians who can play American music can and do improvise, including a schlub fiddler like Reid! Improvisation is the soul of American music. By "American music" we mean Rock, Country, Jazz, Folk, Blues, southern hymnody (black or white), as well as tango, salsa, waltzes, cha-chas, and choros—all of which are forms that depend strongly on improvisation. The musical expression in our churches, including our hymns, can and should be as diverse in tempo, timbre, style, dynamic expression, and harmony as the music we have grown up with and hear all around us every day.

## What's Wrong with the Organ?

We are all used to hearing an organ in church, and playing the organ well requires a great deal of skill and competency. For much Western European sacred music, from Bach to Fauré, as well as for many English and American hymns written in the late nineteenth century through the present, it is the instrument of choice. There is nothing wrong with that. Much of this music is very good, and it is an important part of our heritage. If you have a good instrument and a competent musician, it can and should be used.

Recall, however, that the organ evolved and was brought into churches for the purpose of allowing one musician to fill up a space with sound. It is a mechanical admission that your musical resources and possibilities are limited. If you rely exclusively on the organ for your music, then you are making a theological statement: that there is only one kind of music acceptable to God, that God's ears are western and Eurocentric, that only "schooled" musicians can play in church. Worse, if certain kinds of music are attempted on the organ, you are sending the message to many people that their musical heritage will not be respected in your church, and that you do not care about authentic musical performance.

Some pieces simply should not be attempted on the church organ. Specifically, for example, "Jesu, Jesu," a Ghanaian folksong, "Go Tell It on the Mountain," a nineteenth-century spiritual, "Morning Has Broken," a Gaelic melody. With these examples given, you can doubtless identify many others. Still less does most music found in African-American hymnals or in John Bell's books lend itself to organ performance. Playing an African chant on organ simply continues the embarrassing colonial mindset of the eighteenth- and nineteenth-century church and is in poor musical and theological taste.

Taizé music can be performed on the organ but is much more interesting and participatory if played on other instruments. Listening to the services at Taizé will reveal a sparse use of the organ. At the Taizé community in France, the music is usually accompanied by a very subtle and beautiful synthesized guitar. Consider that at Taizé they have deliberately chosen *not* to use organ for the most part, and they have instructed a trained organist to play a guitar sound on a keyboard. What does this imply?

If worship in your church is limited to the pieces and the style appropriate to the organ, you are certain to be missing a great deal. When you listen to an album of Bob Dylan, there might be an organ player, but it won't be like the one at your church. Ray Charles, Aretha Franklin, Irish fiddle music—no organ! Shape-note music? No instrumentalists at all! Latin American music, African music, folk music, and Jazz—no organ! Reggae music, on the other hand, will often use an organ, but it is too rarely heard in most churches!

The organ is also, too often, discouraging to congregational singing. Because it is capable of playing louder than the human voice, it often drowns out the congregation. Sad to say, it is sometimes purposely used to do so (of course, the same thing can happen with a Rock band). The inevitable message of a loud organ is that the liturgy can be done by one person.

## Okay, Then, How About the Piano?

The piano is often thought of as a folk instrument when played in church. As one who studied and earned a doctorate at a fancy Eastern conservatory, Stephen has a bit of resentment toward that perspective. Piano, perhaps, is found in more homes than the organ; but the piano is nonetheless an icon of Western European classical music. This association is unlikely to go away anytime soon. However, Jazz bars and honky-tonks in New Orleans also have pianos. Thus, the association of the piano with a particular musical tradition—"highbrow" or "lowbrow"—could be mixed, polyglot, even confused. In other words, one should not confuse the medium with the message. It is important to use instrumentation appropriate to the music you select. "Lead Me, Guide Me" will almost always sound better on piano; "All Creatures of Our God and King" will always sound better on the organ; and "Jesu, Jesu" will always sound better *a cappella,* accompanied by drums. Develop the roster of musical palettes and instruments in your church, and don't fake the "sound" of the music. Dare to be authentic. It is shocking to us that any church choir, having taken great pains to master a motet by Thomas Tallis, would in the same service butcher "Halle, Halle, Halle" by singing it "square" or slowly—or worse, by assuming that it needs no rehearsal.

## Okay Then, How About Prerecorded Music or Accompaniment?

As practicing musicians, we have a bias against the use of prerecorded music in liturgical settings. Stephen has worked feverishly to present dance performances with live music (including symphony orchestras). This does not come without great difficulty, but the rewards are vast. Alas, there is a disturbing trend in both dance and musical theatre to use prerecorded music or "midi" versions of the accompaniment. This unfortunate trend is being replicated in churches.

Many churches, especially small congregations, have taken to using prerecorded music or canned accompaniment. They do this because they think they can't find musicians, or worse, as a substitute for "expensive" musicians. Some churches also have taken to presenting "special services," using prerecorded popular music, in the hope that this will attract young people. None of these reasons is satisfactory.

We hope it's clear that saving money by not looking for musicians who can play in your church is false economy, not to say disrespectful of musicians in your congregation who could contribute to your music, or musicians in your community who might be seeking employment.

If the goal is to attract young people, the question is, "Attracting them to what, exactly?" Even if people who experience a canned liturgy tell you afterward that it was good, we suspect that the use of this manner of entertainment accomplishes the wrong objective. As Don Saliers has said, "There is a difference between being made to feel comfortable through immediately accessible forms and styles, and being invited to communal gratitude, awe, delight and hope."[5]

A recording cannot respond to the Holy Spirit, much less to the reaction or mood of the congregation. Nor can the machine respond to the ebb and flow of the congregation's emotions in the singing of a hymn. Nor does a machine know how to maintain silence—an active principle!

## Silence Is Important!

Perhaps the most effective musical instrument you have is one that can be played virtuosically by every congregation, and that is silence.

The constant noise in many contemporary worship services leads to a sort of TV or radio aesthetic. One of the basic tenets in professional radio is the avoidance of "dead air" or silence. It is this aesthetic that competes with the ancient and mystic notion that God is found in silence. In traditional church music, silence is often valued for its evocative quality, rather than its musical or even spiritual effect. Old favorites often make their way into our liturgies by virtue of a merely nostalgic preference, rather than a critical aesthetic or a theological perspective. The same can be said for entire genres of sacred music (nineteenth-century English organ music, for instance). Our first priority needs to be the invitation of the mystic entrance of the Holy Spirit into our liturgy. Silence may be the best way to accomplish this although that is counter to American notions of making noise and doing action.

The seminal American composer John Cage addressed the natural wonders found in silence through his influential composition *4'33"*, a composition in which players literally perform silence. Oddly enough, this blatant rejection of Western values, by allowing anything to happen and calling it organized, was misinterpreted as arrogance and despair, especially by conservative Christians (for example, see Francis Schaeffer's *Where Do We Go From Here,* Intervarsity Press, 1980). This was the opposite of Cage's intent. Cage was a practicing Zen Buddhist, whose work allowed the Holy to be heard openly and without question.[6]

Liturgies must arise from the understanding that the background of our experience is found in the silence of God's Holy presence. From there we can best choose what "noises"—prayers, readings, litanies, music—to make to complement and explore the meaning found in the silence. The Quakers had the right idea: start with no music.

5 "Liturgy and Moral Imagination: Encountering Images in a TV Culture," *Yale Studies in Sacred Music—Musicians for the Churches: Reflections on Vocation and Formation* (New Haven, CT: Institute of Sacred Music, Yale University, 2001), 49.

6 Cage, *Silence: Lectures and Writings* (Middleton, CT: Wesleyan Press, 1961).

# Chapter 9

## Sources

How do we develop musical, artistic, and liturgical literacy? What texts or communities can inform theologically sound and interesting prayer and preaching? We've been saying all along that it's important for priests and musicians to have a deep and collaborative spiritual life. One or the other of us, or both, have read each of the following books and found them meaningful and helpful in leading to sound prayer, preaching, and music making. Add your own favorites to this list. We want to read some more ourselves! We include also a brief discussion of some of our musical and liturgical sources for worship at Canterbury House.

### Books on Creativity in Religion

Madeleine L'Engle, *Walking on Water: Reflections on Faith and Art* (Wheaton, IL: Harold Shaw Publishers, 1980). L'Engle breaks down the division between secular and sacred themes and focuses the artist toward virtuosity. She is a Christian, but that does not dictate the content of her work, which is an appreciation of the sacred in the ordinary and of the ability to turn everyday occurrences into a spiritual and artistic opportunity. "Not long ago," she writes, "a college senior asked if she could talk to me about being a Christian writer. If she wanted to write Christian fiction, how was she to go about it? I told her that if she is truly and deeply a Christian, what she writes is going to be Christian, whether she mentions Jesus or not. And if she is not, in the most profound sense, Christian, then what she writes is not going to be Christian, no matter how many times she invokes the name of the Lord" (pages 121–122).

*The Wisdom of Sun Ra: Sun Ra's Polemical Broadsheets and Streetcorner Leaflets,* John Corbett, ed. (Chicago, IL: Whitewalls, 2006). Sun Ra's writing on the relationship between race and religion is as ecstatic as it is bizarre—historically informed and yet futuristic. As a performer and composer, he used musical styles from Fats Waller and Duke Ellington through the avant-garde with reference to Spirituals and torch songs. Sun Ra's persona, including his insistence that he was not from Earth but rather from Saturn, was an expression both of the black sense of alienation in American culture and the hope of the eschaton, that is, the return of God *to* earth *from* outer space. His religion and philosophy have been criticized as eccentric; but he has a profound sense of the radical otherness of God, and of the deep longing of humanity for justice and liberation.

Liberation and justice on a (perhaps) more practical scale is the theme of Desmond Tutu's *The Rainbow People of God: The Making of a Peaceful Revolution* (NY: Doubleday, 1994). Tutu brought his boundless faith and hope to the seemingly impossible task of confronting apartheid in South Africa and achieved an act of liberation, justice, and mercy literally worthy of a saint. The deepest religion underlies the deepest, most liberating creativity.

Anne Lamott brings an earthiness and a wonderful, wry sense of humor to everyday religion. Her writing pointed to us the value and importance of making a worshiping community a place of welcome and safety for people of every place and condition (*Traveling Mercies: Some Thoughts on Faith* [NY: Pantheon, 1999]). We were particularly moved by her story of walking into St. Andrew Presbyterian Church in Marin City when she was feeling particularly wounded and vulnerable, and sensing that Jesus was there. We try to make Canterbury House like that.

College students have their time altogether filled with social events, volunteer and service opportunities, and "programming," not to mention classes and studies. A campus ministry can expend a great deal of energy and resources in attempting to offer more of what students already have too much of. What we can uniquely offer is a refuge of worship and a discipline of prayer. Kathleen Norris, in her book *The Cloister Walk* (New York: Riverhead, 1996), has much to say of the value of a community of prayer organized around a liturgical cycle. Norris also has the courage to take doubt seriously when speaking of faith. *Amazing Grace: A Vocabulary of Faith* (New York: Riverhead Trade, 1999) is a good resource for preaching.

Annie Dillard, *Pilgrim at Tinker Creek* (New York: Harper's Magazine Press, 1974), integrates Native American spirituality and Christianity in an experiential way. She takes a very realistic, unromantic view of nature and finds there the hand of God. Her solidarity with the natural world had, until recently, almost no expression in contemporary Western European spirituality. Through her inspiration I've learned to acknowledge the presence of God in nature and then search for the music and the prayers that express that same connection. This is very different from the top-down spirituality that is so prevalent in traditional hymnody.

Annie Dillard is actually recovering a tradition of creation spirituality in Western European theological practice that is represented, for example, in the work of medieval humanist Meister Eckhart (1260–1328). Eckhart's sermons, translated by Matthew Fox in *Breakthrough* (New York: Doubleday, 1980), discuss God's nature as Creator, providing a helpful paradigm for college-age seekers who are reorganizing their own thinking about God. Creation spirituality is helpful in providing a nonsexist framework for worshiping and talking about God. Creation is a natural "re-set and re-start" place, as Fox observes: "Eckhart says that the father or creator is a *speaking action* —who truly creates and does not merely cogitate about truth or about creating. So full of mystery and power is this creative Word who is God that we humans are left dumb and speechless by the beauty of creation" (page 60).

## Art and Music as Primary Theology

Hans Küng, in *Art and the Question of Meaning*, trans. Edward Quinn (New York: Crossroad, 1981), describes art as the interplay between God and humans: "a free space for the element of play which leaves open all possibilities" (page 51). This is as good a way of thinking about Harmolodics as if Ornette Coleman had written it! Liturgy is the art of worship, and, if you will, a way of incorporating all of our expression into a celebration of and participation in the presence of God. Küng's *Mozart: Traces of Transcendence*, trans. John Bowden (Grand Rapids, MI: Eerdman's, reprint 1993) is a passionate outcry against the common notion of Mozart as a completely secular composer. Mozart's work is certainly a demonstration that God continues in the business of revelation by coming to us in a language that is beyond and other than words.

Don Postema's *Space for God: The Study and Practice of Prayer and Spirituality* (Grand Rapids, MI: Faith Alive, reprint 1997) is a wonderful discussion of inspiration in the work of two artists:

Rembrandt, an acknowledged Christian, and Van Gogh, a "deeply spiritual" person, in contemporary parlance. Again, we may be surprised by or even skeptical of the human medium; but it is invariably the influence of the Spirit that we recognize in the inspired work of the great artist. As artists, we are vessels of God, as Ravi Shankar and others have said. Henri Nouwen's study, *The Return of the Prodigal Son* (London: Darton, Longman & Todd Ltd., 1994) is a technical discussion of Rembrandt's rendering of the parable from Luke 15. Speaking from a specifically theological perspective, Nouwen makes a careful study of the religious research that the artist undertook in order to create the work. Incidentally, Nouwen was Postema's principal teacher and good friend.

A contemporary musical genius who came to a frank acknowledgment of the importance and the revelatory nature of inspiration is studied in *Ascension: John Coltrane and His Quest* by Eric Nisenson (New York: St. Martin's Press, 1993). Especially interesting is Coltrane's later life, described in chapters ten through thirteen, during which he committed himself completely to a study of Christianity and Hinduism.

## Prayer

Liturgists and musicians must have a prayer life. The visible result of prayer is the ecstasy that pops out in our worship. Prayer and worship also energize and refresh us for social justice. The life of contemplation leads us to the life of action.

Evelyn Underhill writes of prayer and social action. Hers is a work of contextual theology:

> This little book, written during the last months of peace, goes to press in the first weeks of the great war. Many will feel that in such a time of conflict and horror, when only the most ignorant, disloyal, or apathetic can hope for quietness of mind, a book which deals with that which is called the "contemplative" attitude to existence is wholly out of place. (*Practical Mysticism* [London: Hesperides Press, 2006], 11)

This book, first published in 1915, is a frankly technical discussion about how to be a mystic. Her argument is that the most relevant way to be a mystic is to be present in the world. We also like the writings of Thomas Merton, not only because of the very practical things he has to say about contemplation and prayer, but also because of his devotion to social justice and peace (as in *Confessions of a Guilty Bystander* [Garden City, NJ: Doubleday, 1996]). He is often quoted in sermons at Canterbury House.

Simone Weil has been helpful in my approach to campus ministry particularly because of what she has to say about studies and contemplation in her book, *Waiting for God* (New York: Harper Perennial, 2001). Jean LeClerq, also, writes of the relationship between the scholarly life and the life of contemplation in the context of medieval monasticism in *The Love of Learning and the Desire for God: A Study of Monastic Culture*, trans. Catherine Misrahi (New York: Fordham University Press, 1982).

Medieval monasticism raised a tradition of contemplation in the Western tradition that is entirely worthy of the best of Eastern meditative practice. Teresa of Avila and Hildegard of Bingen, for example, have profound things to say about ecstasy and the experience of the Divine. Their writings on the techniques and the experiences of contemplative prayer are as fresh as those of Thomas Keating and Daisetz Suzuki, which are also highly recommended. Hildegard, in particular, was remarkable in her accomplishments not only as a mystic, but also as a musician and an artist. Again, her work demonstrates how music is a primary theological language. We learn from all of these writers that silence is an active, musical principle that is valuable in liturgy in establishing atmosphere and opening communication with God.

Rudolph Otto's *The Idea of the Holy* (Oxford: Oxford University Press, 1958) was profoundly influential on Stephen, especially the appendix on "The Numinous in Poetry, Hymnody, and Liturgy." His description of the numinous as a way of describing God is a contemporary mystical discussion that hearkens back to Julian, Hildegard, and Teresa. Like Merton, Otto was attracted to Eastern approaches to meditation and contemplation and cosmology.

## Preaching

After reading many books on preaching, reading many collections of sermons, and having much experience of hearing preachers both good and bad, I have come to the conclusion that preaching, like music, is learned mostly by practice and by ear. Nevertheless, a good grounding in the fundamentals is helpful and essential. David Buttrick is widely acknowledged as a sound teacher of homiletics. His book, *Homiletic: Moves and Structures* (Philadelphia: Fortress Press, 1987), is a useful introduction to some good practical methods for getting into the text, having a theme, and making the sermon parallel to the scripture being preached. His *Preaching the New and the Now* (Louisville: Westminster John Knox, 1998) is an urgent call to preachers to connect the kingdom of God to genuine, contemporary social issues.

In order to preach prophetically, a preacher needs to be engaged both with scripture and with contemporary issues, just as Karl Barth suggested, by doing theology with a Bible in one hand and a newspaper in the other. All of the books we have discussed so far can help to inform preaching. Anne Lamott, in particular, demonstrates in her writing the importance of telling the truth, however shocking or edgy, and being honest with one's self and one's hearers. Frederick Buechner's sermons, collected in his several books, are down-to-earth, so real, and not about lofty stuff or heady theological concepts.

Barbara Brown Taylor is, of course, very influential to those of us who preach in the Episcopal tradition. She writes very hopefully in *The Preaching Life* (Boston: Cowley, 1993), very constructively in *Speaking of Sin* (Boston: Cowley, 2001), and very honestly in *Leaving Church* (San Francisco: HarperSanFrancisco, 2007).

## Sources for Music: Preludes, Postludes, and Voluntaries

Certainly, the Jazz Mass at Canterbury House does not rely exclusively on Jazz music; nevertheless, we do use Jazz almost exclusively for preludes, postludes, and voluntaries. The music of Ornette Coleman, Sun Ra, John Coltrane, Albert Ayler, and other contemporary Jazz artists—music that some would call "avant-garde" or "Free Jazz"—inspires our musicians most and fits our theology best. Our approach to selecting specific compositions is to correlate the title of a composition with the occasion of the service or the theme identified, sometimes by way of a pun. Thus, a service commemorating Mary Magdalene might employ "Lonely Woman" by Ornette Coleman. Easter is a good occasion for *A Love Supreme* by John Coltrane. For other examples, see the sample services in Appendix A: Service Outlines.

Alas, most of the classics of contemporary Jazz are not available in print. You find them by listening to CDs and albums. I love this music so much that I prepare our charts by transcribing them directly from recordings. If you are looking for a particular piece and need information about where it might be found, you are welcome to contact me directly at srush@umich.edu.

## Sources: Music for Congregational Singing

It takes a lot of musical resources to build diversity in liturgy. A perusal of Appendix B: Musical Resources for Liturgy will show you a long list of our various musical resources. It is by no means an exhaustive list of possibilities. We were excited just this week to discover *Evangelical Lutheran Worship* (2006) with its very diverse sources and up-to-date texts for hymns. We hope to discover yet more new material next week!

John Bell says, in his introduction to *Heaven Shall Not Wait*:

> We live in a Country which has a glorious heritage of folk music, of fiddle and pipe tunes, of vocal melodies all in danger of disappearing into oblivion. But where are the spiritual songs which have clothed themselves in this musical richness? Why is it that Africans, Asians, and Central Americans have allowed the Gospel to take root in their folk music, but we in Britain have, by and large, avoided such an association as if Christ had never joyed to see children piping and dancing in the street? [7]

The same could certainly be said of the United States. Our sources therefore include a great deal of Jazz, blues, folk, and Country tunes, "popular" music, as well as traditional hymnody.

Many of our favorites at Canterbury House include such traditional hymns as "His Eye Is on the Sparrow," "He's Got the Whole World in His Hands," "Abide with Me," "Breathe on me, Breath of God," and "At the Cross." All of these are old warhorses that people in your own congregation are likely to request from time to time. Remember your first and best resource for music may well be your own congregation.

Suggestions from the congregation should always be taken seriously. You might not accede to every request. As mentioned previously, for example, we draw the line at "Faith of Our Fathers." Once, though, a Canterbury House student requested "Rock of Ages." This was not, at the time, a hymn in our normal lexicon. While I was surprised that this request would come from a college-age student, I undertook to do a little research on the tune. The incredible circumstances under which the hymn was written resonated with me so, that I was compelled to use it as soon as possible and it is now a Canterbury House standard.

By honoring the congregation's requests you learn something. You can spark your own intellectual, theological, and musical knowledge, and you may find a new approach to an old favorite hymn that you find invigorating. Check out Ladysmith Black Mambazo's recording of "Leaning on the Everlasting Arms," produced by George Clinton of Funkadelic: *Two Words, One Heart* (Warner Brothers, 1991). You will also gain a great deal of goodwill; the congregation feels included in the process of planning liturgy, and that their spiritual practice or mode of religious expression is being honored. Your openness to this process will also encourage the congregation's openness to new material that you want to share with them: one "Rock of Ages" buys you a Sun Ra tune every time!

Even a hymn you dislike as antiquated or quaint or musically or theologically clumsy has a story behind it, and a theology that you can, in introducing the hymn during the liturgy, either adopt or criticize, providing a preaching opportunity for the musician, if you will. Also, precisely because these pieces are favorites, they have a rich performance history that can be tapped. Find out if James Cleveland or Shirley Caesar did it, listen to their performance, and see if you gain a new appreciation. Look for Gospel recordings by Louis Armstrong, Johnny Cash, Elvis, Aretha Franklin, Al Green, or Albert Ayler.

We like to use hymns from *The Southern Harmony* (Lexington: University Press of Kentucky, 1987). It's a great resource for very singable *a cappella* arrangements of familiar hymn tunes. Similarly, *Rise Up Singing* (Sing Out Publications, 2004) is a wonderful compendium of American folk music, much of which is perfectly applicable to contemporary liturgy.

Our sources include the works of John Bell, a reliable source of singable folk melodies with up-to-

7 John Bell, *Heaven Shall Not Wait* (Chicago: GIA Publications, 1989), 7.

date lyrics. His wonderfully contemporary and humorous lyrics, (as in "Once in Judah's Least Known City") sung to the tune "Once in Royal David's City," are always a hit at Canterbury House: "Mary's Mom and Dad went wild/when they heard their daughter had a child" (*Heaven Shall Not Wait* [Chicago: GIA Publications, 1987]).

Music published by the Taizé community is licensed in the United States to GIA Publications: www.giamusic.com. We use *Music from Taizé, Vols. I and II* and *Taizé Songs for Prayer.* We also use *Taizé 2006–2007*, which is only available in France as far as we know. This relatively small collection of available Taizé music offers us the greatest latitude in terms of languages (yes, our congregation does sing in Swedish). These sources include service music such as Alleluias, Kyries, and helpful segments of psalms. They also have cantor parts and descants. The accompanying instrumental editions have easy-to-play parts for a variety of instruments.

We use two very comprehensive collections of African-American worship music: *Lift Every Voice and Sing* (New York: The Church Pension Fund, 1993) and *Songs of Zion* (Nashville: Abingdon Press, 1981). There remain many other African-American songs and Spirituals not found in commonly used church hymnals, and it is worth looking around to find them. Scholarly collections such as *American Negro Songs,* John W. Work (New York: Dover Publications, Inc.: reprint 1998), and *Ev'ry Time I Feel the Spirit*, Gwendolin Sims Warren (New York: Holt and Company, 1997) are helpful sources. There are also many good recordings of hard-to-find spirituals, and these can be a good resource not only for the songs but also for authentic performance. There is no reason you can't teach your congregation some of this music by rote. An easy way to do this is to simply sing a first verse by yourself or with your choir, and then have your congregation join in. Spirituals and African-American music are continually evolving. Some CDs you will want to hear include *Amazing Grace,* Blind Boys of Alabama (Compendia, 2003); *Dark Was the Night,* Blind Willie Johnson (Columbia Legacy, 1998); *Gospel Soul,* Al Green (Arrival Records, 1993); *Sacred Ground,* Sweet Honey in the Rock (Earthbeat, 1995). Contemporary original African-American and world music may be heard from Stevie Wonder on *Innervisions* (Motown, 1973); Ladysmith Black Mambazo, *Two Worlds, One Heart* (Warner Brothers, 1991); and Bob Marley, *Legend* (Polygram, 1984).

## Liturgical Resources

At Canterbury House our primary liturgical resources are from the Episcopal and Anglican traditions. The *Book of Common Prayer* is a very flexible resource, one underappreciated, in our view, by contemporary liturgists in our own denomination. Its two companions are *The Book of Occasional Services* and *Lesser Feasts and Fasts.* New material, especially using inclusive language, is available in *Enriching Our Worship.* All are available from www.churchpublishing.org. Very popular and influential is *A New Zealand Prayer Book* (San Francisco: HarperCollins, 1989). Common prayer resources from all over the world are found at the resources website of the Society of Archbishop Justus: justus.anglican.org/resources/bcp. The Wild Goose Worship Group of the Iona Community in Scotland and the Taizé Community of France both have resources for creative liturgy available in the United States from GIA Publications, Inc. at www.giamusic.com.

Liturgical resources on the internet are simply too vast to enumerate, but two of my recent favorite places are the website for American Public Media's "Speaking of Faith," at speakingoffaith.publicradio.org, and "Spirituality and Practice" at www.spiritualityandpractice.com.

The internet is also a ready resource for alternative readings. For our service for Constance and Her Companions (see Chapter Three), I used the internet to find a particularly helpful and evocative description of the pathology of Yellow Fever in *Mortality and Morbidity Weekly Report.* The journal of

Marla Ruzicka provided an account of the work of a contemporary martyr, every bit as compelling as the story of Joan of Arc. A letter to the *New York Times* from Eli Thorkelson was a touching statement concerning the role of stress and alienation in suicide on college campuses.

Stephen is continually advocating for the use of texts from other traditions, and these often bring new perspective to our services. Readings from the *Bhaghavad Gita* (an important holy book in the Hindu tradition), Thich Naht Hanh's *Living Buddha, Living Christ* (New York: Riverhead Trade, 1997) and various collections of Zen Koans, translated by D.T. Suzuki and others, have been particularly helpful.

Contemporary liturgy is limited *only* by your own imagination and creativity. If you begin with your own "chart," you will have a place to bring any and every thing you read, see, and hear to bear on the worship of God and the proclamation of God's new creation.

# Chapter 10

## Church Musician—Gig or Calling?

This book on creative liturgy closes with an examination of three great musical contributors to liturgy, what they brought to the Church and how they approached their ministry. While this is not intended to be a comprehensive discussion of "lives of great church musicians," it *is* meant to observe and comment on some of the characteristics of those who have given their musical energies to the church.

A church musician has a prayer life, can improvise and perform well, and can "make it in the secular world, too." Thomas Dorsey, Olivier Messiaen, and Johann Sebastian Bach had faith and skills that church musicians should emulate, admire, and be inspired by. Each of them had an unabashed faith that was public, and not always in their professional best interest. Dorsey had a significant career as a Blues man, accompanying Ma Rainey before devoting his life to the church. Messiaen, as a French academic, operated in an intellectual milieu that was altogether convinced of Sartre's nihilism, and that certainly regarded traditional Catholicism as superstitious, if not embarrassing. Bach clearly preferred to work for the church rather than be employed as a court musician.

### Dorsey, Messiaen, and Bach, a Brief Comparison

Dorsey, Messiaen, and Bach each had a deep faith and a particular perspective they brought to church music: perspectives that will last for centuries. No doubt Messiaen's mystic Catholicism is at perfect odds with Bach's post-Pietistic Lutheranism, and no doubt Messaien and Bach would shrug at Dorsey's bluesy and soulful approach to church music. No matter. By their work, we in the here-and-now are able to eat all manner of foods at a musical smorgasbord, and live in a time when all manner of musics are "acceptable unto Christ." As we have endeavored to prove, all these styles can live happily in one family, one place, one church. Isn't that the spirit of the Creed?

Bach and Dorsey were primarily church musicians. Both had other professional choices available to them, but elected to devote their lives to church music. Bach had a celebrated career as a court composer, and his abstract works will probably survive forever; but the fact remains that he served the majority of his professional life as a church musician. Dorsey simply abandoned a budding career working with two of the founders of the Blues, Ma Rainey and Bessie Smith, in order to serve as a church musician. No question, neither Bach nor Dorsey needed the church economically; rather, they needed the church *spiritually.* This was their point of engagement with reality, where their music could integrate with their spiritual and intellectual beliefs. While Messiaen also had a career at the Paris Conservatoire, he too found his home—musically *and* spiritually—in the church, and no other place would suffice.

In Bach's time the opera was a flourishing form; however, unlike his contemporary Handel, he never wrote a single one. Instead, he wrote highly dramatic musical expositions of biblical texts:

Cantatas, Passions, and settings of the Magnificat. Messiaen took his faith to the concert hall as well, with his deeply inspired St. Francis-style Catholicism. Even his most abstruse and difficult works—*Chronochromie*, for instance—still breathe and seep his adoration of God's wonder, especially through his beloved birdcalls. Dorsey's sobbing Blues-based hymns achieve the same sublimity, using an altogether different syntax. His "Peace in the Valley" and "Precious Lord" moan and sway along with Bessie Smith's early work, but the message is one of a Divine Friend who is there while we suffer, just one step away from the existential sadness often found in the blues. Incidentally, this theology of "Divine Friend" is perhaps the seminal theology for at least one of the authors of this book.

Dorsey, Messiaen, and Bach are examples of church musicians who have completely different styles, while being completely dedicated to the music of the church. In a way, using these three as primary examples illustrates the point that Reid and I have been making all along, namely, that in the end, the style of the music and liturgy should respond to your church's context. The egregious notion that there is *a* style of church music that should somehow be maintained is antithetical to the Gospel mission—the mission of welcomeness. The liturgy should grow organically out of the resources, identity, and tastes of the congregation and community. Hopefully, the resources, identity, and tastes of the congregation and community express a deep unity.

## Thomas A. Dorsey

The author of "Precious Lord, Take My Hand" was born in Villa Rica, Georgia, in 1899. He had an early career as a pianist playing with the legendary Blues singer Ma Rainey, under the name "Georgia Tom." Later, he served as Music Director at Pilgrim Baptist Church in Chicago for about forty years. Thoroughly steeped in both Blues and church music, he synthesized both styles into something called "Gospel Blues." For an excellent thesis on Dorsey's work in this context, read Michael W. Harris's book *The Rise of Gospel Blues: The Music of Thomas Andrew Dorsey in the Urban Church* (New York: Oxford University Press, 1992). Early Blues musicians were already "preachin' it," such as Blind Willie Johnson and Reverend Gary Davis. They used traditional songs and spirituals including "Let My Light Shine" and "John the Revelator." Dorsey chose to write his own works, in response to his own faith and circumstances.

The circumstances that precipitated the writing of "Precious Lord, Take My Hand" bear retelling here. The story is tragic. Dorsey was in St. Louis playing for a convention, when he heard that his wife and child had died in childbirth. On the album *Precious Lord: Recordings of the Great Gospel songs of Thomas A. Dorsey* (Columbia Legacy, 1973), he states his experiences:

> I went out to go to St. Louis one morning to work in a revival. I left my wife asleep in bed, got in my car, and I went along. She was going to become a mother and I was anticipating the great happiness and great joy on my return. I got to St. Louis and about the second night in the meeting the telegraph boy came and brought me a telegram. I opened it and read, "Your wife just died. Come home." I couldn't finish the meeting. Finally I got home to Chicago, the next morning, and it was so. I found it all true. They never moved the body and that chilled me—killed me off—I wanted to go back to Blues. But after putting my wife away, and the baby in the same casket, I went to the old Choral College in the music room there, Mr. Fry and I—and just browsing over the keys and seemingly the words like drops of water from a crevice of a Rock above seemed to drop in line with me on the piano:
>
> *Precious Lord, Take My Hand.*
> *Lead me on, let me stand.*

*I am tired, I am weak, I am worn.*
*Through the storm, through the night,*
*Lead me on to the light.*
*Take my hand, Precious Lord, Lead Me On.*

He says, "I wanted to go back to the Blues." Of course, in a sense, he did! He immediately wrote "Precious Lord," replacing the downright despair so often cried forth in the Blues with the theology of God's grace. Notice that the syntax is not so different, textually or musically, from the blues. The wonderful recording by Marion Williams (*Precious Lord: Recordings of the Great Gospel Songs of Thomas A. Dorsey,* Columbia Legacy, 1973) gives this tune a kind of depth and "soul" that will remind some listeners of Aretha Franklin.

Notice too, that the division between secular and sacred is essentially erased in the work of Thomas Dorsey, and that the soul-force of this music is breathed into the church through his brilliant hands. The music that was moving people on the *outside* of the church continued to move them *inside* the church. Again, to paraphrase Luther, "Why should the Devil have all the great music?" Indeed.

Dorsey had wonderful ideas about the relationship between the preacher and the musician, as well as the spiritual engagement of the musician during the service.

> We feel that the people had forgotten about the old spiritual "Walk All over God's Heaven"; "I'm going to shout all over God's Heaven." We dressed it up, gave it a beat. You hear that in the bass. We put some embellishments and variations there, where the musicians could stand out and be heard. We tried to keep in the deep feeling, the spiritual meaning of the song. We picked a really great artist to do it: Mahalia Jackson.[8]

Of course, he's completely engaged in the text and the spirit of the song, and he's concerned about the engagement of the musicians, the newness of the interpretation, and the excellence of the end result. He says later, in the same interview: "Now a good choirmaster doesn't go into his service unless he knows the text of his pastor—the subject of his text. Then he selects the songs to fit the text." [9]

This is certainly in keeping with what we have been saying all along in this book: service planning means deep connection among all of the members of a worship team. No one is an island. Dorsey also describes the notion of being "caught up in the Spirit" this way:

> Some audiences, I heard them, chant. [He sings] "Lord I want to pray, Lord I want to pray, all night long. Pray for me, pray for me all night long." The minister is continually preaching. Those things spur the minister up, gets him warm, gets him hotter. [Chuckles] There's no separation of the sermon from the congregation. We know they are one. Call and response in Jazz, and we know it's in church music. You'll hear the minister call out, "Do you hear me?" And they say, *"Yes!"* "Do you hear me?" *"Yes!"* There's the use of the symbol, the train, or the arch, or the chariot. Always upwards. Everything looks up so far as the Christian is concerned. You have the song; the old arches are moving. The arch is moving toward God, moving upward.[10]

## Olivier Messiaen

Olivier Messiaen addressed the relationship between the secular and the sacred in a completely different way. For over sixty years, Messiaen—arguably the most important French composer of the

8 Studs Terkel, *And They All Sang: Adventures of an Eclectic Disc Jockey* (New York: New Press, 2006), 178.
9 Ibid., 179–80.
10 Ibid., 180.

twentieth century—served as a church musician at Sainte-Trinité in Paris. In an interview with Claude Samuel originally published in 1967, he says "I have consistently and quite seriously been active there for thirty-three years."[11] Born in 1908, Messiaen worked at Sainte-Trinité (which was actually his mailing address) until his death in 1981.

His description of his duties at Trinité sounds pretty workaday for most church organists:

> Every Sunday I've played for three Masses and Vespers, and often funerals and weddings during the week. I stopped for a few years because, by order of the Paris civic authorities, the organ had to be repaired, but I took up my duties again as soon as the restoration was complete.[12]

Imagine having Olivier Messiaen playing for your wedding! Incidentally, a lovely recording, *Messiaen: par lui Même* (EMI Classics) features Messiaen playing the pre-repaired organ, and is a surreal adventure into how to make lemons out of lemonade. The microtuning that results from the disrepair of the organ is used to full effect in Messiaen's work, and he was known to be as delighted by it as the civic authorities were annoyed.

When asked by Claude Samuel in the same interview about the role of improvisation in his work as a church musician, he responds:

> For the High Mass on Sunday, I played only plainsong, harmonized or not according to circumstances; for the eleven o'clock Mass on Sunday, classical and romantic music; for the Mass at noon, still on a Sunday, I was allowed to play my own music; and finally, for the five o'clock Vespers, I was obliged to improvise because the verses were too short to allow for the playing of pieces between the Psalms and the Magnificat.[13]

Then he elaborates on style:

> I developed the technique of making pastiches on purpose: mock-Mozart, mock-Bach, mock-Schumann and mock-Debussy, in order to continue in the same key and in the same style as the piece just sung. But even so, I improvised in my own style, living on my harmonic and rhythmic "fat"; sometimes I was lucky and had strokes of inspiration.[14]

These words about his employment breathe plenty of real life into the notion of the working church musician.

Messiaen was a pedagogue of monumental importance. At the age of twenty-eight he was teaching at Ecòle Normale de Paris and Schola Cantorum; then he was appointed Professor of Harmony at the Paris Conservatoire at age thirty-two. But was not allowed to teach composition until he was fifty-eight! His students included two of the most important composers of the late twentieth century in their respective countries: Karlheinz Stockhausen of Germany and Pierre Boulez of France.

Messiaen played, by his own account, *four* services each Sunday, with weddings and funerals thrown in, for over sixty years. This is a testament to the faith, the commitment, and the joy of liturgy that Messiaen clearly must have felt. Again, he said to Claude Samuel:

> I've the good fortune to be a Catholic. I was born a believer, and it happens that the Scriptures struck me even as a child. So a number of my works are intended to bring out the theological truths of the Catholic faith. That is the first aspect of my work, the noblest and, doubtless,

11 Olivier Messiaen, *Music and Color: Conversations with Claude Samuel*, trans. E. Thomas Glasow (Portland, OR: Andrews Press, 1994), 5.

12 Ibid., 5.

13 Ibid., 6.

14 Ibid.

> the most useful and valuable; perhaps the only one which I won't regret at the hour of my death.[15]

He continues by making clear the relationship between music-making, faith, and liturgy:

> Truly liturgical music, that which is intended to accompany the Office, is, for all that, an extremely well-founded act of praise in its origin, and those who accomplish this act of praise do so with excellent intention.[16]

Perhaps a better translation might be "with excellent intentionality." Either way, the meaning is clear. Messiaen did not look at liturgical music as "less than" concert work, nor as something that he as an artist had to "put up with in order to get a paycheck," nor something he had to do "so he could do his real work as an artist." The liturgical part of his job was integral to his spiritual and creative life. In a word, it was not *separate*.

Of course, the work of the church organist was not without its ordinary woes. Messiaen carps: "I was exposed to malevolence and the protests of parishioners, above all of the old ladies who heard the devil in the organ pipes." This should sound familiar to the contemporary church music director: "dissonance is evil." Incidentally, my own first exposure to John Cage was in a videotaped workshop by conservative theologian Francis Schaeffer, who argued that Cage's use of chance was a diatribe in favor of atheism, and that his use of dissonance was reflective of his nihilistic stance. Of course, Cage was a strictly observant Zen Buddhist, and extremely fond of the writings of Meister Eckhart. Far from nihilism, Cage's use of chance procedures was, in fact, an affirmation of the natural order of creation.

The playing in church of music that is a bit "modern" can be problematic, certainly. Messiaen's musical response was to write a piece that he frankly expected to please his congregational critics: "My first published organ work, *Le Banquet Céleste*: a very charming, tender, sweet, and springlike piece, which has nothing extraordinary about it!" I have to differ with the master. *Le Banquet Céleste* is one of the most voluptuous pieces ever written for organ, and is perhaps one of the most intensely sensual descriptions of the Eucharist ever translated to music. The formal structure is extremely simple and lovely, and the harmonies are a classic example of his early style (through the 1940s). It is a deeply moving piece that will doubtless endure for centuries. Might this piece, a concession to the "old ladies," be more accurately described as a love letter to them? I feel that these sorts of pieces are needed: fresh, new works, completely appropriate for liturgy, *and* completely modern. New works for liturgy that are rehashing old conventions, mired in harmonic or theological nostalgia, do nothing to bring the presence of Christ into the modern age, but instead perpetuate banality.

## Johann Sebastian Bach

Bach's career is widely known, but like most legends, legend seems to take over after a while and becomes a substitute for reality. Bach did toggle a bit between court and church in his employment, with sojourns in the courts of Weimar and Cöthen, but worked steadily at St. Thomas in Leipzig from 1723 until his death in 1750. In other words, for the majority of his life, Bach was primarily a church musician. The usual music history textbooks (Lang, Grout, and so on) soft-pedal this, and paint him as a freelance composer of the late Baroque. Of course, the first true freelance composer was Ludwig van Beethoven!

Bach's duties were ordinary, in the worst sense of the term. About his job at St. Blasius, Eva Mary and Sydney Grew write,

15 Ibid., 2.
16 Ibid., 8.

> He had no weekday duties. He took the one high service on Sunday and the special services on festivals and saints' days. His salary was what it had been at Arnstadt, with the addition of some corn, wood and fish. He was certainly given responsibilities that were usually undertaken by a cantor. That is, he had to select the music used in the services and, as it would seem, to train the choir. *But this was exactly what he wanted.* (emphasis added)[17]

This sounds like an ordinary church organist to me! Did the congregation recognize this young man for his genius? Hardly. Even in the petition to remove Bach from his post, a public official admitted "the people might *in time* have come to approve" Bach's work (emphasis added). Later, when Bach desperately wanted the job at St. Thomas in Leipzig, he was to find out that the parish preferred Telemann and Graupner (of all people). He was given the job anyway since neither of these two "greater musicians" was available.

One wonders if the opportunity to present as many as fifty-eight Cantatas a year at St. Thomas drew him there, in addition to working with a librettist who would match his non-Pietist theological leanings. It is ironic to think that John Wesley, the consummate Pietist, was firmly opposed to the use of counterpoint in music. Imagine what the parallel church-musical controversy might be today. Drums in church, maybe?

In any event Bach's chores increased in Leipzig. He had to instruct the children in Latin and instrumental music, and was required by his contract to live a "model Christian life."

I review these well-known facts about Bach for a simple reason: So often I hear church organists complaining about their many duties, and how their time is not their own. Interestingly enough, I rarely, if ever, hear a church musician complain about how much music s/he had to write that year, that their copyist quit, or that the resultant music was butchered by the choir—all indignities suffered continually by J. S. Bach. Church musicianship *is* hard! It *is* endless! It doesn't stop at the church door, and it does require composition, improvisation, and literacy, if not study in Latin! We need to expand our notion of what it means to be a church musician, not reduce it. Let it include composition, teaching, singing, playing, improvising, and advising the clergy about the appropriate music. If we, clergy or musician, need to defend this position, we can simply say, "well, this is how *Bach* did it!"

Bach was not without his own foibles and problems, including having to defend naughty but musical children who misbehaved at weddings, but he nonetheless found church work a perfect match for his faith as well as his musicianship. Bach's principal vehicle was the Cantata, not the Opera, as noted above, and this separates him from most of the great Baroque composers. Certainly, Vivaldi, Alessandro and Domenico Scarlatti, and Handel all wrote cantatas—it did pay well! But their primary output was in the area of "secular music," either instrumental music or opera. Bach succeeded no less in the secular domain, and his music was highly regarded though not thought of, even at the time, as progressive or particularly modern. His work, like Jazz, was a synthesis of national tendencies, using elements of Italian, German, and later English styles in Baroque music.

In the end, Bach did not separate his notion of "secular" and "sacred." His style is completely consistent between sacred Cantata and secular Concerto—enough to be a basis for harmonic instruction in every music school today, 260 years after his death. Perhaps Albert Schweitzer said it best:

> For him, art was religion, and so had no concern with the world or with worldly success. It was an end in itself. Bach includes religion in the definition of art in general. All great art, even secular, is in itself religious in his eyes; for him the tones do not perish, but ascend to God like praise too deep for utterance.[18]

17 Eva Mary Grew and Sidney Grew, *Bach* (New York: Collier Books, 1966), 66.

18 Albert Schwitzer, *J. S. Bach* vol. 1, (Library Reprints, 2001), 167.

## My Life as a Church Musician

I have to confess now my own place in this complex world of church musicianship. I have done a few lectures at conferences for the American Guild of Organists on liturgical planning and styles, and I have lectured at improvisation conferences on "playing for church." I started playing church music as a seven-year-old boy in my Southern Baptist congregation. The function of the pianist in this context is one of ornamentation, and at that age I knew a fair amount about ornamentation since I had already plunged deeply into the world of boogie-woogie and Blues (with genuine thanks to my older brother who was a hippie and a Rock musician). By age sixteen, I was either accompanying or singing in the adult choir and was adept at improvisation, which included alternative chord colors, arpeggiation, and often two transpositions in the same hymn. The first transposition only demands rethinking the key signature, the second, if you have perfect pitch, is a sheer act of faith! By seventeen, I was basically expelled from the church for my hairstyle and clothing, and a rather intense love for scripture that made me question some of the theological tenets espoused weekly during services.

I promptly found another community that was more accepting of my gifts, where Hindemith and Stravinsky were played along with Isaac Watts, and discussions of contemporary theological trends were *de riguer*. It was a mind-blowing experience for me that my intellectual self and my spiritual self could coexist!

I was in no position to work as a church musician during my college years nor as a young professor, but when I was hired at the University of Michigan in 1987, I was thrilled to find that Don Postema was working at a campus ministry there, and was in need of a church musician. Don and I became fast and furious friends. I had previously read his excellent book, *Space for God: The Study and Practice of Prayer and Spirituality* (Grand Rapids, MI: Faith Alive, 1997), as well as all of the books listed in his bibliography. I had even taught Sunday school using his book as a text while I was in graduate school in New York. He and I wrote liturgies that were challenging and heavily imbued with improvisation. One service simply had the names for God printed on the cover, while the rest was completely improvised! It was as spiritually honest an experience as any I had had up to that point.

When Don Postema retired, I gathered a band to play for his retirement. The drummer in that band, John Maloney, suggested that we consider "doing this stuff every Sunday." Matthew Lawrence hired me soon after to play at Canterbury House, with the agreement that *a*) the band would be paid better than the lousy Jazz gigs available in town, *b*) a sin-based, guilt-based liturgy would never be offered, *c*) music by Ornette Coleman, Sun Ra, John Coltrane, and Albert Ayler would never be considered problematic or non-liturgical, and *d*) Jazz would never be "special music." Jazz would be played every Sunday. Not once a month. Not "part of a service."

I seem to remember that it took Matthew only about twenty-four hours to get back to me. He had secured a three-year funding commitment from the board, and we were on our way.

In the end, Canterbury House has become the only church I feel I can contribute to (regularly) as a musician. There are no holds barred. There is no sense of exclusion for certain types of music. There is an understanding that we can learn from the world rather than fear it. The understanding that music is a true expression of God's presence is honored here, in a way that I have rarely felt elsewhere. It is also a place where the priest is willing and eager to give the musicians both an artistic and a theological voice. Reid has brought to Canterbury House a sense of joy and exuberance, a sense of journeying into the unknown. Instead of restating tired theology with old code words known only to insiders, Reid has ventured, with me, into the mysterious realms of ecstasy, exuberance, and the numinous. Here, ecstasy collides with deep sadness, and experiments collide with tradition, leading to an unpredictable voyage into the presence of God.

I have found at Canterbury House a home—a place where I can put off my intellectual veneer from the University, and fully bring my spiritual and musical self to a liturgy. I can be, in the words of Matthew Fox, a "Magical, Musical, Mystical Bear." As we said before, great liturgy comes with expertise, faith, and mutual trust on the part of the liturgical planners. I have this and more at Canterbury House. I also have a more-than-equal partner in crime with Reid Hamilton, someone who will challenge me on my silliness (and I am often accused of being too silly) and who will take risks with me, in faith, to achieve the sublimity found in truly great liturgy. We have often said, "If the service doesn't contain an element that might fail, it's just not Canterbury!"

I realize that this situation is unique. I really don't think I could function as a church musician in a large congregation. I am too thin-skinned, and also too busy with my university position. Nonetheless, I know that this liturgy works for this community. That, in the end, is the goal for all of us. I know that the right musician, right clergy, right liturgical planning team, right facility, and right instruments are rarely all found in one place. Even in the most ideal situation, there is the need for constant maintenance. I fret, fume, and worry non-stop over who will be in the band, this year and next. I wept bitterly after the first year when two of the band members left to pursue their musical dreams as road-warrior Rock musicians. We survived; you will too. Great things take a lot of work, and this work is God's. It's worth it.

# Appendix A

## Service Outlines

This appendix includes outlines for several services from 2004 through 2007 at Canterbury House, which were planned and conducted according to the principles set forth in this book. These include services in commemoration of various saints as well as "proper" liturgies for such occasions as All Hallows' Eve, Ash Wednesday, the First Sunday in Lent, Palm Sunday, and the Great Vigil of Easter.

These outlines are based on our service leaflets, which contain the entire "text" of the service: prayers, readings, and music, as well as hagiographies of the respective saints being commemorated (normally reproduced from *Lesser Feasts and Fasts*) and, lately, biographies of composers or lyricists for our music. Our Office Manager, Kathleen Peabody, also incorporates appropriate clip art, with both thoughtfulness and whimsy!

Because the music, scripture texts, and hagiographies we have used can easily be found elsewhere, these have been redacted. We have added commentary concerning how we selected certain texts, music, and preaching themes, and other service notes.

The services outlined here are organized in the order of our academic year—September through April—without regard to what year they might actually have been conducted.

### Jazz Masses

As explained in the Introduction, our usual service is the "Jazz Mass," which generally follows the structure of "The Holy Eucharist: Rite Two" found in the *Book of Common Prayer.* As included in the BCP, that structure would be as follows:

The Word of God
- Salutation and Response
- "Gloria in Excelsis" or "some other song of praise"
- The Collect of the Day
- The Lessons (one or two Lessons, "as appointed")
- The Gospel
- The Sermon
- The Nicene Creed
- The Prayers of the People
- Confession of Sin ("on occasion, the confession may be omitted")
- The Peace

The Holy Communion

The Great Thanksgiving (including the "Sanctus")

The Lord's Prayer

The Breaking of the Bread (after which Communion is served or distributed)

The Post-Communion Prayer

The Blessing

Dismissal

Added to this structure at principal Sunday services in many churches are various preludes, postludes, hymns, anthems, and sung responses. This structure may vary in many particulars from one congregation to another, and Canterbury House also makes several modifications. We usually omit the Nicene Creed and the Confession of Sin, for example, because our services are primarily geared to students who are seekers.

Those working in "liturgical" churches such as Roman Catholic, Lutheran, Presbyterian, and Methodist, will recognize all or most of the elements of this structure athough they might be ordered somewhat differently. "Nonliturgical" churches, too, tend to have some structure of greeting, music, prayers, readings, and sermon that will be familiar to members of their congregations from week to week. The "Jazz Mass," as a principle of improvisation in worship, can be adapted to whatever structure you find or might wish to use. Indeed, our brothers and sisters in nonliturgical churches may be ahead of the others in applying this principle!

Here, then, is the structure of a typical Jazz Mass at Canterbury House in detail, with a description of each element:

**Welcome!**—The Chaplain thanks everyone for being present, comments on the theme of the service, perhaps suggesting an idea for meditation during the opening silence, and invites the Music Director to comment on the music. New or difficult music might be rehearsed with the congregation at this time, in a friendly and welcoming manner.

**Prelude**—Usually, a Jazz composition with a title or a mood that reflects the theme of the service. Our service leaflets contain the instruction: "This music is intended to stretch our boundaries: to disorient or challenge us, or cleanse our interior palate. Some find it helpful to think of it as 'sounds to meditate by.'" Note that preludes and postludes are part of the service, rather than cover music for gathering or exiting. Since our service starts at 5 p.m., this is when the music begins. Note also, the compositions suggested for preludes and postludes are meant to be played live, not "listened to" on CD.

**Silence**—Punctuated by the gong, struck once at the beginning, once during, and once at the end of the silence. The congregation is prepared for an extended silence with a note in the service leaflet: *"Relax, and pray! This could take a while."*

**Opening Sentences**—A formal greeting and response, often appropriate to the season (Advent, Lent, Easter), between the celebrant or leader of the service and the congregation, such as:

*Presider:* Grace and peace to you from God.
*People:* God fill you with truth and joy.

or

*Presider:* Bless the Lord who forgives all our sins.
*People:* God's mercy endures for ever.

or

*Presider:* Alleluia! Christ is risen!
*People:* The Lord is risen indeed! Alleluia!

**Collect of the Day**—Either a collect assigned to the particular saint from *Lesser Feasts and Fasts*, or a seasonal collect from the *Book of Common Prayer.* If your particular tradition does not offer previously written collects, or if you are feeling particularly creative, they can be readily composed. A typical collect includes four parts, namely, the address ("Gracious and loving God"); an attribute of God that relates to the saint or the theme in question ("who gave to your servant Francis an abiding love and respect for all the creatures of the earth"); a petition ("grant that, inspired by his example, we may be good stewards of your creation"); and a doxology (through Jesus Christ our Lord, who lives and reigns with you and the Holy Spirit, one God, now and for ever. *Amen.*).

**Opening Hymn**—Selected to establish a particular mood and corresponding to the theme of the service. Most often, we will select something that gets the congregation "up,"moving and breathing together. The opening hymn is not so much a statement or affirmation of faith as it is an invitation to align with the Spirit.

**First Lesson**—Read by a student assigned by the Chaplain as the congregation gathers. Usually taken from the Hebrew Testament or from the Christian Testament other than the Gospels, and assigned to the particular saint in *Lesser Feasts and Fasts.*

**Psalm**—generally sung according to a tone composed by Stephen (see appendix C). Reid will typically adapt the psalm text to be inclusive (particularly, balancing gender references to God), organize the text to be sung in three to five verses with antiphons, and "point" the psalm—indicating note changes for the singer at the end of each line.

**Second Lesson**—Again read by a student assigned before the beginning of the service, and usually consisting of a reading from material other than scripture, such as the writings of the saint being commemorated, holy writings from other traditions, contemporary newspaper articles, or literary selections.

**Hymn**—Generally having a text, theme, or idea associated with the Gospel reading, and leading to the sermon topic. This might be called a "Sermon Hymn" in some traditions.

**Gospel**—Read by the Chaplain or another ordained person if present. Usually, the reading is that assigned to the particular saint in *Lesser Feasts and Fasts.*

**Sermon or Homily**—If Reid is preaching, this is usually a "Jazz Sermon," as discussed in Chapter Two, delivered without notes. We often have a guest preacher, either a visiting priest, who might or might not preach from a prepared text, or a student, who will almost always have a written text.

**Silence**—A brief time for reflection on what has been said in the sermon or homily. After an interval, the band will begin to extemporize softly as the prayers of the people begin.

**Prayers of the People**—We have adapted a prayer from *A New Zealand Prayer Book* (San Francisco: HarperSanFrancisco, 1997), page 163. The prayers are read by two students assigned before the service begins, and each petition allows for the congregation to respond or offer additional prayer intentions. The band will accompany these prayers with collective improvisation including rattles, whistles, percussive sounds, and quiet musical phrases. This is the band's "sonic response" to the text and mood of the spoken prayers. Care is taken to accompany rather than drown out those who are leading the prayers. As the prayers are drawing to a close, the band segues into the prayer response.

**Prayer Response**—A meditative Taizé composition, chanted by the congregation. See Chapter Seven for notes concerning performance of Taizé music.

**The Peace**—The celebrant greets the people with the phrase "The peace of the Lord be always with you." The people respond with "And also with you!" and then greet one another in the name of God. At Canterbury House this invariably involves some joyful chaos, which tends to continue until the band begins to play the Offertory.

**Offertory and Dancing**—The band strikes up an African chant, or a chant from the developing world, almost always with a clave groove on agogo bells. The congregation joins in, singing and dancing. Offerings of money, written prayer requests or intentions, and pledges of service are placed in a basket. The bread and wine for Communion are brought (danced!) forward to the altar. Everyone sings, dances, claps, stomps, and shouts until the altar has been prepared for Communion.

**The Holy Communion**—Introduced by "The Great Thanksgiving" or Eucharistic prayer, selected from the *Book of Common Prayer* or *A New Zealand Prayer Book*, or from other traditions or sources, or, on occasion, offered extemporaneously. The prayer includes the hymn of praise attributed to the angels in glory: the "Sanctus" or "Holy, Holy, Holy," which at Canterbury House is sung.

**Sanctus**—From among several possible selections: "Blues Sanctus," by Stephen, or "Halle, Halle, Halle," from *Many and Great,* ed. & arr. John Bell (Chicago: GIA Publications, Inc., 1990), "Wholy, Holy" by Marvin Gaye (*What's Going On,* Motown Records, 1971). There are many other possibilities, of course!

**Lord's Prayer**—We alternate the address to "Our Father" and "Our Mother" from week to week. Sometimes we will sing this prayer.

**Breaking of the Bread**—May be accompanied by an acclamation and response such as "Christ our Passover is sacrificed for us / Therefore let us keep the feast," or an anthem such as "Agnus Dei (*Lamb of God*)." See Stephen's "Blues Agnus Dei" at Appendix D: Blues Mass.

**Communion Hymn**—A Taizé composition so that those present do not have to refer to paper while communion is being distributed.

**Post-Communion Prayer**—A prayer of thanks to God for communion and community, asking for grace for the congregation to go forth in joy and service to the world. It may be selected from among many possibilities in various prayer books and liturgy sources or composed or improvised on the theme of the service.

**Blessing**—This might be a seasonal blessing from *The Book of Occasional Services* or some other source.

**Closing Hymn**—Again, selected to continue or reverse the mood established up to this point in the service, with a text that comments on or is congruent with the theme.

**Dismissal**—A formal ending to the service such as:

*Deacon:* Go in peace to love and serve the Lord.
*People:* Thanks be to God.

or

*Deacon:* Alleluia, alleluia! Let us go forth into the world, rejoicing in the power of the Spirit!
*People:* Thanks be to God. Alleluia, alleluia!

**Postlude**—Again, a Jazz composition performed by the band, with a title that states or comments on the theme of the service. At Canterbury House, everyone sticks around to listen to this!

## Taizé Services

The Taizé Community in France is an ecumenical Christian community whose worship emphasizes prayer and meditation. Their music, written mostly by Brother Jacques Berthier, consists of simple, repetitive phrases using lines from psalms or other scripture, repeated or sung in canon. They attract thousands of visitors every year, and a single service will include hundreds of people. Stephen has visited Taizé, has studied their music for twenty years, and has led numerous workshops on Taizé music. Creating this faithful replication of the Taizé service for Canterbury House naturally required some adaptation for our small space, as well as some other minor adjustments for our context.

A typical Taizé service at Canterbury House is structured as follows:

**Prelude and Invocation (instrumental)**—When led by a director who has studied and mastered it, Taizé music can be easily played by musicians who have only a little experience. We invite students who play an instrument to join a pickup rehearsal that Stephen conducts during the hour before the service. Pieces are rehearsed in reverse order, so that as the congregation assembles, the prelude is being rehearsed. The same tune is used for the first congregational chant—a very easy and painless way of teaching the music to the congregation.

**Introduction and Welcome**—The Chaplain, or just as often, the student who is leading the service, thanks everyone for being present, comments on the saint being commemorated, and invites the Music Director to comment on the music. Music for our Taizé services is also selected according to a theme appropriate to the saint or the liturgical occasion. The Taizé Community does not organize their liturgy around a saint, of course, but we have found this is a useful and enjoyable way to structure and develop our service.

**Chant**—Usually, the same tune that has been used as the prelude. The congregation can very quickly pick this up, having already heard the piece being played for several minutes as a prelude.

**Alleluia**—During Lent or on solemn occasions, we may use a Kyrie rather than an Alleluia.

**Psalm**—Psalms for Taizé services at Canterbury House are spoken, for a change. We read them "like the monks," alternating whole verses between two groups ("by choirs") and taking a long breath at the half verse. This meditative way of reading psalms gets everyone breathing together.

**Silence**

**Chant**—Yet another Taizé composition in keeping with the theme of the service.

**Silence**—These intervals of silence early in the service are brief, usually about one minute.

**Chant**—Several different Taizé compositions will be used during a single service.

**Gospel Reading**—At Taizé, readings from scripture are particularly brief, usually only one or two sentences read in three or four languages. At Canterbury House, since we are generally commemorating a specific saint, we'll typically use the Gospel lesson associated with that saint. If it is particularly long it might be edited down; but this is not usual for us.

**Chant**—Often, though not always, the Gospel reading is "framed" by the chant. That is, the same tune will be used before and after the reading.

**Silent Meditation**—This meditation is long—about ten minutes—and punctuated by the gong at the beginning, middle, and end of the meditation.

**Chant**

**The Prayers of the People**—Usually, our adaptation from the Prayers of the People, from *A New Zealand Prayer Book* (San Francisco: HarperSanFrancisco, 1997), page 163, chanted, with a Taizé Kyrie between petitions.

**Prayer Response**—Usually, the same Kyrie that we have been using as a chant tone for the prayer.

**Chant**

**Benediction**

**Postlude**—Generally an instrumental rendition of the chant that closed the service. Very often, the congregation will spontaneously sing along.

## Other Services

Services for specific occasions such as the Blessing of the Animals for St. Francis' Day, the Liturgy for All Hallows' Eve, or liturgies for Ash Wednesday, Maundy Thursday, Palm Sunday, or the Easter Vigil are also planned by Reid and Stephen together, from beginning to end, using available sources. Presented here are the outlines of services for All Hallows' Eve, adapted from The *Book of Occasional Services,* and the liturgies for Ash Wednesday, Palm Sunday, and the Great Vigil of Easter, all adapted from the *Book of Common Prayer.*

## Services, with Commentary

September 3, 2006: Jazz Mass—Albert Schweitzer
September 12, 2004: Jazz Mass—Constance and Her Companions
September 17, 2006: Taizé Service—Hildegard of Bingen
September 25, 2006: Jazz Mass—St. Michael and All Angels
October 31, 2006: Service for All Hallows' Eve
November 19, 2006: Jazz Mass—Elizabeth of Hungary
February 21, 2006: Liturgy for Ash Wednesday
March 5, 2006: Jazz Mass—The First Sunday in Lent
April 1, 2007: Jazz Mass—Palm Sunday
April 7, 2007: Easter Jazz Vigil

## September 3, 2006: Jazz Mass—Albert Schweitzer

*Albert Schweitzer is not (yet) included as an observance in* Lesser Feasts and Fasts. *His views of Jesus and the Christ were not particularly orthodox. Nevertheless, we decided to observe a commemoration of him at Canterbury House because the date he entered into glory, September 4, occurs early in the semester, and his life was a model of service, scholarship, and devotion—values we like to encourage in our students.*

*Schweitzer was an unusual blend of (very progressive) theologian and musician, as well as a doctor of medicine. A true genius, he abandoned the refinement and "civilization" of Europe to be a lover of the whole world. The music for the service reflects this.*

Welcome!

Prelude: "Garden of Souls"—Ornette Coleman, *New York is Now* (Blue Note)
*"Garden of Souls" is a lovely mid-tempo tune whose title could easily describe Schweitzer's view of all humanity.*

Silence

Opening Sentences

Collect of the Day

*Since Schweitzer is not included in* LFF, *I composed a collect:* Heavenly Father, whose Son Jesus Christ came, not to be served, but to serve: Give us the grace to follow in his footsteps, and to show forth your love by loving and serving our neighbors, and coming, as did Albert Schweitzer, to the rescue of those in need; for the sake of the same Jesus Christ our Lord, who lives and reigns with you and the Holy Spirit, one God, now and for ever. Amen.

Invocation: "He Came Down" in John Bell, ed., *Many and Great* (Chicago: GIA Publications, Inc., 2002), 14
*Since Schweitzer served in Africa, we selected this tune from Cameroon: "He came down that we might have love/joy/peace!"*

First Lesson: Deuteronomy 15:10–11
*The Hebrew Testament's commandment to serve the poor.*

Psalm 150: Nature Tone (*see* Appendix C: Psalm Tones)
*Psalm 150 revels in the praise of God with music and sound. We coupled this text with Stephen's "Nature Tone." The text "The Earth Is Yours, O Giver of Life!" is an evangelical expression of the theme of the service. Note in the setting of the psalm text the references to God in masculine, feminine, and gender-neutral terms. Psalms for chanting to Stephen's Psalm Tones are paraphrased by Reid, usually based on a combination of the translations from the* Book of Common Prayer *and* The Psalms: An Inclusive Langage Version Based on the Grail Translation from the Hebrew *(Chicago: GIA Publications, Inc., 1986).*

Hallelujah! Praise God in his holy **temple;**
Praise him in the mighty **heavens.**
Praise him for his powerful **deeds,**
praise him for his excellent **greatness.** *Antiphon*

Praise God with the sounds of the **trumpet,**
praise her with lute and **harp.**
Praise her with timbrel and **dance;**
praise her with strings and **pipes.** *Antiphon*

Praise God with resounding **cymbals,**
praise God with clashing **cymbals.**
Let everything that lives and has **breath,**
give praise to God, **Hallelujah!** *Antiphon*

Second Lesson: A Reading from Albert Schweitzer

For that reason it is a good thing that the true historical Jesus should overthrow the modern Jesus, should rise up against the modern spirit and send upon earth, not peace, but a sword. He was not a teacher, not a casuist; He was an imperious ruler. It was because He was so in His inmost being that He could think of Himself as the Son of Man. That was only the temporally conditioned expression of the fact that He was an authoritative ruler. The names in which men expressed their recognition of Him as such, Messiah, Son of Man, Son of God, have become for us historical parables. We can find no designation which expresses what He is for us.

He comes to us as One unknown, without a name, as of old, by the lakeside. He came to those men who knew Him not. He speaks to us the same word: "Follow thou me!" and sets us to the tasks which He has to fulfill for our time. He commands. And to those who obey Him, whether they be wise or simple, He will reveal Himself in the toils, the conflicts, the sufferings which they shall pass through in His fellowship, and as an ineffable mystery, they shall learn in their own experience Who He is.

*The Quest of the Historical Jesus* (New York: Collier, 1968), 403.

*I chose from Schweitzer's own writings an alternative reading that expresses the imperative nature of Christ, the radical presence of Christ in the world, whose existence* requires *us to respond.*

Hymn: "Sleepers wake" in *The Hymnal 1982* (New York: The Church Pension Fund, 1985), 61.

*It seemed appropriate to include a Bach work in a service commemorating this great scholar of Bach. This wonderful harmonization is perfect for congregational singing in parts, and begs for* a cappella *singing.*

Gospel: Matthew 25:31–46

*Again, this selection was made "in-house," and chosen because in this lesson Jesus clearly sets forth the standard for our treatment of the poor, the stranger, the prisoner.*

Homily

Silence

Prayers of the People, adapted from *A New Zealand Prayer Book* (San Francisco: HarperSanFrancisco, 1997), 163.

Prayer Response: "Beati voi poveri" in *Taizé 2006–2007* (Taizé: Ateliers et Presses de Taizé, 2007), 124

*The English translation of this Taizé piece is "Blessed Are the Poor, for Theirs Is the Kingdom of Heaven."*

The Peace

Offertory and Dancing: "Jesu Tawa Pono" (Zimbabwe), in John Bell, ed., *Many and Great* (Chicago: GIA Publications, Inc., 2002), 51.

*This chant from Zimbabwe, easy to learn and upbeat, always gets the congregation to move their feet.*

The Holy Communion

Blues Sanctus—Stephen Rush (*see* Appendix D: Blues Mass)

Lord's Prayer

Breaking of the Bread

Communion Hymn: "Ubi Caritas," from *Taizé 2006–2007* (Taizé: Ateliers et Presses de Taizé, 2007), 4.
*"Where there Is Charity and Love, God Is There."*

Post-Communion Prayer

Blessing

Closing Hymn: "S/He's got the Whole World," *Lift Every Voice and Sing II: An African American Hymnal* (New York: The Church Pension Fund, 1993), 217.

*A Canterbury House favorite, with a very "up" mood and with the gender reference to God alternated by verse.*

Dismissal

Postlude: D Minor Fugue, *The Well-Tempered Clavier, Book I,* J. S. Bach
"Lookout for Hope"— Bill Frisell (*Lookout for Hope,* Impulse)

*In another acknowledgement of Schweitzer's status as an influential Bach scholar and performer, the band played a Jazz version of the D-Minor Fugue as an introduction to the title track to Bill Frisell's 1987 album.*

## September 12, 2004: Jazz Mass—Constance and Her Companions
(See chapter 3 for an in-depth discussion of this service)

Welcome!

Prelude: "Who Does She Hope to Be"—Sonny Sharrock, *Ask the Ages* (Axiom, 1991)

Silence

Opening Sentences

Collect of the Day, from *Lesser Feasts and Fasts*

Invocation: "Abide with me," from *The Hymnal 1982* (New York: The Church Pension Fund, 1985), 662.

First Lesson: 2 Corinthians 1:3–5

Psalm 116: Compassion Tone (*see* Appendix C: Psalm Tones)

The LORD has heard the voice of my **supplication,**
he inclined his ear to me when I called upon **him.**
The cords of death **entangled me;**
I came to grief and **sorrow.** *Antiphon*

Then I called upon the Name of the **LORD:**
"O LORD, I pray you save my **life.**"
Gracious is the LORD and **righteous**;
our God is full of **compassion.** *Antiphon*

The LORD watches over the **innocent;**
I was brought very low, and he **helped me.**
Turn again to your rest, O **my soul,**
for the LORD has treated you **well.** *Antiphon*

For you have rescued my life from **death,**
my eyes from tears, and my feet from **stumbling.**
I will walk in the presence of the **LORD**
in the land of the **living.** *Antiphon*

How shall I repay the **LORD**
for all the good things he has done for **me**?
I will lift up the cup of **salvation**
and call upon the Name of the **LORD.** *Antiphon*

I will fulfill my vows to the **LORD**
in the presence of all his **people.**
Precious in the sight of the **LORD**
is the death of his **servants.** *Antiphon*

I am your servant and the child of your **handmaid;**
you have freed me from my **bonds.**
I will offer you the sacrifice of **thanksgiving**
and call upon the Name of the **LORD.** *Antiphon*

I will fulfill my vows to the **LORD**
in the presence of all his **people,**
in the courts of the LORD'S **house,**
in the midst of you, O Jerusalem. **Hallelujah!** *Antiphon*

*This service was done early in my tenure at Canterbury House. Since then I have learned to use only three to five "verses," as edited, for the Psalm—this might represent as many as six to ten verses of the Psalm text—and to balance the gender references.*

Second Lesson: A Reading from *Morbidity and Mortality Weekly Report,* April 19, 2002:

Yellow fever is a mosquito borne viral disease that has caused deaths in U.S. and European travelers to sub-Saharan Africa and tropical South America. Although no specific treatment exists for yellow fever and the case-fatality rate for severe yellow fever is approximately 20%, and effective vaccine is available.

On return from Brazil on March 10, 2002, a previously healthy man aged 47 years from Texas presented to an emergency department with a 4-day history of crampy abdominal pain and a 1-day history of fever of 102.8 degrees and severe headache. At the emergency department, he received symptomatic treatment and an antibiotic and was discharged. His fever and headache worsened, and on March 12 he was hospitalized for intractable vomiting. On admission, physical examination revealed an ill-appearing, febrile man. Laboratory tests documented anemia, abnormal coagulation, renal failure, and liver failure.

The patient was presumptively treated for malaria. Three days after admission, the patient developed shock, seizures, and excessive bleeding at venipuncture sites; he died the following day.

*I found this article on the internet as I was looking for information on yellow fever. I was particularly fortunate to find this brief account that not only described the symptoms of yellow fever, but also highlighted the point that it is now rare in the developed world even as it remains endemic in sub-Saharan Africa and tropical South America. It is adapted for public reading.*

Hymn: "A Woman's Care," in John Bell, *Heaven Shall Not Wait* (Chicago: GIA Publications, Inc., 1989), 24.

Gospel: John 12:20–28

*The readings assigned for Constance and Her Companions in* Lesser Feasts and Fasts *call for the reading of John 12:24–28. When we read this pericope in preparation for planning this service, we felt that the introductory account of the Greeks who said to Philip "Sir, we wish to see Jesus" (vv. 20–21) should not be omitted. Those who "wish to see Jesus" in the most direct and meaningful way cannot find a more direct path than to emulate Constance and her Companions in their self-sacrificial devotion.*

Homily

Silence

Prayers of the People—adapted from *A New Zealand Prayer Book* (San Francisco: Harper-SanFrancisco, 1997), 163.

Prayer Response: "In Manus Tuas, Pater,"from *Taizé 2006–2007* (Taizé: Ateliers et Presses de Taizé, 2007), 30.

The Peace

Offertory and Dancing: "I Walk the Line," Johnny Cash, *The Essential Johnny Cash, 1955–1983* (Columbia/Legacy, 1992).

The Holy Communion

Sanctus: "Halle, Halle, Halle" (Puerto Rico), in John Bell, ed., *Many and Great* (Chicago: GIA Publications, Inc., 2002), 18.

Lord's Prayer

Breaking of the Bread

Communion Hymn: "Ubi Caritas," from *Taizé 2006–2007* (Taizé: Ateliers et Presses de Taizé, 2007), 4.

Post-Communion Prayer

Blessing

Closing Hymn: "There is a Balm in Gilead," from *Lift Every Voice and Sing II: An African American Hymnal* (New York: The Church Pension Fund, 1993), 203.

Dismissal

Postlude: "Memphis Blues"—W. C. Handy

*W. C. Handy, a Memphis native, is often called the "Father of the Blues." He collected and transcribed many Blues melodies while traveling with dance bands during the 1890s. Historically, then, this tune comes from virtually the same time and place as Constance. The sheet music for "Memphis Blues," published in 1912, quickly sold out, making it arguably the first "hit" Blues song ever. A scan of the first page of this composition was found on eBay, from which Stephen prepared an arrangement. Sometimes having the "right" music takes some considerable effort!*

## September 17, 2006: Taizé Service—Hildegard of Bingen

*The service for Hildegard of Bingen was a Taizé service. As explained above, Taizé services at Canterbury House follow the structure of services at the Taizé Community as our space and context permit. In this service we added some chants by Hildegard herself, a remarkable saint who was a mystic, a musician, an artist, and a healer. We sought to convey, through the music for this service, the vision of God as the creator of all, both the external world of natural beauty and the interior realm of ecstasy and the Numinous.*

Prelude and Invocation: Sanctum Nomen Domini (instrumental), from *Taizé 2006–2007* (Taizé: Ateliers et Presses de Taizé, 2007), 56.

Introduction and Welcome

Chant: Sanctum Nomen Domini
*The congregation chants the same piece that was played as a prelude. A new chant can quickly be taught this way. The text of this chant invokes the Magnificat and the voice of Mary, queen among saints.*

Alleluia: Alleluia 3, from *Taizé 2006–2007* (Taizé: Ateliers et Presses de Taizé, 2007), 74.
*This Alleluia, in a minor key, is based on Orthodox chant. Since the words are the same in any language, we can sing it in Russian!*

Psalm 104: Benedic, *anima mea*
*Psalms for Taizé services at Canterbury House are spoken. We read them "like the monks," alternating whole verses by choirs, and taking a long breath at the half verse. This meditative way of reading psalms gets everyone breathing together.*

Silence

Choral Chant: O Virtus Sapientiae—Hildegard von Bingen, transcribed by Stephen Rush from *Hildegard Von Bingen-Symphoniae, Geistliche Gesange* (Harmonia Mundi, 1985).

> O moving force of Wisdom, encircling the wheel of the cosmos, encompassing all that is, all that has life. You have three wings: The first unfurls aloft in the highest heights. The second dips its way dripping sweat on the Earth. Over, under, and through all things whirls the third. Praise to you, O Wisdom, worthy of praise!

*This complicated piece of music was sung by Reid and me together with a few congregants with exceptional reading ability.*

Silence
*This meditation is brief (about one minute).*

Chant: Laudate omnes gentes, from *Music from Taizé, Vol. I* (Chicago: GIA Publications, Inc., 1978), 12.
*This piece moves away from the more personal notion of praise expressed in the preceding chants and toward an expression of praise by "all nations."*

Reading: John 3:16–17

Chant: Laudate omnes gentes, from *Music from Taizé, Vol. I* (Chicago: GIA Publications, Inc., 1978), 12.

*The Gospel reading is framed by the chant.*

Silent Meditation

*This meditation is long (about ten minutes).*

Chant: There is no darkness or trouble (not in print)

*"Aucune Ombre" is a somber and meditative piece, though written in a major key.*

Prayers of the People, adapted from *A New Zealand Prayer Book* (San Francisco: HarperSanFrancisco, 1997), 163, and chanted with Kyrie 20, from *Taizé 2006–2007* (Taizé: Ateliers et Presses de Taizé, 2007), 90.

Prayer Response: Kyrie 20, from *Taizé 2006–2007* (Taizé: Ateliers et Presses de Taizé, 2007), 90.

*Kyrie 20 is a more upbeat Kyrie. Chanting the prayers with this Kyrie as a refrain holds the congregation's attention.*

Choral Chant: O Felix Anima—Hildegard von Bingen, transcribed by Stephen Rush from *Hildegard Von Bingen-Symphoniae, Geistliche Gesange* (Freiburg: Harmonia Mundi, 1985).

O happy soul, whose body has risen from the Earth which you wander and tread
on during your sojourn in this world.
Made to be the very mirror of Divinity, you have been crowned
with divine imagination and intelligence.
The Holy Spirit looks upon you and discovers its very own dwelling place.
Made to be the mirror of Divinity, you have been crowned
with divine imagination and intelligence.
Therefore—glory to the Father, to the Son, and to the Holy Spirit.

*Again, a complex work of art by Hildegard, expressing the beauty of the human soul as created by God.*

Benediction

Chant: Vieni Spirito Creatore, from *Taizé 2006–2007* (Taizé: Ateliers et Presses de Taizé, 2007), 57.

*A lovely Taizé chant praising God as Creator. The English translation of this piece does not do it justice!*

## September 25, 2006: Jazz Mass—St. Michael and All Angels

*By the end of the first month of the semester, the freshmen are starting to see what they have gotten themselves into at this major university! The Commemoration of St. Michael and All Angels is an opportunity to send up the call for divine aid. Calling upon the angels is a practice as old as our faith. We considered that for scholars, calling for divine aid is a plea for enlightenment; so enlightenment became the theme of our service. It seemed to us also that enlightenment or spiritual awareness should and does lead to action and commitment in the world through acts of compassion and justice. Note that we do not engage in these things for themselves or even merely for the service of others. Rather, they are a way of translating the divine gift of enlightenment into the divine imperative of service.*

Welcome!

Prelude: "Compassion"—John Coltrane (*First Meditations,* Impulse, 1965)
*The title of this classic late Coltrane composition underscored for us that enlightenment is not merely mental or ideal, but physical and practical.*

Silence

Opening Sentences

Collect of the Day; from *Lesser Feasts and Fasts*

Invocation: "Siyahamba" (South Africa), from *Wonder, Love and Praise* (New York: The Church Pension Fund, 1997), 787.

First Lesson: Revelation 12:7–12

Psalm 103: Shelter Tone (*see* Appendix C: Psalm Tones)
*The idea of appealing to the angels for protection led us to the notion of "shelter" for the Psalm tone.*

Bless the Lord, O my **soul,**
and all that is within me, bless his holy **Name.**
Bless the Lord, O my **soul,**
and forget not all his **benefits.** *Antiphon*

The Lord executes **righteousness**
and judgment for all who are **oppressed.**
He made his ways know to **Moses**
and his works to the children of **Israel.** *Antiphon*

Bless the Lord, you angels who do his **bidding,**
and hearken to the voice of his **word.**
Bless the Lord, all you his **hosts,**
you ministers of his who do his **will.** *Antiphon*

Second Lesson: A reading from *The Sayings of the Desert Fathers*

It happened that Abba Moses was struggling with the temptation of fornication. Unable to stay any longer in the cell, he went and told Abba Isidore. The old man exhorted him to return to his cell, but he refused, saying, "Abba, I cannot." Then Abba Isidore took Moses out onto the terrace and said to him, "Look towards the west." He looked and saw hordes of demons flying about and making a noise before launching an attack. Then Abba Isidore said to him, "Look toward the east." He turned and saw an innumerable multitude of holy angels shining with glory. Abba Isidore said, "See, these are sent by the Lord to the saints to bring them help, while those in the west fight against them. Those who are with us are more in number than they are." Then Abba Moses gave thanks to God, plucked up courage and returned to his cell.

*The Sayings of the Desert Fathers,* trans. Benedicta Ward, rev. ed. (Kalamazoo: Cistercian Publications, 1984), 138.

*Nowadays we tend to think of angels and demons metaphorically; but they remain useful and instructive metaphors nonetheless. I thought the reference to the temptation of fornication, for a congregation of college students, was both subtle and appropriate.*

Hymn: "Didn' My Lord Deliver Daniel," from *Lift Every Voice and Sing II: An African American Hymnal* (New York: The Church Pension Fund, 1993), 182.

*This spiritual is a direct appeal to God and the hope that God will respond, in character, to the need for deliverance.*

Gospel: Luke 4:16–21

Homily

Silence

Prayers of the People: Adapted from *A New Zealand Prayer Book* (San Francisco: Harper-SanFrancisco, 1997), 163.

Prayer Response: "Our darkness," from *Taizé 2006–2007* (Taizé: Ateliers et Presses de Taizé, 2007), 26.

*The text of this song is "Our darkness is never darkness in your sight, the deepest night is clear as the daylight." It brought to my mind a line from the "Student's Prayer" of St. Thomas Aquinas: "Graciously let a ray of your light penetrate the darkness of my understanding."*

The Peace

Offertory and Dancing: "Jesu Tawa Pano" (Zimbabwe), in John Bell, ed., *Many and Great* (Chicago: GIA Publications, Inc., 2002), 51.

*This African chant invites the congregation to dance, singing "Jesus we are here* for you," *again bringing together enlightenment and action.*

The Holy Communion

Blues Sanctus—Stephen Rush (*see* Appendix D: Blues Mass)

Lord's Prayer

Breaking of the Bread

Communion Hymn: "The Lord Is My Light," from *Music from Taizé, Vol. II* (Chicago: GIA Publications, Inc., 1982), 50.

*Light and salvation are expressly brought together in this text.*

Post-Communion Prayer

Blessing

Closing Hymn: "This Little Light of Mine," from *Lift Every Voice and Sing II: An African American Hymnal* (New York: The Church Pension Fund, 1993), 160.

*We do this tune as a laid back shuffle-boogie with its various verses encouraging the members of the congregation to show their light all around the world. It invites the students to reflect the light of the Holy Spirit in an academic setting—a controversial and challenging endeavor!*

Dismissal

Postlude: "Acknowledgement" from "A Love Supreme," John Coltrane (*A Love Supreme,* Atlantic, 1964)

*This portion of the Suite, in which the band chants "A love supreme" over and over, is actually very Taizé-like in performance. The students at Canterbury House are so familiar with this tune that they join the band in the singing.*

## October 31, 2006: Service for All Hallows' Eve

*This service was adapted from* The Book of Occasional Services, *which provides "a visit may be made to a cemetery or burial place." In a campus ministry setting, we're not going to miss an invitation like that! Because this service was held in a graveyard, the instruments had to be portable. Also, we expected a small congregation on account of the competition with Halloween as a secular and commercial holiday, so congregational music had to be quite simple. I admit that I prayed for good weather because we would have lost the bass player if there was any chance of rain at all. The scaled down orchestration, with trombone, sax, acoustic guitar and bass, and drums, gave a strange and haunting tone to the service.*

Welcome and Procession

Prelude: "Witches and Devils," Albert Ayler, *Witches and Devils,* (Freedom/Black Saint, 1964).
*Albert Ayler is one of our musical "patron saints" at Canterbury House. For this arrangement of his fabulous recording "Witches and Devils," I was able to use trombone for a lead instrument rather than piano.*

Silence

*According to* The Book of Occasional Services *"the rite begins with the Service of Light, page 109 of the* Prayer Book, *using the Prayer for Light appointed for Festivals of Saints. Our service begins as follows:*

Presider: Bless the Lord who forgives all our sins;
People: God's mercy endures for ever.

Presider: If I say, "Surely the darkness will cover me, and the light around me turn to night," darkness is not dark to you, O Lord; the night is as bright as the day; darkness and light to you are both alike. *(Psalm 139:10–11)*

Let us pray: Lord Christ, your saints have been the lights of the world in every generation: Grant that we who follow in their footsteps may be made worthy to enter with them into that heavenly Country where you live and reign for ever and ever. *Amen.*

Phos Hilaron: *The Hymnal 1982* (New York: The Church Pension Fund, 1985), S 59.
*This ancient hymn was sung to the chant setting in* The Hymnal 1982 *and was very effective using a saxophone "voice" for accompaniment.*

The Witch of Endor: 1 Samuel 28:3–25
*We set this story for reading in parts. Spooky musical accompaniment included chains, drums, rattles, and tapping a gravestone.*

Hymn: "Somebody's Buried in the Graveyard," American Traditional, from *American Negro Songs* (Mineola, NY: Dover Publications, Inc., 1998), 127.
*This Spiritual is in a simple Blues form. As the light diminished, it was a good thing to have a simple, repetitive tune that grew, as we sang it, in familiarity and in dynamic level. The more repetitions, the more rowdy and wonderful the hymn became.*

Prayer

The Valley of Dry Bones: Ezekiel 37:1–14

*Read with yet more spooky musical accompaniment. The reaction was one of good cheer, of course, for these are college students, not grade school children. The fun of the context and the weirdness of these stories and the way we told them all contributed to a liturgical experience that was quite out of the ordinary.*

Hymn: "Soon-a Will Be Done," from *Songs of Zion* (Nashville: Abingdon Press, 1981), 158.

*In a different context, "Dem Dry Bones" might have seemed a logical choice, but it is too complicated to sing with these instruments in this (outdoor) setting. Instead, we sang yet another spiritual, this time* a cappella *with improvised harmonies (*à la *Blind Boys of Alabama) and clapping. This required talent from our musical leaders as well as bravery and good humor from the congregation.*

Prayer

Homily

Silence

Te Deum laudamus: Blues Setting—Stephen Rush

*The Te Deum was improvised over a traditional Blues line (such as used by Muddy Waters in "Hoochie Coochie Man" on his* Live at Newport *album):*

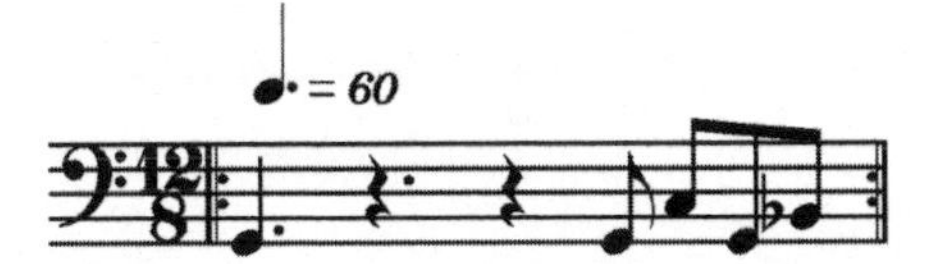


*Against this bass line and groove, Reid sang the Te Deum in verses, and between each verse, replied with Stephen's "Blues Sanctus" (see* Appendix D: Blues Mass) *which everyone at Canterbury House knows very well. This was all done basically in pitch darkness. Observe the pragmatics of this: only the priest and one of the musicians needs a bit of light to see the text (the music is easily memorized) and the congregation can simply chime in at the appropriate moment.*

Lord's Prayer

Collect for All Saints' Day, taken from the *Book of Common Prayer*

Prayer

The Blessing

Postlude: "Ghosts," Albert Ayler (*Love Cry,* Impulse!, 1967)

*In addition to being one of Albert Ayler's most famous pieces, "Ghosts" is really a very fun New Orleans-style march, or Calypso, and musically hearkens back to Mardi Gras. Our musicians have this piece memorized, so darkness was not a problem.*

## November 19, 2006: Jazz Mass—Elizabeth of Hungary

*There is a lovely legend of St. Elizabeth of Hungary, that having been forbidden by her family to give further relief to the poor, she attempted to smuggle bread out of the palace in her apron. When she was caught by surprise and required to reveal what she was carrying, she dropped her apron to display that it was filled with roses. This magical story captures my heart: from a position of tremendous wealth she gave it all away to serve the poor. As such, every piece of music pointed toward the idea of service. One question that our students do, in fact, ask themselves, is "How can I use this fancy education to serve something or someone other than myself?" The theme of this service was "poverty." When we talk about "poverty" at Canterbury House, we mean not only the call to the service of the poor, but also the liberation to be found in rendering ourselves poor before God.*

Welcome!

Prelude: "Who Does She Hope to Be?"—Sonny Sharrock, *Ask the Ages* (Axiom, 1991)
*This lovely tune, from the amazing* Ask the Ages *album, is a Canterbury House favorite, and we use it often in association with female saints. It happens that it was especially appropriate to use for Elizabeth in conjunction with Sharrock's "Promises Kept" as our postlude.*

Silence

Opening Sentences

Collect of the Day, taken from *Lesser Feasts and Fasts*

Invocation: "You Hear the Lambs a-Crying," taken from *Lift Every Voice and Sing II: An African American Hymnal* (New York: The Church Pension Fund, 1993), 110.
*This song could be sung about Elizabeth as well as Jesus. Perhaps the salient feature of all the saints is their emulation of Christ. With its call and response structure, this spiritual is fun to sing and easy to learn.*

First Lesson: Tobit 12:6b–9
*Raphael's litany of "good things to do," and particularly to give alms, is a helpful bit of formation for our college students, who, we hope, will remember later in life for the benefit of others the difficulties of their present, but temporary, poverty.*

Psalm 112: Enlightenment Tone (*see* Appendix C: Psalm Tones)
*"The righteous are merciful and full of compassion."*

Hallelujah!
Happy are those who fear the **LORD,**
and have great delight in her **commandments.**
Their descendants will be mighty in **the land;**
the generation of the upright will be **blessed.** *Antiphon*

Wealth and riches will be in their **houses,**
and their righteousness will last for **ever.**
Light shines in the darkness for the **upright;**
the righteous are merciful and full of **compassion.** *Antiphon*

It is good for them to be generous in **lending,**

and to manage their affairs with **justice.**
For they will never be **shaken;**
the righteous will be kept in everlasting **remembrance.** *Antiphon*

They have given freely to the **poor;**
and their righteousness stands fast for **ever.**
The wicked will see it and be **angry;**
they will gnash their teeth and pine **away.** *Antiphon*

Second Lesson: A Reading from St. Bonaventure:

It happened that the young Francis of Assisi, dressed in his fine clothes, met a certain knight who was of noble birth, but poor and badly clothed. Moved to compassion for his poverty, Francis took off his own garments and clothed the man on the spot. At one and the same time he fulfilled the two-fold duty of covering over the embarrassment of a noble knight and relieving the poverty of a poor man.

The following night, when he had fallen asleep, God in his goodness showed him a large and splendid palace full of military weapons emblazoned with the insignia of Christ's cross. Thus God vividly indicated that the compassion he had exhibited toward the poor knight for love of the supreme King would be repaid with an incomparable reward. And so when Francis asked to whom these belonged, he received an answer from heaven that all these things were for him and his knights. When he awoke in the morning, he judged the strange vision to be an indication that he would have great prosperity; for he had no experience in interpreting divine mysteries nor did he know how to pass through visible images to grasp the invisible truth beyond. Therefore, still ignorant of God's plan, he decided to join a certain count in Apulia, hoping in his service to obtain the glory of knighthood, as his vision seemed to foretell.

He set out on his journey shortly afterwards; but when he had gone as far as the next town, he heard during the night the Lord address him in a familiar way, saying: "Francis, who can do more for you, a lord or a servant, a rich man or a poor man?" When Francis replied that a lord and a rich man could do more, he was at once asked: "Why, then, are you abandoning the Lord for a servant and the rich God for a poor man?" And Francis replied: "Lord, what will you have me do?" And the Lord answered him: "Return to your land, because the vision which you have seen foretells a spiritual outcome which will be accomplished in you not by human but by divine planning." In the morning, then, he returned in haste to Assisi, joyous and free of care; already a model of obedience, he awaited the Lord's will.

(*Bonaventure: The Soul's Journey Into God; The Tree of Life; The Life of St. Francis,* trans. Ewert Cousins [New York: Paulist Press, 1978]).

Hymn: "We Belong to God" (Mexico) in John Bell, ed., *One Is the Body* (Chicago: GIA Publications, Inc., 2002), 64.

*Rather than follow this story of St. Francis with any of several hymns with texts attributed to St. Francis, we sang this lovely Mexican tune with a text by John Bell. Several of our Canterburians have worked on the U.S.–Mexico border and points south, and it seemed important that we sing about giving our lives to God from a Latin American perspective, musically and theologically.*

Gospel: Luke 12:32–34

Homily

Silence

Prayers of the People—adapted from *A New Zealand Prayer Book* (San Francisco: Harper-SanFrancisco, 1997), 163.

Prayer Response: "Wait for the Lord," from *Music from Taizé, Vol. II* (Chicago: GIA Publications, Inc., 1982), 78.

*"Wait for the Lord" is a reminder to the congregation that as we are giving help to others, our own help comes from the Lord.*

The Peace

Offertory and Dancing: "He Came Down" (Cameroon), in John Bell, ed., *Many and Great* (Chicago: GIA Publications, Inc., 2002), 14.

*A perennial Canterbury House favorite, emphasizing the heart of Christ's ministry—Love, Joy, Peace—the message of saints from Elizabeth to Mother Teresa.*

The Holy Communion

Sanctus: Franz Schubert, *The Hymnal 1982* (New York: The Church Pension Fund, 1985), S 130.

*A nice aesthetic contrast to the Mexican and African music, Spirituals, and Jazz used heretofore in the service.*

Lord's Prayer

Breaking of the Bread

Communion Hymn: "O Poverty," from *Music from Taizé, Vol. II* (Chicago: GIA Publications, Inc., 1982), 47.

*A reminder that Jesus himself came from poverty.*

Post-Communion Prayer

Blessing

Closing Hymn: "The Word of Life" in John Bell, *Heaven Shall Not Wait* (Chicago: GIA Publications, Inc. 1989), 64.

*The tune, originating from Ireland, is "Wild Mountain Thyme." The song tells of the whole ministry of Jesus, ending the chorus with, "And he's here when we call him, bringing health and love and laughter." It is an exuberant reiteration of the message of Love, Peace, and Joy heard earlier in "He Came Down."*

Dismissal

Postlude: "Promises Kept," Sonny Sharrock, *Ask the Ages* (Axiom, 1991)

*We have to confess that "Promises Kept" is a frequent coda to services at Canterbury House not only because we love the tune, but also because it expresses so well our own best understanding of who God is.*

## February 21, 2006: Ash Wednesday Liturgy

*The text of the liturgy is taken more or less directly from the* Book of Common Prayer. *Stephen and I are the only musicians for the service (he on piano and recorder, I on fiddle). Nearly all of the music is in D minor. The following year we changed some of the musical selections to put the whole liturgy in this key.*

The Salutation and Collect of the Day

Invocation: "Amazing Grace" (tune: "House of the Rising Sun")
*Lyrics to "Amazing Grace" are found, among many other places, in* The Hymnal 1982 *(New York: The Church Pension Fund, 1985), 671. "House of the Rising Sun" is a traditional Blues tune.*

First Lesson: Joel 2:1–2, 12–17

Chant: "Bless the Lord My Soul," from *Music from Taizé, Vol. II* (Chicago: GIA Publications, Inc., 1982), 9.

Second Lesson: 2 Corinthians 5:20b–6:10

Chant: "O Poverty," from *Music from Taizé, Vol. II* (Chicago: GIA Publications, Inc., 1982), 47.

Third Lesson: Matthew 6:1–6,16–21

Homily

Invitation to Observe a Holy Lent

Silence

Imposition of Ashes

Chant: "Stay with Me," from *Music from Taizé, Vol. II* (Chicago: GIA Publications, Inc., 1982), 67.
*Chanting this piece during the Impoistion of the Ashes creates an appropriately solemn mood.*

Psalm 51

Silence

Litany of Penitence

Chant: "Kyrie Eleison" (Ghana), in John Bell, ed., *Many and Great* (Chicago, GIA Publications, Inc., 2002), 23.

Lord's Prayer

The Absolution

Closing Hymn: "What Wondrous Love Is This," from *The Hymnal 1982* (New York: The Church Pension Fund, 1985), 439.
*It is especially effective to sing this hymn* a cappella.

Blessing and Dismissal

## March 5, 2006: Jazz Mass—The First Sunday in Lent

*For certain Sundays, particularly the First Sunday of Advent and the First Sunday in Lent, we will use the proper lessons from the Lectionary appointed for use in the Episcopal Church.*

*We struggled with this service because we did not want to go down the "sin" road so very much, but wanted to try to understand the deeper need for redemption. The water themes in the readings suggested a theme of baptism—renewal after all!*

*This service "kicks off" the Lenten season in an ironically celebratory way. At Canterbury House we follow an older tradition that Sundays in Lent should be considered "little Easters"—Sundays are not counted in the forty days that comprise the season. This service is therefore less penitential than Lenten services in many churches; but the point of Easter is joy in resurrection. There is no reason for moroseness about our finiteness, nor that of Jesus!*

Welcome

Prelude: "Purity," James "Blood" Ulmer, *In the Name of . . .* (DIW)

*This tune is interesting for its polyrhythmic nature (two simultaneous grooves) and its funky ostinato—a remarkable "earthy" beginning for this almost anti-sober service. It also points to the two readings referring to either literal (Noah) or metaphysical (1 Peter) baptism.*

Silence

Opening Sentences

Collect of the Day, from the *Book of Common Prayer*

Invocation: "I've Got Peace Like a River," from *Lift Every Voice and Sing II: An African American Hymnal* (New York: The Church Pension Fund, 1993), 201.

First Lesson: Genesis 9:8–17

Psalm 25:3–9: Shelter Tone (*see* Appendix C: Psalm Tones)

Show me your ways, O **LORD,**
And teach me your **paths.**
Lead me in your truth and **teach me,**
for you are the God of my **salvation.** *Antiphon*

Remember not the sins of my youth and my **transgressions;**
Remember me according to your love, **O LORD;**
Gracious and upright is **the LORD;**
Therefore he teaches sinners in his **way.** *Antiphon*

She guides the humble in doing **right**
and teaches her way to the **lowly.**
All the paths of God are love and **faithfulness**
To those who keep her covenant and her **testimonies.** *Antiphon*

Second Lesson: 1 Peter 3:18–22

Hymn: "Down by the Riverside," from *Lift Every Voice and Sing II: An African American Hymnal* (New York: The Church Pension Fund, 1993), 210.

Gospel: Mark 1:9–13

Homily

Silence

Prayers of the People: The Great Litany—from the *Book of Common Prayer*
*The Great Litany was chanted, and accompanied by the band playing "In a Silent Way" by Miles Davis.*

Prayer Response: Blues Kyrie, Stephen Rush (*see* Appendix D: Blues Mass)

The Peace

Offertory: "The Blood of Jesus Makes Me Whole," Blind Willie Johnson, from *Dark Was the Night* (Columbia, 1998)
The Holy Communion

Sanctus: "Wholy Holy," Marvin Gaye, from *What's Going On* (Motown Records, 1971)
*During Lent we used Marvin Gaye's "Wholy Holy" as the Sanctus, with his plea for self and world renewal.*

Breaking of the Bread

Lord's Prayer

Communion Hymn: "Spirit of the Living God," from *Lift Every Voice and Sing II: An African American Hymnal* (New York: The Church Pension Fund, 1993), 115.
*The activator for change, in the Christian life, is the Holy Spirit, and we praise her with this hymn. The text could be the ultimate expression of the whole Lenten theme: "Melt me, mold me, fill me, use me."*

Post-Communion Prayer

The Blessing

Closing Hymn: "Lead Me, Guide Me," from *Lift Every Voice and Sing II: An African American Hymnal* (New York: The Church Pension Fund, 1993), 194.
*The congregation asks for God's assistance through the Lenten journey with this great Gospel standard.*

Dismissal

Postlude: "Waiting for an Answer," Charles Hayden/Pat Metheny, *Rejoicing* (ECM, 1983)
*"Waiting for an Answer" is an open-ended tune, but ecstatic and beautiful. It underscores that the Lenten journey is never over: we are waiting for God's help every minute, every day.*

## April 1, 2007: Jazz Mass—Palm Sunday

*The Palm Sunday Liturgy found in the* Book of Common Prayer *seems to assume that the congregation will not be present for worship again until Easter Sunday. Thus, the liturgy starts with a strongly festival atmosphere and proceeds through a reading of the Passion Gospel.*

*We have elected* not *to do this at Canterbury House. Instead, we observe the services of Holy Week: the Maundy Thursday liturgy, and the Good Friday liturgy, including a choral reading of the Passion Gospel by the female students of the House. The mood of this Palm Sunday service grows darker as it progresses, but only the closing hymn refers directly to the Passion.*

*Palm Sunday is simply a difficult service in every way. Since we have no processional space at all, the liturgy of the Palms makes sense only if done outdoors. Of course, the problems with this are myriad: acoustics, weather, gawkers, musical instruments—a Music Director's nightmare. The best way to respond is to make the procession as festive and even goofy as possible—a "parade of fools," if you will.*

Welcome!

Opening Sentences

Collect

The Blessing of the Palms

The Procession

Hymn in Procession: "Klezmer Gloria," Stephen Rush

*We led the students to a little open spot on the campus, singing and accompanied by drums, trombone, and shakers as we went. For congregational singing in procession, it's important to have musicians at the front and back, and to encourage the congregation's best singers to stand or march in the middle. We used what I call my "Klezmer Gloria." It was written for Don Postema's church, Campus Chapel, in 1990, and is meant to have a strong Hasidic feel in tone, mode, and mood. With clarinet, tambourine, trombone, and fiddle we came close!*

Collect

Opening Hymn: "He Came Down" (Cameroon), in John Bell, ed., *Many and Great* (Chicago: GIA Publications, Inc., 2002), 14.

*After the Collect, we sang a Canterbury favorite, "He Came Down" (in services with great awkwardness, we lean toward the familiar). Of course, this tune, from Cameroon, was designed to be sung* a cappella *or with drum accompaniment, so it fit our instrumentation and situation perfectly. Obviously, the words hit the theme of Palm Sunday with the refrain: "Why did He come?"*

First Lesson: Zechariah 9:9–10

Psalm 118:1–2, 19–29

*We chose not to sing the Psalm, because of the difficulties outdoors, but instead read it, like monks, with bold pauses between sentences.*

Second Lesson: Philippians 2:5–11

Hymn: "Ride On, King Jesus," from *Lift Every Voice and Sing II: An African American Hymnal* (New York: The Church Pension Fund, 1993), 97.

*Following the Philippians reading, with its dangerously colonial phrase, "Let every tongue confess that Jesus Christ is Lord," we sang "Ride On, King Jesus." We all improvised harmonies to this classic Spiritual, and the results were fun and joyous.*

Gospel: Luke 19:28–40

Hymn in Procession: "Klezmer Gloria," Stephen Rush

*Following the Gospel reading of the Palm Sunday story, we sang the "Klezmer Gloria" all the way back to the church with a reignited exuberance. By now the tune was completely familiar, so once we got back indoors, we sped up the Gloria to the point of absurdity. Finally, the band and the whole congregation collapsed in laughter during the last verse, which at last was too hard to sing, play, or dance!*

Homily

Silence

Prayers of the People—adapted from *A New Zealand Prayer Book* (San Francisco: HarperSanFrancisco, 1997), 163.

Prayer Response: "Stay With Us, O Lord Jesus Christ," from *Music from Taizé, Vol. II* (Chicago: GIA Publications, Inc., 1982), 69.

*By the end of this chant, we were making the mood shift toward Good Friday, with this chant that inverts Jesus' plea to the disciples, "Could you not stay awake with me one hour? Stay awake and pray that you may not come into the time of trial."*

The Peace

Offertory: "I Shall Be Released," Bob Dylan, *The Definitive Bob Dylan Songbook* (Amsco Publishing, 2001).

*Bob Dylan's "I Shall Be Released" has become a recent Canterbury favorite, and the students chime in on the chorus with gusto and harmony. The text of this Rock standard could be a retelling of the Easter Week story, and Jesus could be the singer of the text, "I see my light come shining / From the west unto the east / Any day now, any day now / I Shall Be Released." Many tears were shed, to put it mildly.*

The Holy Communion

Sanctus: "Blues Sanctus," Stephen Rush (*see* Appendix D: Blues Mass)

*The mood for the Eucharist was dark now, and we used the Blues Sanctus at a much slower tempo than normally.*

Lord's Prayer

Breaking of the Bread

Communion Hymn: "Laudate, omnes gentes," from *Music from Taizé, Vol. I* (Chicago: GIA Publications, Inc., 1978), 12.

*The text of this chant, translated "Praise the Lord, all ye peoples," is richly ironic in the context of Palm Sunday. The tempo is extremely slow, with its throbbing Sarabande groove. Irony capped upon irony, this little masterpiece is in a major key. It's an amazing composition!*

Post-Communion Prayer

The Blessing

Closing Hymn: "An Emperor of Fools," in John Bell, *Enemy of Apathy* rev. ed. (Chicago: GIA Publications, Inc., 1990), 50.

*John Bell's masterful "Emperor of Fools" simply retells the story one more time, and sets up Holy Week in a somber tone. This tune, incidentally, is harmonically ambiguous until the very end, a perfect metaphor for Holy Week.*

Dismissal

Postlude: "Troublemaker," James "Blood" Ulmer, *Original Phalanx* (Moers Music, 1994).

*The postlude took a curveball approach with the funk tune by James "Blood" Ulmer "Troublemaker." Jesus described himself as someone who was not bringing peace, but a sword! Notice that our Palm Sunday service does not include the reading of the Passion. We assume that the students will come back for our Good Friday service and hear it then. Nevertheless, we are establishing the mood for the drama that plays out in the coming Holy Week.*

# April 7, 2007: Easter Jazz Vigil

*This service again follows the Easter Vigil found in the* Book of Common Prayer.

The Lighting of the Pascal Candle

*The* BCP *instructs: "In the darkness, fire is kindled"* (BCP, 285). *We started our service at sunset, in the parking lot. We roped off the parking lot with caution tape—almost like a police "crime scene"—with flashing lights and sirens, and the invitatory prayer read through a megaphone. This brought together many ideas established in the Passion story: Jesus treated as a dangerous criminal, his tomb placed under guard, and his resurrection as an astonishing* event.

*For the past two years, we have had the good fortune to have a fire juggler in our band, so the lighting of the fire is especially festive. When we don't have a fire juggler, we use a pyrophone (a musical instrument that involves literally playing with fire).*

*The Easter Vigil can easily turn into a "showcase for the band," with its myriad readings followed by music. It is bad liturgy, in my opinion, for a service to confuse itself with a concert. Thus, after the Lighting of the Pascal Candle, we make an explicit transition from "unruly mob in a parking lot" to "expectant congregation in a church" by moving into a darkened indoor worship space. As people enter, they hear silence. Once seated, the gong sounds. Our gong is a two-foot model. It's loud and deep!*

"Love Supreme" Exultet—Tone "A Love Supreme"—John Coltrane, *A Love Supreme* (Atlantic, 1964)

*The sound of the gong is the first note in one of the real Jazz anthems of Canterbury House, "A Love Supreme." On the "Easter Jazz Vigil" recording, available from Canterbury House, you can hear Chaplain Matt Lawrence speaking the text of the Exsultet as the band plays the tune. It occurred to me, however, that it should be possible to sing the chant setting of the Exsultet on key with "A Love Supreme." Stephen was initially skeptical of this approach; but a good singer and a good band can make it happen!*

The Liturgy of the Word

*In this segment, this service was a structural mapping of hymn or Jazz tune to the several scripture readings appointed for the Vigil. From among many choices, the selected readings all pointed to the difficult semester—a semester in which suicides on campus, war, and miserable Michigan weather had brought us all down. God's faithfulness through it all (in the spirit of the Passover Feast) was celebrated.*

Abraham's Sacrifice of Isaac: Genesis 22:1–18

Hymn: "Precious Lord," from *Lift Every Voice and Sing II: An African American Hymnal* (New York: The Church Pension Fund, 1993), 106.

*Abraham's near sacrifice of his own son was answered with "Precious Lord":*

*When my way grows drear,*
*precious Lord, linger near,*
*When my life is almost gone;*
*Hear my cry, hear my call,*
*Hold my hand, lest I fall,*
*Take my hand, precious Lord,*
*Lead me on.*

Israel's Deliverance at the Red Sea: Exodus 14:10–15:2

Hymn: "Wade in the Water," from *Lift Every Voice and Sing II: An African American Hymnal* (New York: The Church Pension Fund, 1993), 143.

*"Wade in the Water" is a delicious combination of minor key and upbeat tempo, which responds, we think, very appropriately to the story of Israel's deliverance at the Red Sea.*

The Gathering of God's people: Zephaniah 3:12–20

Anthem: "Praise God, I'm Satisfied," Blind Willie Johnson, *Dark Was the Night* (Columbia Legacy, 1998)

*The Zephaniah reading about the "Gathering of God's People" was answered with "Praise God, I'm Satisfied" by Blind Willie Johnson. The text seems a bizarre and troubling confessional:*

*Praise God I'm Satisfied*
*But I may have let him die.*
*Well I'm glad to know that he loves me so*
*That He was crucified.*

*It seems the singer is saying he is better off now that Jesus has died. This medieval theological convention seems strange to modern liberal Christians, but it does at least acknowledge that we, through our sin, have a hand in the crucifixion.*

The Holy Eucharist

Hymn: "Hallelujah, We Sing Your Praises," from *Wonder, Love and Praise* (New York: The Church Pension Fund, 1997), 784.

*Quickly (please!) after "Praise God, I'm Satisfied," we lit the candles on the altar, brought up the lights, and moved to "Hallelujah, We Sing Your Praises" from South Africa. This was the first exclamation of Hallelujah after the long, dark period of Lent. Dance and Sing your way to the Altar!*

Collect

The First Reading: Romans 6:3–11

Psalm 114: Liberation Tone—Stephen Rush (*see* Appendix C: Psalm Tones)

Hallelujah! When Israel came out of **Egypt,**
the house of Jacob from a people of strange **speech,**
Judah became God's **sanctuary**
and Israel his **dominion.** *Antiphon*

The sea beheld it and **fled:**
Jordan turned and went **back.**
The mountains skipped like **rams,**
and the little hills like young **sheep.** *Antiphon*

Tremble, O earth, at the presence of the **Lord,**
at the presence of the God of **Jacob,**
Who turned the hard Rock into a pool of **water**
and flint-stone into a flowing **spring.** *Antiphon*

*After the Romans reading, we sang the Liberation Tone to accompany Psalm 114, "Hallelujah! When Israel came out of Egypt!" Psalm 114 is a litany of thanks and praise.*

Gospel: Luke 24:1–12

Sermon

The Renewal of Baptismal Vows

Tone: "Beati," from *Music from Taizé, Vol. I* (Chicago: GIA Publications, Inc., 1978), 3.

Prayers of the People, adapted from *A New Zealand Prayer Book* (San Francisco: HarperSanFrancisco, 1997), 163.

Prayer Response: "Beati," from *Music from Taizé, Vol. I* (Chicago: GIA Publications, Inc., 1978), 3.
*During the Baptismal Vows we sang the simple Taizé chant "Beati." We played the pulsing groove (very similar to Coltrane's "A Love Supreme—Acknowledgement") under the vows, and then chanted the Beatitudes at the end of this beautiful litany while folding in the Prayers of the People. This is a long section of the service (about 10 minutes), but it had plenty of dynamic fluctuation and color change, as well as space for spoken text, sung text (the Beatitudes), and improvisation. Any tune with a haunting pulse will work here, including Aaron Siegel's "Aperture" (found on the Canterbury Easter Vigil recording).*

The Peace

Offertory: "One Love," Bob Marley, *Songs of Freedom* (Hal Leonard Publishing, 1992).
*This happy, hopeful tune is a Canterbury House favorite.*

The Holy Communion

Sanctus: "Halle, Halle, Halle" (Puerto Rico), in John Bell, ed., *Many and Great* (Chicago: GIA Publications, Inc., 2002), 18.
*At the Communion we sang an extended version of the lively Calypso Alleluia, "Halle, Halle." Indeed, bursting into a New Orleans-style dance at the communion might seem a bit sacrilegious. Nonetheless, after all the dismal, depressing darkness of Lent, this was a needed release. No question, the fact that our Easter lands right in the middle of the last week of classes, or often, exams, makes this release somehow topical or (if possible?) more poignant.*

Lord's Prayer

The Breaking of the Bread

Communion Hymn: "Ubi Caritas," from *Taizé 2006–2007* (Taizé: Ateliers et Presses de Taizé, 2007), 15.
*The chant during Communion, "Ubi Caritas," reminds us that Jesus' death was an act of love. There is a subtle and seasonal connect here as well since our simple Maundy Thursday service consists of singing two Taizé chants, "Ubi Caritas" and the often-overlooked "Ubi Caritas Deus Ibi Est," combined with a few short readings, a foot washing, and an agapé meal. The "Ubi Caritas" in the Easter Vigil hearkens back to this "last supper." Maundy Thursday is, of course, the Passover Seder, adapted to the Holy Week story. The Easter Vigil has a similar structure, with it's retelling of God's faithfulness to us.*

Post Communion Prayer

The Blessing

Closing Hymn: "Redemption Song," Bob Marley, *Songs of Freedom* (Hal Leonard Publishing, 1992).

*The service ends with "Redemption Song" by Bob Marley, with his "song of freedom" and redemption. We openly admit that it is partly absurd to think of a largely white and well-to-do student population singing "O pirates, yes, they rob I; Sold I to the merchant ships"—no more true for them than it was for Bob Marley. But these stories bear repeating and, to the extent possible, internalizing. The question "How long shall they kill our prophets, while we stand aside and look" must still be asked, as we know from the assassinations of prophets in our own lifetime.*

Dismissal

Postlude: "Promises Kept," Sonny Sharrock, *Ask the Ages* (Axiom, 1991).

*In the spirit of the Seder (the retelling of God's faithfulness to Israel), we finished this rocky journey with Sonny Sharrock's fabulous "Promises Kept."*

*The diversity of the music in our Easter Vigil, including African music, African-American songs and Spirituals, Blues, postmodern Jazz, Calypso dance-chant, and Reggae, is intentional. We are making a statement from within our context and to our congregation that God's love is all inclusiveand that God died and rose again for every person on the planet. In gratitude, we offer to God the whole planet's very best music.*

# Appendix B

## Musical Resources for Liturgy

### How to Use This Appendix

The purpose of this music index is to offer examples of what we have found to be useful music for services, organized according to liturgical theme. The purpose is not to provide the reader with pat solutions for a "musically diverse service." What is appropriate for Canterbury House may or may not be appropriate for your congregants, musicians, and demographic.

Again, our recommended approach to creative liturgy is to meet together, pray about the texts for the given service, determine a theme, and then search for the most appropriate music to support that theme. Each one of the pieces listed below has been used in a service at Canterbury House with these principles in mind.

We do not, and you will not want to, use the categories suggested below in a rigid or inflexible manner. Clearly, a given piece of music might work well for any of several themes. Moreover, one theme might lead to or suggest another.

Say, for example, that you are planning a service for the Fourth Sunday in Lent, and your scripture lessons are Joshua 5:9–12, Psalm 32, 2 Corinthians 5:16–21, and Luke 15:1–3; 11b–32 (these are the Revised Common Lectionary Readings for Lent IV, Year C). You might decide, particularly based on the Gospel parable of the Prodigal Son, that an appropriate theme is "Grace." You could as easily conclude that a good theme is "Enlightenment," or "Deliverance," or even "Death/Resurrection." You may decide that some of these themes relate closely to one another, or provide a movement through the service from one idea to another.

In any event, it is only after reading, reflecting upon, and discussing the readings for the service, that you will be ready to select a category or categories from those listed below—or make your own categories. We strongly encourage you to create your own categories, and to take the time and research to find your own music to complement them. Our theology and our themes have grown out of our own context. You will want to use your own context, and consequently your own themes and your own musical and theological inclinations.

That said, with this Appendix, you can use the suggested music as a starting point for making your decisions about music for your service. Take note of your reactions: "That's too weird!" "That's too hard!" "We don't have that!" "We did that last week!" "Our musicians would never play that!" "Why does that fit this category?" All of these reactions are vital and helpful in learning about how you do liturgy. The compositions suggested below for preludes and postludes are meant to be played live by your musicians, not played on CD for passive listening by the congregation. See Chapter Eight for a discussion on why we discourage the use of prerecorded music in liturgy.

We hope that these resources and the choices you and your congregation make will help you develop not only a creative and diverse liturgy, but a creative and diverse worship community.

This index can also serve as a way to introduce yourself and your liturgical planning team to some music that may be unfamiliar. Again, many of the classics of Jazz since 1960 are unavailable in sheet music form; please contact the authors if you want scores (transcriptions) of these pieces: srush@umich.edu.

## Key

"Hymnal Collection" (hymnals frequently in use at Canterbury House):

- CRC *Psalter Hymnal* (Grand Rapids: CRC Publications, 1987)
- H *The Hymnal 1982* (New York: The Church Pension Fund, 1985)
- LEVAS *Lift Every Voice and Sing II: An African American Hymnal* (New York: The Church Pension Fund, 1993)
- WLP *Wonder, Love and Praise* (New York: The Church Pension Fund, 1997)
- Z *Songs of Zion* (Nashville: Abingdon Press, 1981)

Taizé music:

- T *Taizé 2006–2007* (Taizé: Ateliers et Presses de Taizé, 2007)
- T/V1 *Music from Taizé, Vol. I* (Chicago: GIA Publications, Inc., 1978)
- T/V2 *Music from Taizé, Vol. II* (Chicago: GIA Publications, Inc., 1982)
- T/SaP *Songs & Prayers from Taizé* (Chicago: GIA Publications, Inc., 1991)
- T/SfP *Taizé: Songs for Prayer* (Chicago: GIA Publications, Inc., 1998)
- P Stephen Rush, personal collection

John Bell:

- Heaven *Heaven Shall Not Wait* (Chicago: GIA Publications, Inc., 1989)
- EoA *Enemy of Apathy* (Chicago: GIA Publications, Inc., 1988, rev. ed. 1990)
- Sent *Sent by the Lord* (Chicago: GIA Publications, Inc., 1991)
- Love *Love From Below* (Chicago: GIA Publications, Inc., 1989)
- Many *Many and Great* (Chicago: GIA Publications, Inc., 2002)
- One *One is the Body* (Chicago: GIA Publications, Inc., 2002)

Bob Dylan, *The Definitive Bob Dylan Songbook* (New York: Amsco Publications, 2001)

Bob Marley, *Songs of Freedom* (Milwaukee: Hal Leonard Publishing, 1992)

Other music is referenced to recordings or other collections as indicated.

## Themes and Suggested Music

### Advent/Christmas/Incarnation/Revelation/"End Times"

Hymnal Collection:

- In Christ There Is No East or West—LEVAS 62
- Go Tell It on the Mountain—LEVAS 21
- Christ Is Coming (Advent)—LEVAS 6
- Wade in the Water—LEVAS 143
- Soon and Very Soon—LEVAS 14
- Salamu Maria—LEVAS 51

Sleepers Awake (*Wachet Auf*)—H 61, 62
Come Thou Long Expected Jesus (Advent)—H 66
I Want to Be Ready (Advent)—LEVAS 7
Saviour of the Nations Come—H 54
That Boy-Child of Mary (Ghana)—LEVAS 25

Taizé:
Prepare the Way (Advent)—T/V2 50
The Lord Is my Light—T/V2 73
Our Soul Is Waiting for God (*Notre Ame Attend le Signeur*)—T/SfP 36
Wait for the Lord—T/V2 78

Bell:
Word of Life—Heaven 64
God Bless Us and Disturb Us (Advent)—Heaven 58
Once in Judah's Least Known City—Heaven 54
Cloth for the Cradle—Heaven 52
Son of Mary—Heaven 75
Go Home by Another Way—EoA 80
Heaven on Earth—EoA 108
He Comes—EoA 70
Deo Gratias (Wise Men)—Heaven 56
Finding God—EoA 12
He Came Down (Cameroon)—Many 14

Coltrane, John:
Cousin Mary (*Giant Steps,* Atlantic)

Crumb, George:
A Little Suite for Christmas (*A Little Suite for Christmas,* Bridge Records)

Frisell, Bill:
Hope and Fear (*Is That You?,* Elektra Musician Records)
Lookout for Hope (*Lookout for Hope,* Impulse)

House, Son:
John the Revelator (*The Original Delta Blues,* Columbia Legacy)

Ives, Charles:
Christmas Song, *114 Songs* (Associated Music Publishers)

Kirk, Rahsaan Roland:
Three for the Festival (*Kirk's Works,* Mercury Records)

Mayfield, Curtis:
People Get Ready (*People Get Ready: The Curtis Mayfield Story,* Rhino Records)

Mengelberg, Misha (with Eric Dolphy):
Hypochrismustreefuzz (*Last Date,* Limelight)

Mingus, Charles:
The Man Who Never Sleeps (Advent) (*Statements,* Lotus Jazz)

Sun Ra:

Moonship Journey (*Cosmos,* Sun Ra's Inner City)
For the Sunrise (*Live at Montreux,* Sun Ra's Inner City)
Rocket #9 (*Singles Collection,* ESP)
Brainville (*Sun Song,* Delmark)
Future (*Sun Song,* Delmark)

Ulmer, James "Blood":

Baby Talk (*No Wave,* Moers Music)
Revelation March (*In the Name of . . . ,* DIW)

Waits, Tom:

Jesus Gonna Be Here (Advent) (Blind Boys of Alabama, *Spirit of the Century,* Real World)

**All Saints' Day:** *see* **Death/Resurrection**

**Baptism:** *see* **Water/Baptism**

**Blessedness:** *see* **Grace/Blessedness/Thanksgiving**

**Christmas:** *see* **Advent/Christmas/Revelation/Incarnation/"End Times"**

**Communion (Eucharist)** (*see also* **Community of Saints/Diversity**)**:**

Hymnal Collection:

I'm Going to Eat at the Welcome Table—LEVAS 148
In Christ There Is no East or West—LEVAS 62
The Blood Will Never Lose Its Power—Z 184
Let Us Break Bread Together on Our Knees—Z 88

Taizé:

Eat This Bread—T/V2 30
Da Pacem Domine—T/V1 94
Dona Nobis Pacem Domine—T/V2 26
Aucune Ombre—P
By Night (*De noche iremos*)—T 12
Beati—T/V1 3

Bell:

Lord of All—EoA 64
He Comes—EoA 70

**Community of Saints/Diversity:**

Hymnal Collection:

I'm Going to Eat at the Welcome Table—LEVAS 148
One Bread, One Body—LEVAS 151
Sign Me Up—LEVAS 142
My Shepherd Is the Lord (*El Señor es Mi Pastor*)—CRC 162
Blessed Martin—LEVAS 46

In Christ There Is no East or West—LEVAS 62
Jesus We Love to Meet (Mali)—CRC 245

Taizé:
Ubi Caritas Deus Ibi Est—T 4
Ubi Caritas—T 15, T/V1 28

Bell:
Gifts of the Spirit—Heaven 86
Word of Life—Heaven 64
Love of God Comes Close—EoA 96
Strangest of Saints—Heaven 101

Dylan, *The Definitive Bob Dylan Songbook* (Amsco Pub.)
Forever Young
I Dreamed I Saw St. Augustine

Marley:
One Love (*Songs of Freedom,* Hal Leonard Pub.)

Beatles:
All Together Now (*Yellow Submarine,* Capitol)

Coleman, Ornette:
Song X (*Song X* with Pat Metheny, Nonesuch)
Congeniality (*The Shape of Jazz to Come,* Atlantic)
In All Languages (*In All Languges,* Harmolodic/Verve)

Coltrane, John:
Offering (*Expression,* Impulse)
Naima (*Giant Steps,* Atlantic)

Davis, Miles:
Tutu (*Tutu,* Warner Bros.)

Frisell, Bill:
Strange Meeting (*This Land,* Elektra Nonesuch Records)
Unsung Heroes (*Where in the World,* Nonesuch Records)

Kirk, Rahsaan Roland:
from Bechet, Byas and Fats (*Kirk's Works,* Mercury)

Sharrock, Sonny:
As We Used to Sing (*Ask the Ages,* Axiom)

Shorter, Wayne:
Sanctuary (Miles Davis, *Bitches Brew,* Columbia)

Taylor, Cecil:
E.B. (*The World of Cecil Taylor,* Candid Records)
Chorus of Seeds (*Dark to Themselves,* Enja Records)

Traditional:

When the Saints Go Marchin' In

Tyner, McCoy:

Blues on the Corner (*The Real McCoy,* Blue Note)

**Death/Resurrection** (*see also* **Easter**):

Hymnal Collection:

My Faith Looks Up to Thee—H 691
Lord I Want to Be a Christian—LEVAS 138
Breathe on Me, Breath of God—H 508
Noel Nouvelet (Now the Green Blade Riseth)—H 204
Deep River—LEVAS 8
Soon-a Will Be Done with the Troubles of the World—Z 158
I Wanna Be Ready—LEVAS 7
My Lord, What a Morning—LEVAS 13
I Want Jesus to Walk with Me—Z 95

Taizé:

Jesus, Remember Me—T/V1 9
Misericordias Domini—T/V1 21

Traditional:

Somebody's Buried in the Graveyard, (*American Negro Songs* (Dover Publications, Inc., 1988), 127

Bell:

Kyrie Eleison (Ghana)—Many 23
Last Journey—EoA 88

Bryars, Gavin:

Jesus' Blood Never Failed Me Yet (*Jesus' Blood Never Failed Me Yet,* Point Records)

Coleman, Ornette:

Tears Inside (Pat Metheny, *Rejoicing,* ECM)

Coltrane, John:

Cousin Mary (*Giant Steps,* Atlantic)

Frisell, Bill:

Cold, Cold Ground (*Good Dog, Happy Man*, Nonesuch Records)

Johnson, Blind Willie:

Dark Was the Night, Cold Was the Ground (*Dark Was the Night,* Columbia Legacy)
Praise God I'm Satisfied (*Praise God I'm Satisfied,* Yazoo)

Mingus, Charles:

Goodbye Porkpie Hat (*Passions of a Man,* Atlantic)

Rush, Stephen:

See Ya!—P

Stanley, Ralph

O Death (*O Brother Where Art Thou,* UMG)

Waits, Tom:

Cold Cold Ground (*Big Time,* Island Records)

**Deliverance** (*see also* **Liberation**)**:**

Hymnal Collection:

Deep River—LEVAS 8
O Freedom!—LEVAS 225
Precious Lord—LEVAS 106
Glory Glory, Hallelujah (Since I Laid My Burden Down)—LEVAS 130
Salamu Maria—LEVAS 51

Taizé:

Libera Nos Domine—T/V1 60
When the Night Becomes Dark—T/SaP 25
Beati voi Poveri—T 124
Lajuda en Vindrà—T 134

Bell:

Somos Pueblo Que Camina (Nicaragua)—Sent 26
Kyrie (Ghana)—Many 23

Marley:

Redemption Song (*Songs of Freedom,* Hal Leonard Pub.)

Coleman, Ornette:

Endangered Species (*Song X* with Pat Metheny, Nonesuch Records)
Feet Music (*In All Languges,* Harmolodic/Verve)
Song X (*Song X* with Pat Metheny, Nonesuch Records)

Holiday, Billie:

God Bless the Child (*God Bless the Child,* MCA)

Johnson, Blind Willie:

Praise God I'm Satisfied (*Praise God I'm Satisfied,* Yazoo)

Sharrock, Sonny:

Promises Kept (*Ask the Ages*, Axiom)

Sun Ra:

El Is the Sound of Joy (*Live at Montreux*, Sun Ra's Inner City)

**Discipleship:** *see* **Work/Obedience/Will of God**

**Diversity:** *see* **Community of Saints/Diversity**

**Doubt:** *see* **Fear/Doubt/Trouble**

**Easter:**

Hymnal Collection:

For the Beauty of the Earth—H 416, alternative tune H 119

Bell:

Enemy of Apathy—EoA 94
Dance and Sing—Heaven 19

Coleman, Ornette:

The Veil (*Song X* with Pat Metheny, Nonesuch Records)

Mingus, Charles:

Pithecanthropus Erectus (*Passions of a Man,* Atlantic)

Sun Ra:

For the Sunrise (*Live at Montreux,* Sun Ra's Inner City)
Sun Song (*Sun Song,* Delmark)

**Ecstasy** (*see also* **Light/Epiphany/Enlightenment):**

Taizé:

Vieni Spirito Creatore—T 57

Bell:

O God You Made Us All Unique—One 74

Coleman, Ornette:

Space Church (*In All Languges,* Harmolodic/Verve)

Coltrane, John:

Father Son and Holy Ghost (*Meditations,* Impulse)
Reflection (*A Love Supreme,* Atlantic)

Kirk, Rahsaan Roland:

I Talk with the Spirits (*Kirk's Works,* Mercury)

Mitchell, Roscoe:

Ninth Room (*The Paris Session,* Arista Freedom)
Spiritual (*The Paris Session,* Arista Freedom)

Sun Ra:

Enlightenment (*Concert for the Comet Kohoutek,* ESP)
Brainville (*Sun Song,* Delmark

von Bingen, Hildegard (*Hildegard von Bingen—Symphonize, Geistlich Gesanger,* Harmonia Mundi)

O Sapientiae
Felix Anima

**"End Times":** *see* **Advent/Christmas/Revelation/Incarnation/"End Times"**

**Enlightenment:** *see* **Light/Epiphany/Enlightenment**

**Epiphany:** *see* **Light/Epiphany/Enlightenment**

**Eucharist:** *see* **Communion**

**Faith:** *see* **Trust/Faith**

**Fear/Doubt/Trouble:**

Hymnal Collection:

Precious Lord—LEVAS 106
Lead Me, Guide Me—LEVAS 194
Nobody Knows the Trouble I've Seen—LEVAS 172
What a Friend We Have in Jesus—LEVAS 109
Wayfaring Stranger—LEVAS 19
Didn' My Lord Deliver Daniel?—LEVAS 182
Sometimes I Feel Like a Motherless Chile—LEVAS 169
I Shall Not Be Moved—Z 35
I Couldn't Hear Nobody Pray—Z 78
I Want Jesus to Walk with Me—Z 95
We Shall Overcome—LEVAS 227

Taizé:

There Is no Darkness or Trouble—P
O Poverty—T/V2 47
L'ajuda em Vindrà—T 134
My Peace—T/V2 39
Da Pacem Cordium—T 55
Dona Nobis Pacem Domine—T/V2 26

Bell:

How Long O Lord?—Heaven 30
A Woman's Care—Heaven 24
Finding God—EoA 12
O Lord My God—EoA 38
Contemporary Reproaches—EoA 42
The Sorrow—EoA 73
Sing My Soul—EoA 61

Dylan:

Desolation Row

Blind Boys of Alabama:

Sometimes I Feel Like a Motherless Chile (*Spirit of the Century,* Real World)

Bowie, Lester:

Zero (*Third Decade,* ECM)

Coleman, Ornette:

Lonely Woman (*The Shape of Jazz to Come,* Atlantic)

Frisell, Bill:
Hope and Fear (*Is That You?,* Elektra Musician Records)

Garbarek, Jan:
It's OK to Listen to that Grey Voice (*Rites,* ECM)

Indian Bhajan:
Ye Mise Thura—P

Kirk, Rahsaan Roland:
Slippery, Hippery, Flippery (*Kirk's Works,* Mercury)

Metheny, Pat, and Charlie Haden:
Waiting for an Answer (*Rejoicing,* ECM)

Rush, Stephen:
Akimbo (*Hymn for Roscoe,* MMC)

Sun Ra:
Outer Space Emergency (*Concert for the Comet Kohoutek,* ESP)
Transition (*Sun Song,* Delmark)

Wonder, Stevie:
Jesus Children (*Innervisions,* Motown)

**Freedom** (*see also* **Deliverance; Liberation; Poverty/Mercy**)**:**
Hymnal Collection:
Deep River—LEVAS 8
Glory, Glory, Hallelujah (Since I Laid My Burden Down)—LEVAS 130
Lift Every Voice and Sing—LEVAS 1
Oh, Freedom—LEVAS 225
Precious Lord—LEVAS 106
I Shall Not Be Moved—Z 35

Taizé:
Beati voi Poveri—T 124
O Poverty—T/V2 47
The Lord Is My Light—T/V2 73
Libera Nos Domine—T/V1 60

Bell:
If You Believe and I Believe (Zimbabwe)—Sent 51

Marley:
Redemption Song

Coleman, Ornette (*In All Languges,* Harmolodic/Verve):
Feet Music
In All Languages

Mingus, Charles (*The Black Saint and the Sinner Lady,* Impulse):
Freewoman

Oh, This Freedom Slave Cries
Stop! Look! And Sing Songs of Revolutions!

Ulmer, James "Blood":
Justice for us All (*Blues Preacher,* DIW/Columbia)

**Gospel:**

Hymnal Collection:
Go Tell It on the Mountain—LEVAS 21
Ain'-a That Good News—LEVAS 180
Wayfaring Stranger—LEVAS 19
Get On Board Little Children—Z 116

Ayler, Albert:
Spirits Rejoice (*Live in Greenwich Village,* Impulse!)
Spirits (*Witches and Devils,* Freedom/Black Saint)
Spiritual Unity (*Spiritual Unity,* ESP)
Ghosts (*Love Cry,* Impulse!)

Coleman, Ornette:
The Good Life (*Song X* with Pat Metheny, Nonesuch)

House, Son:
John the Revelator (*The Original Delta Blues,* Columbia Legacy)

Mayfield, Curtis:
People Get Ready (*People Get Ready: The Curtis Mayfield Story,* Rhino Records)

Sun Ra:
New Horizons (*Sun Song,* Delmark)
Future (*Sun Song,* Delmark)

Waits, Tom:
Jesus Gonna Be Here (Blind Boys of Alabama, *Spirit of the Century,* Real World)

**Grace/Blessedness/Thanksgiving:**

Hymnal Collection:
Precious Lord—LEVAS 106
Amazing Grace—H 671
What Wondrous Love Is This—H 439

Taizé:
Bless the Lord, My Soul—T/V2 9
Beati—T/V1 3
Tui Amoris Ignem—T 14
In the Lord I'll be Ever Thankful—T/SfP 20
Confetimini Domini—T 18
Laudate Omnes Gentes—T/V1 12

Blind Boys of Alabama:

Amazing Grace (*Spirit of the Century,* Real World)

Bell:

Gifts of the Spirit—Heaven 86
The Song—Heaven 20

Dylan:

Saving Grace

Marley:

Thank You Lord

Coleman, Ornette:

Chronology (*The Shape of Jazz to Come,* Atlantic)

Dolphy, Eric:

The Madrig Speaks, the Panther Walks (*Last Date,* Limelight)

Ulmer, James "Blood":

Abundance (*In the Name of . . . ,* DIW)
Purity (*In the Name of . . . ,* DIW)
High Time (*Freelancing,* CBS Records)

**Guidance/Searching** (*see also* **Trust/Faith; Work/Obedience/Will of God**):

Hymnal Collection:

His Eye Is on the Sparrow—LEVAS 191
Lead Me, Guide Me—LEVAS 194
Precious Lord—LEVAS 106
Go Down, Moses—LEVAS 228
I Want Jesus to Walk with Me—Z 95

Taizé:

Wait for the Lord—T/V2 78
Stay with Me—T/V2 67
Stay with Us—T/V2 69
Bless the Lord, My Soul—T/V2 9

Bell:

Finding God—EoA 12

Ayler, Albert:

Prophecy (*Prophecy,* ESP)

Coleman, Ornette:

Space Church (*In All Languges,* Harmolodic/Verve)

Coltrane, John:

Pursuance (*A Love Supreme,* Atlantic)

Johnson, Blind Willie:

It's Nobody's Fault But Mine (Blind Boys of Alabama, *Spirit of the Century,* Real World)

Kirk, Rahsaan Roland:
    Old Rugged Cross Rant (*Blacknuss,* Atlantic)

Sun Ra:
    Enlightenment (*Concert for the Comet Kohoutek,* ESP)
    Outer Space Incorporated (*Calling Planet Earth,* Freedom Records)

**Healing:** *see* **Peace/Healing**

**Hope:**

Hymnal Collection:
    I Shall Not Be Moved—Z 35
    S/He's Got the Whole World in Her/His Hands—LEVAS 217

Taizé:
    Esprit Consolateur—T 136
    *Dans Nos Obscurities* (Within Our Darkest Night)—T 1
    *Aucune Ombre* (There Is No Darkness Nor Trouble)—P

Bell:
    Heaven on Earth—EoA 108

Dylan:
    Desolation Row

Coleman, Ornette:
    Kathelin Gray (*Song X* with Pat Metheny, Nonesuch Records)

Frisell, Bill:
    Lookout for Hope (*Lookout for Hope,* Impulse)
    Things Will Never Be the Same (*Blues Dream,* Nonesuch Records)
    Where Do We Go from Here? (*Blues Dream,* Nonesuch Records)

Garbarek, Jan:
    When the Ying Meets the Yang (*Rites,* ECM)

Johnson, Blind Willie:
    Praise God I'm Satisfied (*Praise God I'm Satisfied,* Yazoo)

Kirschenmann, Mark:
    Other Planes of Here (Quartex, *Cerebral*, Canterbury House)

Lennon, John:
    Imagine (*Imagine*, Capitol Records)

Rush, Stephen:
    Countin' (*Hymn for Roscoe*, MMC)

Sharrock, Sonny:
    Promises Kept (*Ask the Ages*, Axiom)
    Who Does She Hope to Be? (*Ask the Ages*, Axiom)

Siegel, Aaron:

Aperture (*Easter Vigil*; Quartex, *Cerebral*, Canterbury House)

**Incarnation:** *see* **Advent/Christmas/Incarnation/Revelation/"End Times"**

**Joy:**

Hymnal Collection:

We Shall Overcome—LEVAS 227
Clap Your Hands, O Ye People—CRC 166
The Trees of the Field—CRC 197
Oh Freedom!—LEVAS 225

Taizé:

O Jesus Ma Joie—T 145
Jesus Christ, O Clart d'en Haut—T 146
Vous Qui Sur la Terre Habitez—T 147

Ayler, Albert:

Spirits Rejoice (*Live in Greenwich Village,* Impulse)

Bach, J.S.

Jesu, Joy of Man's Desiring

Coleman, Ornette:

Rejoicing (Pat Metheny, *Rejoicing,* ECM)

Coltrane, John:

Joy (*First Meditations,* Impulse)

Jackson, Ronald Shannon:

Dancers of Joy (*Eye on You,* About Time Records)

Sun Ra:

El is the Sound Of Joy (*Live at Montreux,* Sun Ra's Inner City)

**Justice** (*see also* **Kingdom of God**)**:**

Hymnal Collection:

Listen to Your Children Praying—CRC 625
The Old Rugged Cross—LEVAS 38
You Hear the Lambs a-Cryin'—LEVAS 110
Blessed Martin—LEVAS 46
We Shall Overcome—LEVAS 227
Ride On, King Jesus—LEVAS 97

Taizé:

O Poverty—T/V2 47
Beati voi Poveri—T 124

Bell:

Ride On, Ride On—EoA 20
Contemporary Reproaches—EoA 42
Enemy of Apathy—Enemy 94
Inspired by Love and Anger—Heaven 108
The Savior—Heaven 94
Heaven Shall Not Wait—Heaven 92
O Great God and Lord of the Earth (El Salvador)—One 94
We Belong to God (*Somos del Señor*) (Mexico)—One 64

Dylan:

The Times they are a Changin'
I Shall Be Released
Señor
Positively Fourth Street

Marley:

Get Up, Stand Up
Exodus
Redemption
The Son Is Shining
Who the Cap Fit?

Anderson, Laurie:

O Superman (*United States Live,* Warner Bros.)

Ayler, Albert:

Prophecy (*Prophecy,* ESP)

Bowie, Lester:

Ja (*Nice Guys,* ECM)

Coleman, Ornette:

Endangered Species (*Song X* with Pat Metheny, Nonesuch Records)
Mob Job (*Song X* with Pat Metheny, Nonesuch Records)
Song X (*Song X* with Pat Metheny, Nonesuch Records)

Coltrane, John:

India (*Impressions,* Impulse)
Consequences *(First Meditations,* Impulse)

Davis, Miles:

Tutu (*Tutu,* Warner Bros.)
Sanctuary (Wayne Shorter, *Bitches Brew,* Columbia)
Pharoah's Dance (*Bitches Brew,* Columbia)
Miles Runs the Voodoo Down (*Bitches Brew,* Columbia)

Guthrie, Woody:

This Land Is Your Land (*Woody Guthrie,* Warner Bros.)

Holiday, Billie:

God Bless the Child (*God Bless the Child,* MCA)

Jackson, Ronald Shannon:

Rough Traders (James "Blood" Ulmer/George Adams, *Phalanx,* Moers Music)

Kirk, Rahsaan Roland:

Old Rugged Cross Rant (*Blacknuss,* Atlantic)

Mingus, Charles:

Prayer for Passive Resistance (*Mingus at Antibes,* Atlantic)

Tyner, McCoy:

Blues on the Corner (*The Real McCoy,* Blue Note)

Ulmer, James "Blood":

Justice For Us All (*Blues Preacher,* DIW/Columbia)

Wonder, Stevie:

Saturn (*Songs in the Key of Life,* Tamla)
Visions (*Innervisions,* Motown)

Dolphy, Eric:

The Madrig Speaks, The Panther Walks (*Last Date,* Limelight)

**Kingdom of God** (*see also* **Justice**)**:**

Hymnal Collection:

In Christ There Is no East or West—LEVAS 62
We're Marching to Zion—LEVAS 12
Glory Glory, Hallelujah (Since I Laid My Burden Down)—LEVAS 130
Ain-a That Good News—LEVAS 180
S/He's Got the Whole World in Her/His Hand—LEVAS 217
Jesu Jesu (Ghana)—H 602
*Tú Has Venido a La Orilla* (You Have Come Down to the Lakeshore) (Puerto Rico)—WLP 758

Taizé:

The Kingdom of God Is Justice and Peace—T 125
Cantate Domino—P
Salvator Mundi—T/V1 110
Laudate Omnes Gentes—T/V1 12
Jubilate, Alleluia—T 27
Vous Qui Sur la Terre Habitez—T 147

Bell:

Heaven on Earth—EoA 108

Marley:

Get Up, Stand Up
One Love

Lennon, John:

Imagine (*Imagine,* Capitol Records)

Ulmer, James "Blood":

Justice for us All (*Blues Preacher,* DIW/Columbia)
Are You Glad to Be in America? (*Are You Glad to Be in America?,* DIW/Columbia)

Wonder, Stevie:

Saturn (*Songs in the Key of Life,* Tamla)

**Lent and Sacrifice:**

Hymnal Collection:

You Hear the Lambs a-cryin'—LEVAS 110
At the Cross—LEVAS 30
O Sacred Head Sore Wounded—H 168, 169
Sleepers Awake! (*Wachet Auf*)—H 61, 62
Were You There—H 172
He Never Said a Mumbalin' Word—LEVAS 33
I Know the Lord—LEVAS 131
Christ Is Coming, Prepare the Way—LEVAS 6

Taizé:

Adoramus Te Christe—T/V2 2
Jesus, Remember Me—T/V1 9

Bell:

Pawnbroker—EoA 26
Emperor of Fools (Palm Sunday)—EoA 50
The Temptations—Heaven 74

Dylan:

The Lonely Death of Hattie Carroll
In the Garden
Positively 4th St.

Blind Boys of Alabama:

The Last Time (*Spirit of the Century*, Real World)

Bryars, Gavin:

Jesus' Blood Never Failed Me Yet (*Jesus' Blood Never Failed Me Yet,* Point Records)

Cash, Johnny:

What Is Truth (*The Essential Johhny Cash,* Columbia Legacy)

Coleman, Ornette:

Mob Job (*Song X* with Pat Metheny, Nonesuch Records)

Lennon, John:

Instant Karma (*Shaved Fish,* Capitol)

Mingus, Charles:

Pithecanthropus Erectus (*Passions of a Man,* Atlantic)

Rush, Stephen:

Trompa—P

Sun Ra:
For the Sunrise (*Live at Montreux,* Inner City)

Traditional Blues:
Nobody Knows When You're Down and Out

Ulmer, James "Blood":
Troublemaker (*Original Phalanx,* Moers Music)
Big Tree (*No Wave,* Moers Music)

Waits, Tom:
Way Down in the Hole (Blind Boys of Alabama, *Spirit of the Century,* Real World)

**Liberation** (*see also* **Deliverance; Light/Epiphany/Enlightenment):**
Hymnal Collection:
Deep River—LEVAS 8
O Freedom!—LEVAS 225
Precious Lord—LEVAS 106
Glory, Glory, Hallelujah (Since I Laid My Burden Down)—LEVAS 130
Salamu Maria—LEVAS 51

Taizé:
Libera Nos Domine—T/V1 60
When the Night Becomes Dark—T/SaP 25
Beati voi Poveri—T 124
L'ajuda em Vindrà—T 134

Bell:
Somos Pueblo que Camina—Sent 26
Kyrie (Ghana)—Many 23

Marley:
Redemption Song

Coleman, Ornette:
Endangered Species (*Song X* with Pat Metheny, Nonesuch)
Feet Music (*In All Languges,* Harmolodic/Verve)
Song X (*Song X* with Pat Metheny, Nonesuch)

Holiday, Billie:
God Bless the Child (*God Bless the Child,* MCA)

Sharrock, Sonny:
Promises Kept (*Ask the Ages,* Axiom)

Sun Ra:
El Is the Sound of Joy (*Live at Montreux,* Inner City)

**Life** (*see also* **Water/Baptism):**
Hymnal Collection:
Oh Freedom—LEVAS 225

Wade in the Water—LEVAS 143
Breathe on Me, Breath of God—H 508

Taizé:
Kristus, din Ande—T 138

Coleman, Ornette:
The Good Life (*Song X* with Pat Metheny, Nonesuch Records)
Rejoicing (Pat Metheny, *Rejoicing,* ECM)

**Light/Epiphany/Enlightenment** (*see also* **Hope**)**:**
Hymnal Collection:
Lord Speak to Me That I May Speak—CRC 528
Christ Is the World's True Light—H 542
How Bright Appears the Morning Star—H 496, 497
Sleepers Awake (*Wachet Auf*)—H 61, 62
This Little Light of Mine—LEVAS 160
Let the Heaven Light Shine on Me—LEVAS 174
Siyahamba (We Are Marching) (South Africa)—WLP 787

Taizé:
Jésus le Christ—T 9
The Lord Is My Light—T/V2 73
O Light of Every Heart—T 100
Christe Lux Mundi—T 135
C'est Toi Ma Lampe Signeur—T 8
*La Ténebrè* (Our Darkness)—T 26
There Is No Darkness or Trouble—P
When the Night Becomes Dark—T/SaP 25
Veni Sancte Spiritu—T/V1 90

Coltrane, John:
Seraphic Light (*Stellar Regions,* Impulse)

Johnson, Blind Willie:
Let Your Light Shine (*Dark Was the Night,* Columbia Legacy)

Sun Ra:
Enlightenment (*Concert for the Comet Kohoutek,* ESP)
For the Sun Rise (*Live at Montreux,* Inner City)
Sun Song (*Sun Song,* Delmark)

Williams, Hank:
I Saw the Light (*Hank Williams, The Hits,* Mercury Nashville)

**Love:**
Hymnal Collection:
O Freedom—LEVAS 225
What Wondrous Love Is This—H 439

Jesu Jesu—H 602
In Christ There Is No East or West—LEVAS 62
Abide with Me—H 662
Noel Nouvelet (Now the Green Blade Riseth)—H 204

Taizé:

Wyslawiajcie Pana—T 131
Tui Amoris Ignem—T 14
Ubi Caritas—T 15, T/V1 28
Ubi Caritas Deus Ibi Est—T 4
Esprit Consolateur—T 136
*El Alma Que Anda en Amor* (The Soul Filled by Love)—T 132

Bell:

The Savior—Heaven 94
A Woman's Care—Heaven 24
The Song—Heaven 20
I'll Love the Lord—Heaven 88
Heaven Shall Not Wait—Heaven 92

Marley:

Could You Be Loved
One Love

Coleman, Ornette:

Kathelin Gray (*Song X* with Pat Metheny, Nonesuch Records)
Space Church (*In All Languages,* Harmolodic/Verve)

Coltrane, John:

Acknowledgement, Pursuance, Resolution, Psalm (*Love Supreme Suite,* Atlantic Records)
Compassion (*First Meditations,* Impulse)

Mingus, Charles:

Reincarnation of a Lovebird (*Passions of a Man,* Atlantic)
Of Love, Pain and Passioned Revolt (*The Black Saint and the Sinner Lady,* Impulse Records)

Siegel, Aaron:

Aperture (*Easter Vigil*, Canterbury House)

Sun Ra:

Love in Outer Space (*Singles Collection,* ESP)

Wonder, Stevie:

I Am Singing (*Songs in the Key of Life*, Tamla)
Love's in Need of Love Today (*Songs in the Key of Life*, Tamla)

**Mercy:** *see* **Poverty/Mercy**

**Mystery:** *see* **Spirit/Mystery**

**Nature** (*see also* **Life; Water/Baptism**):

Hymnal Collection:

For the Beauty of the Earth—H 416, alternative tune H 119
Amazing Grace—H 671
Lead Me, Guide Me—LEVAS 194
Spirit of the Living God—LEVAS 115
Higher Ground—LEVAS 165
I've Got Peace Like a River—LEVAS 201
Lord Make Us Servants of Your Peace (St. Francis)—H 593
The Trees of the Field—CRC 197
Noel Nouvelet (Now the Green Blade Riseth)—H 204
S/He's Got the Whole World in Her/His Hand—LEVAS 217

Taizé:

In Manus Tuas, Pater—T 30
The Kingdom of God Is Justice and Peace—T 125
Surrexit Christus—T 40
Vieni Spirito Creatore—T 57

Bell:

Dance and Sing—Heaven 19
Maker and Mover, Light and Life—One 76
I'll Love the Lord—Heaven 88
Heaven Shall Not Wait—Heaven 92
Enemy of Apathy—EoA 94
Lord of the Morning—EoA 67
Many and Great (Navajo)—Many 36

Blind Boys of Alabama:

Amazing Grace (*Spirit of the Century,* Real World)

Coleman, Ornette:

Garden of Souls (*New York Is Now,* Blue Note)

Gaye, Marvin:

Mercy, Mercy Me (*What's Going On,* Motown Records)

Jackson, Ronald Shannon:

Dancers of Joy (*Eye on You,* About Time Records)

Mingus, Charles:

Pithecanthropus Erectus (*Passions of a Man,* Atlantic)

Sun Ra:

For the Sunrise (*Live at Montreux,* Inner City)

Ulmer, James "Blood":

Abundance (*In the Name of . . .,* DIW)

von Bingen, Hildegard (*Hildegard von Bingen—Symphonize, Geistlich Gesanger,* Harmonia Mundi):
Virtus Sapientiae
Felix Anima

Weber, Eberhard:
Yellow Fields (*Yellow Fields,* ECM)

Wonder, Stevie:
Higher Ground (*Innervisions,* Motown)

**Obedience:** *see* **Work/Obedience/Will of God**

**Peace/Healing:**

Hymnal Collection:
Lord Make Us Servants of Your Peace (St. Francis)—H 593
Down By the Riverside—LEVAS 210
Glory, Glory, Hallelujah (Since I Laid My Burden Down)—LEVAS 130
I've Got Peace Like a River—LEVAS 201
We Shall Overcome—LEVAS 227
There Is a Balm in Gilead—LEVAS 203

Taizé:
Christe Salvator—T 21
Da Pacem Cordium—T 55
Kingdom of God—T 125
Dona La Pace—T 53
My Peace—T/V2 39
Nunc Dimittis—T/V1 22

Bell:
Lo I Am with You 'til the End of the Days—EoA 98
Jesu Tawa Pono (Zimbabwe), Many 51

Dylan:
Man of Peace
Masters of War

Coleman, Ornette:
Peace (*The Shape of Jazz to Come,* Atlantic)

Coltrane, John:
Selflessness (*Selflessness,* MCA/Impulse)
Softly, as in a Morning Sunrise (composed by Sigmund Romberg)
(*"Live" at the Village Vanguard,* Impulse)
Peace on Earth (*Live in Japan,* Impulse)

Davis, Miles:
Shhh/Peaceful (*In a Silent Way,* Columbia)

Evans, Bill:
Peace Piece (*Everybody Digs Bill Evans,* Verve)

Lennon, John:

Imagine (*Imagine,* Capitol)

Silver, Horace:

Peace (*Blowin' the Blues Away,* Blue Note)

Tyner, McCoy:

Search for Peace (*The Real McCoy,* Blue Note)

Waits, Tom:

Jesus Gonna Be Here Soon (Blind Boys of Alabama, *Spirit of the Century*, Real World)

**Poverty/Mercy:**

Hymnal Collection:

S/He's Got the Whole World in Her/His Hand—LEVAS 217
Glory, Glory, Hallelujah (Since I Laid My Burden Down)—LEVAS 130
I Want Jesus to Walk with Me—Z 95
We Shall Overcome—LEVAS 227
Abide With Me—H 662
Jesu Jesu (Ghana)—H 602

Taizé:

O Poverty—T/V2 47
Beati voi Poveri—T 124
Stay with Me—T/V2 67
Kyrie 12—T 85
L'ajuda em Vindrà—T 134
Wyslawiajcie Pana—T 131
Ubi Caritas—T 15, T/V1 28
Ubi Caritas Deus Ibi Est—T 4
Misercordias Domini—T/V1 121
Gospodi B—T 104
El Alma que Anda en Amor—T 132

Bell:

Kyrie Eleison (Ghana)—Many 23
Kyrie Guarany (Paraguay)—Sent 28
Somos Pueblo que Camina (Nicaragua)—Sent 26

Dylan:

Hard Times
Positively 4th St.
Tombstone Blues
Like a Rolling Stone
Desolation Row

Marley:

Belly Full
Ja
One Love

Ayler, Albert:

Love Cry (*Love Cry,* Impulse!)

Coleman, Ornette:

Endangered Species (*Song X* with Pat Metheny, Nonesuch Records)
Lonely Woman (*The Shape of Jazz to Come,* Atlantic)
Tears Inside (Pat Metheny, *Rejoicing,* ECM)

Coltrane, John:

Love Supreme Suite (*Love Supreme Suite,* Atlantic Records)
Compassion (*First Meditations,* Impulse)
Compassion (*Meditations*, Impulse)
Love (*First Meditations,* Impulse)

Frisell, Bill:

Child at Heart (*Live,* Gramavision)

King, Ben E.:

Stand by Me (*The Ultimate Collection,* East/West Records)

Rush, Stephen:

Blues Kyrie (Blues Mass, see Appendix D)

Sanders, Pharoah:

The Creator Has a Master Plan (*The Creator Has a Master Plan,* Tokuma Japan Comm.)

Silver, Horace:

Lonely Woman (Pat Metheny, *Rejoicing,* ECM)

Sun Ra:

Outer Space Emergency (*Concert for the Comet Kohoutek,* ESP)

Taylor, Cecil:

Of What (*Looking Ahead,* Contemporary)

Waits, Tom:

On the Nickel (*Heartattack and Vine,* Elektra Records)

Wonder, Stevie:

Living for the City (*Innervisions,* Motown)

**Praise:**

Hymnal Collection:

Pange Lingua—H 166
How Great Thou Art—LEVAS 60
Hallelujah, We Sing Your Praises (South Africa)—WLP 784

Taizé:

Alleluias—T 71, 94, 96, 97
Laudate Omnes Gentes—T/V1 12
Gloria, Deo—T 109
O Christe Domine Jesu—T/V2 42

Sanctum nomen Domini—T 56
Cantate Domino—P
Jubilate, Alleluia—T 27
Singt dem Herrn—T 24

Bell:
We Need You, God—EoA 52
Lord of the Morning—EoA 67
The Song of the Crowd—Heaven 82
Halle, Halle, Halle (Puerto Rico)—Many 18

Coleman, Ornette:
Rejoicing (Pat Metheny, *Rejoicing,* ECM)

Coltrane, John:
Leo (*Interstellar Space,* Impulse Records)
Father, Son, and Holy Ghost (*Meditations,* Impulse)

Frisell, Bill:
Rag (*Is That You?,* Elektra Musician Records)

Gaye, Marvin:
Wholy Holy (*What's Going On,* Motown Records)

Jackson, Ronald Shannon:
Dancers of Joy (*Eye on You,* About Time)

Johnson, Blind Willie:
Praise God I'm Satisfied (*Praise God I'm Satisfied,* Yazoo)

Rush, Stephen:
Klezmer Gloria—P
Blues Gloria (see Appendix D)

Sun Ra:
El Is the Sound of Joy (*Live at Montreux,* Inner City)

**Prayer:**

Hymnal Collection:
Nearer, My God, To Thee—LEVAS 54
What a Friend We Have in Jesus—LEVAS 109
King Jesus Is a-Listenin'—LEVAS 84
I Couldn't Hear Nobody Pray—Z 78

Taizé:
Wait for the Lord—T/V2 78
Stay with Us—T/V2 69
Stay with Me—T/V2 67
By Night (De Noche Iremos)—T/SaP 46

Marley:
Natural Mystic

Coltrane, John:
Serenity (*First Meditations,* Impulse)

Indian Bhajan:
Ye Mise Thura—P

Metheny, Pat, and Charlie Haden:
Waiting for an Answer (*Rejoicing,* ECM)

Mingus, Charles:
Man Who Never Sleeps (*Statements,* Lotus Jazz)
Prayer for Passive Resistance (*Mingus at Antibes,* Atlantic)
Wednesday Night Prayer Meeting (*Passions of a Man,* Atlantic)

Rush, Stephen:
Lord's Prayer (style of Taizé)—P
Hymn for Roscoe—(*Hymn for Roscoe,* MMC)

Sun Ra:
Journey Outward (*Out There a Minute,* Blast First Records)

Taylor, Cecil:
Streams (*Dark to Themselves,* Enja)

Wonder, Stevie:
Have a Talk with God (*Songs in the Key of Life,* Tamla
Higher Ground (*Innervisions,* Motown)

**Resurrection:** *see* **Death/Resurrection**

**Scholarship** (*see also* **Light/Epiphany/Enlightenment):**
Hymnal Collection:
Lord Speak to Me That I May Speak—CRC 528
Higher Ground—LEVAS 165

Coleman, Ornette:
Trigonometry (*Song X* with Pat Metheny, Nonesuch Records)

Sun Ra:
Brainville (*Sun Song,* Delmark)
Discipline (*Concert for the Comet Kohoutek,* ESP)

Wonder, Stevie:
Higher Ground (*Innervisions,* Motown)

**Sin:**
Hymnal Collection:
There Is a Balm in Gilead—LEVAS 203
Forgive Our Sins as We Forgive—H 674
Take Up Your Cross—H 675

Ayler, Albert:

Witches and Devils (*Witches and Devils*, Freedom/Black Saint)
Spirits (*Witches and Devils*, Freedom/Black Saint)
Ghosts (*Love Cry*, Impulse!), (*Prophecy*, ESP)

Mingus, Charles (*Black Saint and the Sinner Lady,* Impulse):

Saint and Sinner Join in Merriment on Battle Front
Stop! Look! And Listen, Sinner Jim Whitney

Sun Ra (*Sun Song,* Delmark):

Street Named Hell
Call for All Demons
Possession

**Spirit/Mystery:**

Hymnal Collection:

Spirit of God, Descend Upon My Heart—LEVAS 119
Spirit of the Living God—LEVAS 115
There's a Sweet, Sweet Spirit in This Place—LEVAS 120
I'm Gonna Sing When the Spirit Says Sing—LEVAS 117
Everytime I Feel the Spirit—LEVAS 114

Taizé:

Veni Sancte Spiritus—T/V1 6
Tui Amoris—T 14
Spiritus Jesu Christi—T 36
Vieni Spirito Creatore—T 57
Tu Sei Sorgente Viva—T 39

Ayler, Albert:

Spirits Rejoice (*Live in Greenwich Village,* Impulse!)
Spirits (*Witches and Devils,* Freedom/Black Saint)
Witches and Devils (*Witches and Devils,* Freedom/Black Saint)
Holy Ghost (*Live in Greenwich Village,* Impulse!)
Ghosts (*Love Cry,* Impulse!), (*Prophecy,* ESP)

Coltrane, John:

Father, Son, and Holy Ghost (*Meditations,* Impulse)
Reflection (*A Love Supreme,* Atlantic Records)

Kirk, Rahsaan Roland:

I Talk with the Spirits (*Kirk's Works,* Mercury)

Mingus, Charles:

Man Who Never Sleeps (*Statements,* Lotus Jazz)
Better Get Hit in Your Soul (*Passions of a Man,* Atlantic)

Mitchell, Roscoe (*The Paris Session,* Arista Freedom):

Ninth Room
Spiritual

Rush, Stephen:

Breathe in the Spirit (*Catch Your Breath*, Don Postema, Grand Rapids: CRC Publishing, 1997)

Waits, Tom:

Jesus Gonna Be Here (*Spirit of the Century,* Blind Boys of Alabama, Real World)

Sun Ra:

Sun Song (*Sun Song,* Delmark)

**Thanksgiving:** *see* **Grace/Blessedness/Thanksgiving**

**Trouble:** *see* **Fear/Doubt/Trouble**

**Trust/Faith** (*see also* **Hope**):

Hymnal Collection:

Amazing Grace—H 671
Just a Closer Walk with Thee—LEVAS 72
Lead Me, Guide Me—LEVAS 194
I Want Jesus to Walk with Me—Z 95
We Shall Overcome—LEVAS 227
King Jesus Is a-Listenin'—LEVAS 84
Didn' My Lord Deliver Daniel?—LEVAS 182
I Don't Feel No Ways Tired—LEVAS 199
I'm Gonna Sing When the Spirit Says Sing—LEVAS 117
I Will Trust in the Lord—LEVAS 193
Ain'a That Good News—LEVAS 180
S/He's Got the Whole World in Her/His Hand—LEVAS 217
I Shall Not Be Moved—Z 35
Get on Board Little Children—Z 116

Taizé:

Bonum Est Confidere—T 35
Bendigo al Señor—T 133
Salvator Mundi—T/V1 110

Bell:

Lo I Am with You 'til the End of the Days—EoA 98
I'll Love the Lord—Heaven 88

Dylan:

Are You Ready?

Blind Boys of Alabama:

Amazing Grace (*Spirit of the Century,* Real World)

Cash, Johnny:

I Walk the Line (*The Essential Johnny Cash,* Columbia Legacy)

Coleman, Ornette:

Macho Woman (*Body Meta,* Artists House)

Coltrane, John:

Father, Son, and Holy Ghost (*Meditations,* Impulse)

Frisell, Bill:

Have a Little Faith (John Hyatt) (*Live,* Gramavision)
Lookout for Hope (*Lookout for Hope,* Impulse)
Throughout (*Live,* Gramavision)

Johnson, Blind Willie:

Praise God I'm Satisfied (*Praise God I'm Satisfied,* Yazoo)

Lennon, John:

Instant Karma (*Shaved Fish,* Capitol)

Sharrock, Sonny:

Promises Kept (*Ask the Ages*, Axiom)

Wonder, Stevie:

Saturn (*Songs in the Key of Life,* Tamla)

**Water/Baptism:**

Hymnal Collection:

Shall We Gather at the River—LEVAS 141
Wade in the Water—LEVAS 143
Down by the Riverside—LEVAS 210
I've Got Peace Like a River—LEVAS 201
Deep River—LEVAS 8
Take Me to the Water—LEVAS 134

Taizé:

By night (De Noche Iremos)—T/SaP 46
Kristus, din Ande—T 138

Coleman, Ornette:

The Good Life (*Song X* with Pat Metheny, Nonesuch Records)

Garbarek, Jan:

Where the Waters Meet (*Rites,* ECM)

Green, Al:

Take Me to the River (*More Greatest Hits,* The Right Stuff)

Ives, Charles:

At the River, *114 Songs* (out of print)

**Will of God:** *see* **Work/Obedience/Will of God**

**Work/Obedience/Will of God:**

Hymnal Collection:

Wayfaring Stranger—LEVAS 19
Sign Me Up—LEVAS 142

Higher Ground—LEVAS 165
Lead Me, Guide Me—LEVAS 194
Lord Speak to Me That I May Speak—CRC 528
Jesu Jesu (Ghana)—H 602
I Shall Not Be Moved—Z 35
Get on Board Little Children—Z 116

Taizé:
In Manus Tuas, Pater—T 30
By Night (De Noche Iremos)—T/SaP 46

Bell:
Jesus Christ Is Waiting—EoA 78
Sing Hey for the Carpenter—Heaven 77
I'll Love the Lord—Heaven 88
Heaven Shall Not Wait—Heaven 92
Gifts of the Spirit—Heaven 86
Christ in the Stranger's Guise—EoA 83
The Strangest of Saints—Heaven 101
The Summons—Heaven 102

Dylan:
John Wesley Harding

Coltrane, John:
India (*Impressions,* Impulse)
Africa (*Africa Brass Sessions, vol. 2,* Impulse)
Compassion (*First Meditations,* Impulse)
Compassion (*Meditations,* Impulse)

Coleman, Ornette:
Feet Music (*In All Languges,* Harmolodic/Verve)
Trigonometry (*Song X* with Pat Metheny, Nonesuch Records)
Word from Bird (*Song X* with Pat Metheny, Nonesuch Records)

Frisell, Bill:
Things Will Never Be the Same (*Blues Dream,* Nonesuch Records)

Kirk, Rahsaan Roland:
From Bechet, Byas and Fats (*Kirk's Works,* Mercury)

Metheny, Pat:
The Calling (*Rejoicing,* ECM)

Metheny, Pat, and Charlie Haden:
Waiting for an Answer (*Rejoicing,* ECM)

Rush, Stephen:
Breathe in the Spirit (*Catch Your Breath*, Don Postema, Grand Rapids: CRC Publications, 1997)
Change Up—P
Play Tough (*Easter Jazz Vigil,* Canterbury House)

Sanders, Pharoah:

The Creator Has a Master Plan (*The Creator Has a Master Plan,* Tokuma Japan Comm.)

Sun Ra:

Discipline (*Concert for the Comet Kohoutek,* ESP)
Brainville (*Sun Song,* Delmark)

Wonder, Stevie:

Higher Ground (*Innervisions,* Motown)

## A Note Concerning Spirituals:

It is best to consult recordings for authentic performances of this music. Listen, at least, to Mississippi John Hurt, Rev. Gary Davis, Blind Willie Johnson, and Son House. These versions have an accuracy and an immediacy lacking in printed versions.

## Highly Recommended Recordings for an Introduction to the Jazz and Blues Used at Canterbury House:

Art Ensemble of Chicago, *The Paris Session* (Arista Freedom)
Art Esemble of Chicago, *Nice Guys* (ECM)
Albert Ayler, *Witches and Devils* (Freedom/Black Saint)
Blind Boys of Alabama, *Spirit of the Century* (Real World)
Ornette Coleman, *Song X* with Pat Metheny (Nonesuch)
Ornette Coleman, *The Shape of Jazz to Come* (Atlantic)
John Coltrane, *Love Supreme* (Atlantic)
John Coltrane, *Meditations* (Impulse)
John Coltrane, *First Meditations* (Impulse)
Rev. Gary Davis, *Say No to the Devil* (Bluesville)
Miles Davis, *Bitches Brew* (Columbia)
Miles Davis, *Filles des Kilamanjaro* (Columbia)
Miles Davis, *In a Silent Way* (Columbia)
Bill Frisell, *Live* (Gramavision)
Jan Garbarek, *Rites* (ECM)
Blind Willie Johnson, *Dark Was the Night* (Columbia)
Blind Willie Johnson, *Praise God I'm Satisfied* (Yazoo)
Rahsaan Roland Kirk, *Kirk's Works* (Mercury)
Bob Marley, *Legend* (Def Jam)
Sonny Sharrock, *Ask the Ages* (Axiom)
Sun Ra, *Concert for the Comet Kohoutek* (ESP)
Sun Ra, *Live at Montreux* (Inner City)
Cecil Taylor, *Dark Unto Themselves* (Inner City)
McCoy Tyner, *The Real McCoy* (Blue Note)
James "Blood" Ulmer, *Are You Glad to Be in America?* (DIW/Columbia)
Various Artists, *The Original Delta Blues* (Columbia Legacy)
Stevie Wonder, *Innervisions* (Motown)

# Appendix C

## Psalm Tones by Stephen Rush

These Psalm Tones were created in order to imbue the chanting of the psalms with a deeper and clearer emotive content due to mood, harmonic intensity, and melodic contour. Traditional Psalm Tones (such as those found in the *Liber Usualis*) were not written to instill a particular mood, but were simply a tool for reciting and chanting the psalms, hopefully letting the emotional impact of the psalm emerge on its own. These Psalm Tones allow the singers emotional engagement *in simpatico* with the psalms. My feeling is that the psalms are the most emotional texts in the Bible, why not sing them that way?

In order to use these, simply chant the psalm (or the portion prescribed by the lectionary), using the upper tone of the "chant chords" as the **reciting tone**. Follow the instructions for each Psalm Tone for groove, pulse, and form. Sound samples of the Psalm Tones are provided free at www.churchpublishing.com. This guide can also be used for personal prayer and study, matching the various themes to various psalms. Of course, there are myriad themes to the psalms. The tones below are merely the few that seem to hit the author the hardest.

### Psalm Tones

Praise (Ps. 48:1)
Justice and Peace (Ps. 72:1)
Where is God? (Ps. 130:1)
Thanks (Ps. 111:2)
Shelter (Ps. 142:1)
Nature and Creation (Ps. 24:1)
Compassion (Ps. 119:39)
Enlightenment (Ps. 112:5)
Community (Ps. 133:1)
Liberation (Ps 103:6)
Trust (Ps. 37:3)

Texts for these Psalm Tones are from *Psalms for Praying* by Nan C. Merrill (New York: Continuum, 1996).

# Psalm Tone 1

## *Praise*

**Stephen Rush**

*Performance Directions:*

For the verses sing words in the first line of the psalm text to the first note, moving to the second note at the bold word. Move to the third note for the second line, proceeding to the fourth note at the bold word, etc.

Example of psalm text:
Rejoice in the Lord, you **righteous;**
*(sing to the 1st note) /(move to the second note)*

it is good for the just to sing **praises.**
*( to third note) /(to fourth note)*

Use the groove from "In a Silent Way" by Miles Davis to support it. The tempo should allow the cantor to sing the text of the psalm without feeling rushed. Alternate between verse and antiphon as needed for the performance of the psalm.

# Psalm Tone 2

*Justice and Peace*

**Stephen Rush**

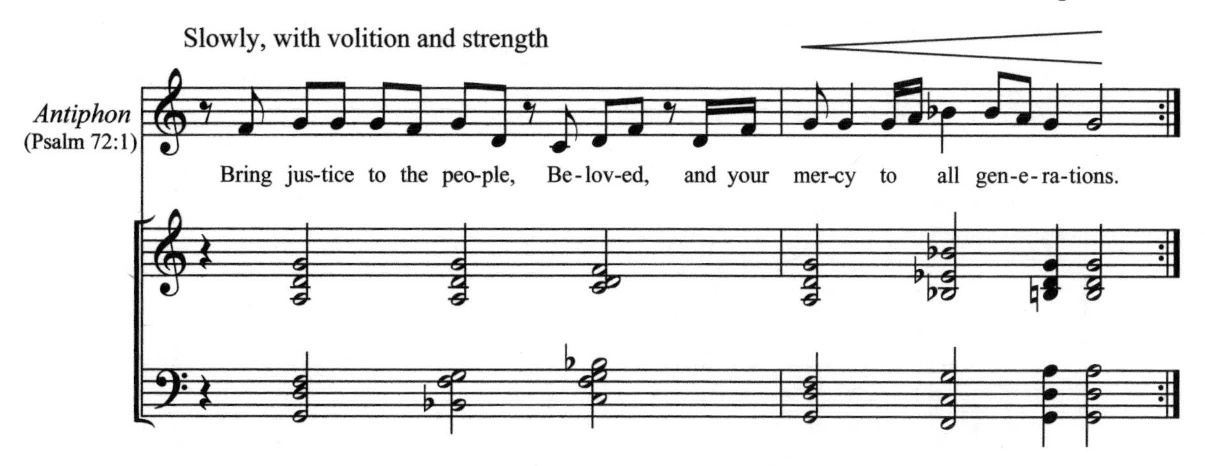


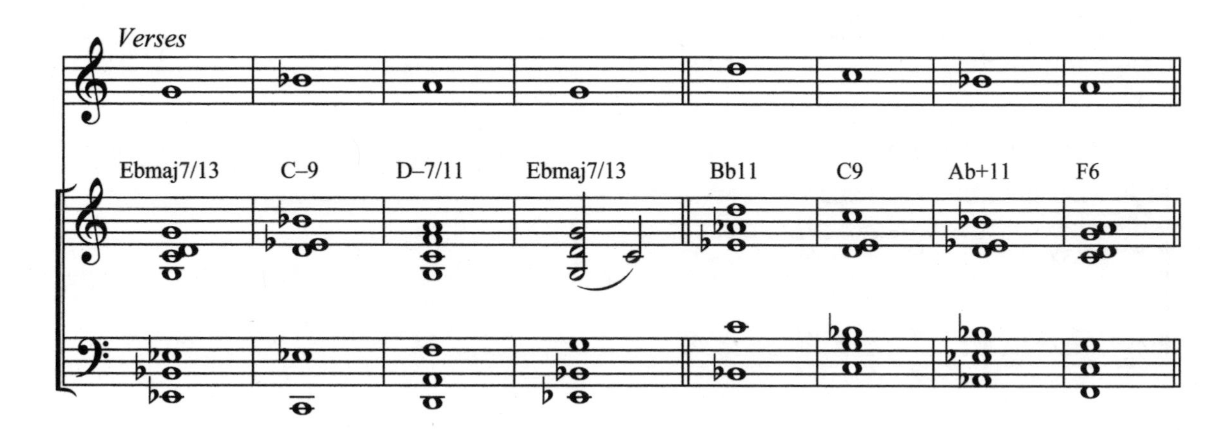


*Performance Directions:*

For the antiphon, use a slow ecstatic pulse, and deliver it loudly with intensity.

For the verses sing words in the first line to the first note, moving to the second note at the bold word. Move to the third note for the second line, proceeding to the fourth note at the bold word, etc.

Use the groove from "In a Silent Way" by Miles Davis to support it. The tempo should allow the cantor to sing the text of the psalm without feeling rushed. Alternate between verse and antiphon as needed for the performance of the psalm.

# Psalm Tone 3

*Where Is God?*

Stephen Rush

*Performance Directions:*

For the antiphon, use a deliberate and plodding pulse. Should be sung in an angry, menacing way.

For the verses sing words in the first line to the first note, moving to the second note at the bold word. Move to the third note for the second line, proceeding to the fourth note at the bold word, etc.

Use the groove from "In a Silent Way" by Miles Davis to support it. The tempo should allow the cantor to sing the text of the psalm without feeling rushed. Alternate between verse and antiphon as needed for the performance of the psalm.

# Psalm Tone 4

*Thanks*

**Stephen Rush**

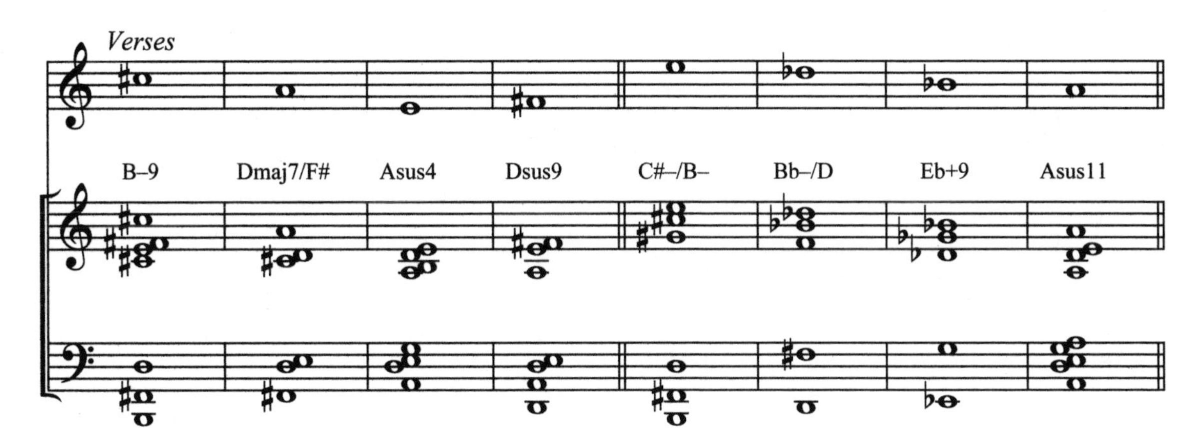


*Performance Directions:*

Use the same pulse and groove for the verses as for the antiphon.

For the verses sing words in the first line to the first note, moving to the second note at the bold word. Move to the third note for the second line, proceeding to the fourth note at the bold word, etc.

The tempo should allow the cantor to sing the text of the psalm without feeling rushed. Alternate between verse and antiphon as needed for the performance of the psalm.

# Psalm Tone 5

## *Shelter*

**Stephen Rush**

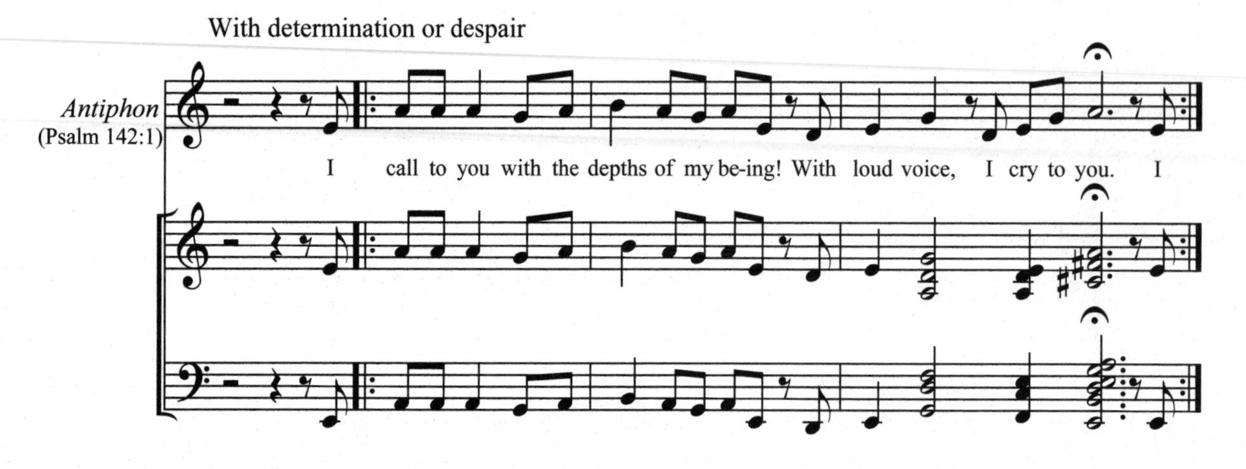


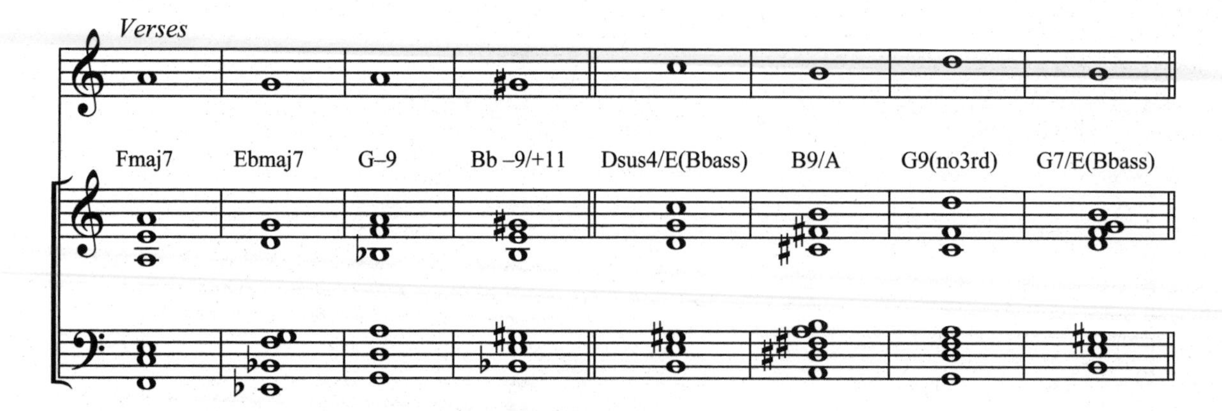


*Performance Directions:*

For the antiphon, use a determined pulse, deliver loudly with desperate urgency or confidence.

For the verses sing words in the first line to the first note, moving to the second note at the bold word. Move to the third note for the second line, proceeding to the fourth note at the bold word, etc.

Use the groove from "In a Silent Way" by Miles Davis to support it. The tempo should allow the cantor to sing the text of the psalm without feeling rushed. Alternate between verse and antiphon as needed for the performance of the psalm.

# Psalm Tone 6

*Nature/Creation*

**Stephen Rush**

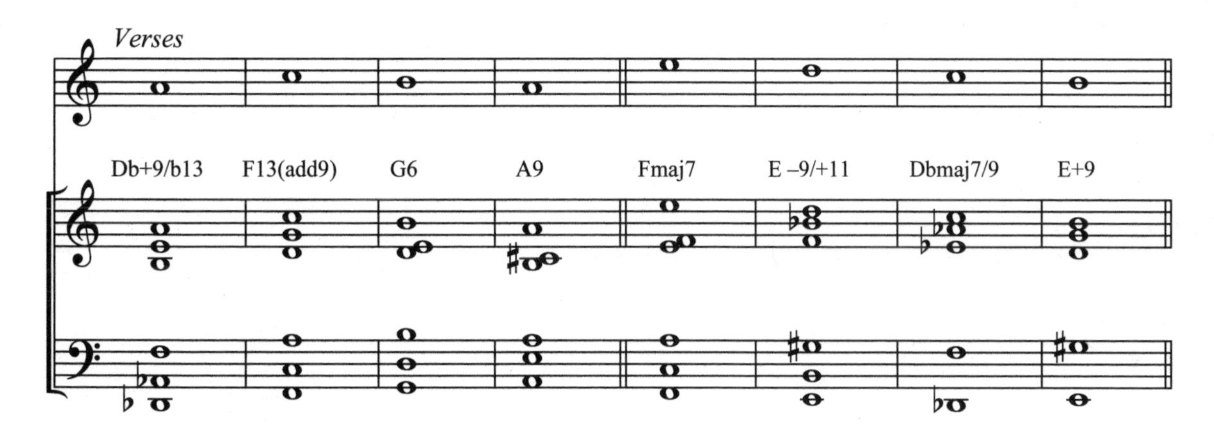


*Performance Directions:*

For the antiphon, use a slow ecstatic pulse and deliver it loudly with intensity.
If the congregation really gets excited, continue the antiphon many times at the end.

For the verses sing words in the first line to the first note, moving to the second note at the bold word.
Move to the third note for the second line, proceeding to the fourth note at the bold word, etc.

Use the groove from "In a Silent Way" by Miles Davis to support it. The tempo should allow the cantor to sing the text of the psalm without feeling rushed. Alternate between verse and antiphon as needed for the performance of the psalm.

# Psalm Tone 7

## *Compassion*

Stephen Rush

*Verses*

*Performance Directions:*

For the antiphon, use a steady slow rock groove. Use the same groove for the verses.

For the verses sing words in the first line to the first note, moving to the second note at the bold word. Move to the third note for the second line, proceeding to the fourth note at the bold word, etc.

The tempo should allow the cantor to sing the text of the psalm without feeling rushed. Alternate between verse and antiphon as needed for the performance of the psalm.

# Psalm Tone 8

*Enlightenment*

**Stephen Rush**

*Performance Directions:*

For the antiphon use a quick 3/4 rock groove, played and sung gently. Use the same groove for the verses, but extend the harmonic rhythm as indicated.

For the verses sing words in the first line to the first note, moving to the second note at the bold word. Move to the third note for the second line, proceeding to the fourth note at the bold word, etc.

# Psalm Tone 9

*Community*

Stephen Rush

*Performance Directions:*

For the antiphon use a quick 6/8 rock groove, played in an excited way (see Bob Dylan's "Death of Hattie Carroll"). Use the same groove for the verses, buat extend the harmonic rhythm as indicated.

For the verses sing words in the first line to the first note, moving to the second note at the bold word. Move to the third note for the second line, proceeding to the fourth note at the bold word, etc.

The tempo should allow the cantor to sing the text of the psalm without feeling rushed. Alternate between verse and antiphon as needed for the performance of the psalm.

# Psalm Tone 10

*Liberation*

*for Reid Hamilton*

**Stephen Rush**

*Performance Directions:*

For the antiphon, use a swift jazz waltz lilt, played and sung gently. Use the same groove for the verses, but extend the harmonic rhythm as indicated. For the verses sing words in the first line to the first note, moving to the second note at the bold word. Move to the third note for the second line, proceeding to the fourth note at the bold word, etc.

The tempo should allow the cantor to sing the text of the psalm without feeling rushed.
Alternate between verse and antiphon as needed for the performance of the psalm.

# Psalm Tone 11

*Trust*

Stephen Rush

*Performance Directions:*

For the antiphon, play in a deep, slow funky groove (see Miles Davis's *Tutu*).

For the verses sing words in the first line to the first note, moving to the second note at the bold word. Move to the third note for the second line, proceeding to the fourth note at the bold word, etc.

Use the groove from "In a Silent Way" by Miles Davis to support it. The tempo should allow the cantor to sing the text of the psalm without feeling rushed. Alternate between verse and antiphon as needed for the performance of the psalm.

## Psalms According to Theme:

| | |
|---|---|
| Psalm 1 | Justice and Peace |
| Psalm 2 | Justice and Peace |
| Psalm 3 | Where Is God?, Liberation |
| Psalm 4 | Where Is God?, Liberation, Shelter |
| Psalm 5 | Shelter, Justice and Peace |
| Psalm 6 | Where Is God?, Compassion |
| Psalm 7 | Shelter, Justice and Peace |
| Psalm 8 | Thanks, Nature, Praise |
| Psalm 9 | Thanks, Justice and Peace |
| Psalm 10 | Where Is God? |
| Psalm 11 | Shelter, Justice and Peace |
| Psalm 12 | Where Is God?, Compassion |
| Psalm 13 | Where Is God?, Trust |
| Psalm 14 | Liberation, Justice and Peace |
| Psalm 15 | Justice and Peace, Shelter |
| Psalm 16 | Shelter, Praise, Justice and Peace |
| Psalm 17 | Justice and Peace, Shelter |
| Psalm 18 (I and II) | Shelter, Praise, Trust |
| Psalm 19 | Praise, Justice and Peace |
| Psalm 20 | Shelter, Trust |
| Psalm 21 | Shelter, Trust, Liberation |
| Psalm 22 | Where Is God?, Praise |
| Psalm 23 | Shelter, Trust |
| Psalm 24 | Shelter, Nature, Praise |
| Psalm 25 | Trust, Shelter, Enlightenment |
| Psalm 26 | Enlightenment, Community |
| Psalm 27 | Shelter |
| Psalm 28 | Shelter, Where Is God?, Justice and Peace |
| Psalm 29 | Praise |
| Psalm 30 | Praise, Trust |
| Psalm 31 | Shelter, Trust |
| Psalm 32 | Compassion |
| Psalm 33 | Praise |
| Psalm 34 | Praise, Shelter, Liberation |
| Psalm 35 | Justice and Peace, Praise |
| Psalm 36 | Justice and Peace |
| Psalm 37 | Justice and Peace, Trust, Enlightenment |
| Psalm 38 | Enlightenment, Trust |
| Psalm 39 | Where Is God?, Liberation |
| Psalm 40 | Where Is God?, Trust |
| Psalm 41 | Shelter, Trust, Praise |
| Psalm 42 | Where Is God?, Nature |
| Psalm 43 | Justice and Peace |

| | |
|---|---|
| Psalm 44 | Justice and Peace, Trust |
| Psalm 45 | Thanks, Praise |
| Psalm 46 | Justice and Peace, Shelter, Nature |
| Psalm 47 | Praise |
| Psalm 48 | Praise |
| Psalm 49 | Trust, Enlightenment, Liberation |
| Psalm 50 | Justice and Peace |
| Psalm 51 | Compassion, Liberation, Justice and Peace |
| Psalm 52 | Justice and Peace, Thanks |
| Psalm 53 | Enlightenment, Shelter, Liberation |
| Psalm 54 | Shelter, Liberation |
| Psalm 55 | Shelter, Where Is God? |
| Psalm 56 | Trust, Praise, Shelter |
| Psalm 57 | Shelter, Enlightenment |
| Psalm 58 | Justice and Peace, Liberation, Trust |
| Psalm 59 | Shelter, Liberation |
| Psalm 60 | Shelter, Liberation |
| Psalm 61 | Shelter, Nature, Justice |
| Psalm 62 | Enlightenment, Shelter, Trust |
| Psalm 63 | Where Is God?, Justice and Peace |
| Psalm 64 | Enlightenment, Where Is God? |
| Psalm 65 | Praise, Nature |
| Psalm 66 | Praise, Community, Shelter |
| Psalm 67 | Thanks, Compassion, Praise |
| Psalm 68 | Justice and Peace, Liberation, Nature, Praise |
| Psalm 69 | Where Is God?, Praise, Justice and Peace |
| Psalm 70 | Liberation, Enlightenment |
| Psalm 71 | Shelter, Praise |
| Psalm 72 | Justice and Peace, Compassion, Nature, Praise |
| Psalm 73 | Shelter, Enlightenment |
| Psalm 74 | Shelter, Where Is God? |
| Psalm 75 | Thanks, Justice and Peace, Praise |
| Psalm 76 | Praise, Justice and Peace |
| Psalm 77 | Where Is God?, Liberation, Nature |
| Psalm 78:I | Justice and Peace, Enlightenment |
| Psalm 78:II | Liberation, Justice and Peace |
| Psalm 79 | Justice and Peace, Community |
| Psalm 80 | Enlightenment, Liberation, Trust |
| Psalm 81 | Praise |
| Psalm 82 | Justice and Peace |
| Psalm 83 | Where Is God? |
| Psalm 84 | Shelter, Praise, Trust |
| Psalm 85 | Thanks, Compassion |
| Psalm 86 | Where Is God?, Compassion |
| Psalm 87 | Shelter, Enlightenment |
| Psalm 88 | Where Is God? |

| | |
|---|---|
| Psalm 89: I | Compassion, Praise |
| Psalm 89: II | Community, Enlightenment, Where Is God? |
| Psalm 90 | Shelter, Enlightenment, Liberation |
| Psalm 91 | Shelter |
| Psalm 92 | Thanks, Praise |
| Psalm 93 | Nature, Praise |
| Psalm 94 | Justice and Peace |
| Psalm 95 | Praise, Thanks |
| Psalm 96 | Praise, Community, Nature |
| Psalm 97 | Praise, Thanks, Nature |
| Psalm 98 | Praise, Nature |
| Psalm 99 | Enlightenment, Praise |
| Psalm 100 | Praise, Trust |
| Psalm 101 | Justice and Peace, Compassion |
| Psalm 102 | Where Is God?, Justice and Peace |
| Psalm 103 | Praise, Thanks, Compassion |
| Psalm 104 | Praise, Nature |
| Psalm 105: I | Thanks |
| Psalm 105: II | Justice and Peace, Compassion |
| Psalm 106: I | Praise, Justice and Peace |
| Psalm 106: II | Justice and Peace, Liberation |
| Psalm 107: I | Thanks, Compassion |
| Psalm 107: II | Nature, Compassion |
| Psalm 108 | Praise, Thanks |
| Psalm 109 | Compassion, Justice and Peace, Where Is God? |
| Psalm 110 | Nature, Justice and Peace |
| Psalm 111 | Praise, Thanks |
| Psalm 112 | Praise, Justice and Peace |
| Psalm 113 | Praise, Thanks |
| Psalm 114 | Shelter, Nature |
| Psalm 115 | Community, Trust, Where Is God? |
| Psalm 116 | Shelter, Trust, Liberation |
| Psalm 117 | Liberation, Praise, Thanks |
| Psalm 118 | Thanks, Liberation, Shelter |
| Psalm 119 | |
| 1–8 Aleph: | Thanks |
| 9–16 Beth: | Enlightenment |
| 17–24 Gimel: | Justice |
| 25–32 Daleth: | Enlightenment, Liberation |
| 33–40 He: | Enlightenment |
| 41–48 Waw: | Compassion |
| 49–56 Zayin: | Compassion, Shelter |
| 57–64 Heth: | Trust |
| 65–72 Teth: | Justice |
| 73–80 Yodh: | Compassion |
| 81–88 Kaph: | Compassion |

| | |
|---|---|
| 89–96 Lamedh: | Trust, Nature |
| 97–104 Mem: | Enlightenment |
| 105–112 Nun: | Enlightenment |
| 113–120 Samekh: | Shelter, Compassion |
| 121–128 Ayin: | Justice |
| 129–136 Pe: | Compassion, Liberation |
| 137–144 Sadhe: | Justice |
| 145–152 Qoph: | Shelter |
| 153–160 Resh: | Liberation |
| 161–168 Shin: | Shelter |
| 169–176 Taw: | Liberation, Shelter |
| Psalm 120 | Shelter, Liberation |
| Psalm 121 | Liberation, Shelter |
| Psalm 122 | Community, Liberation, Shelter |
| Psalm 123 | Justice and Peace, Shelter |
| Psalm 124 | Liberation, Justice and Peace |
| Psalm 125 | Trust, Justice and Peace |
| Psalm 126 | Compassion |
| Psalm 127 | Shelter, Compassion |
| Psalm 128 | Compassion, Shelter, Praise |
| Psalm 129 | Praise |
| Psalm 130 | Where Is God?, Praise |
| Psalm 131 | Enlightenment |
| Psalm 132 | Shelter |
| Psalm 133 | Community |
| Psalm 134 | Praise |
| Psalm 135 | Praise, Thanks |
| Psalm 136 | Compassion, Praise, Thanks, Liberation |
| Psalm 137 | Compassion, Liberation, Where Is God? |
| Psalm 138 | Thanks, Liberation |
| Psalm 139 | Shelter, Enlightenment |
| Psalm 140 | Shelter, Liberation |
| Psalm 141 | Shelter, Liberation |
| Psalm 142 | Shelter, Liberation |
| Psalm 143 | Where Is God? |
| Psalm 144 | Enlightenment, Liberation, Nature |
| Psalm 145 | Shelter, Praise |
| Psalm 146 | Praise, Justice and Peace |
| Psalm 147 | Praise, Nature, Thanks |
| Psalm 148 | Praise, Community, Nature, Justice and Peace |
| Psalm 149 | Praise, Community, Justice and Peace |
| Psalm 150 | Praise |

# Appendix D

## Blues Mass by Stephen Rush

### The Blues as a Deep Expression of Christ's Love

The Blues contains an important, contemporary message for us as followers of Christ. The Blues invites us to embrace the full experience of human reality, the dark as well as the light side, and reminds us that whenever we are in trouble, God is with us. In the words of "Blind" Gary Davis, we can "hold to God's unchanging hand." Lent is an obvious good and appropriate time for the Blues, but there are many times in the church year your congregation may "have the Blues." These are the times, to quote John Lee Hooker, to use "Blues as a Healer."

To sing the Blues in church is to acknowledge two things:

1) We are living in post-Victorian times. We are a culture of many cloths and colors. We acknowledge that the message of this music from the United States and from the black south is an important musical tradition that has its place in worship as well as culture.
2) We are living in an existential age whose prophets include Kafka, Dostoyevsky, Camus, and Sartre. We acknowledge that life is truly hard. Yet we know that Jesus suffers with us.

Listen to just the *words* of the Blues:

"I Know His Blood Can Make Me Whole"
*I was a gambler, I was sick and couldn't get well, I know His blood can make me whole.*

"Nobody's Fault But Mine"
*If I don't read (the Bible) my soul'll be lost.*

"I Just Can't Keep from Cryin' Sometimes"
*My mother she's in Glory, my father he's gone too, Alabama put him away. I thought that as I got older—I think that's what I told her—I just can't keep from cryin' sometimes. My heart's full of sorrow, and my eyes full of tears.*

—*Blind Willie Johnson*

*You know His voice is like a rushing waterfall—a double-edged sword from his mouth. He said I am the first and the last. I hold the keys to DEATH and HELL. The lamp, he said, now here I am: I stand at the door and knock. If anyone hears and opens the door, then I'll come on in and talk.*

—*Son House* (who said he was "saved by the Blues")

*They call it Stormy Monday, but Tuesday's just as bad; Wednesday's worse baby, and I tell you Thursday's oh, so sad. Lord the eagle flies on Friday, and Saturday I go out to play. Sunday I go to church and I have to get on my knees and pray: Lord have mercy, my life is so hard, come help me get through the day.*

*—T-Bone Walker*

*Blues is a healer, all over the world*
*Blues is a healer, healer, all over the world, all over the world*
*It healed me, it can heal you.*

*—John Lee Hooker*

The Blues express, not only in words but in their very musical form, the Christian message of God coming down to earth and then even further: God, through Jesus, descending into the land of the dead. Even the harmonic structure of the Blues reinforces this idea of descent into hell, and then rising up.

Technically speaking: in a G (key) Blues the first four bars are basically G, with a slight move away to C toward the beginning. Then we move to IV or C—a move that symbolizes progress away, up, and out. The last four bars go all the way up to D, the highest chord in the progression, then back to C, then sink all the way back down to G again, usually accompanied with a crescendo to lead us back to the return of G.

This is a musical, emotional, and theological way of saying that it's okay to sink back down—as we say in the Apostles' Creed, to "descend into hell." The Blues chord progression lifts us *out* of the depths (G major) and into the heights (D major), then returns us back down again. This is what B.B. King described as "lifting you up with the blues." We sing a sad song to make us feel, if not happy, then at least okay with our sadness! The Blues reflects an emotional/spiritual cycle, and what's delightful about the Blues is that it happens over and over and over again—one Blues song can easily include one hundred cycles of this lifting up and setting back down.

All of these Blues musicians—Blind Willie Johnson, Son House, T-Bone Walker, John Lee Hooker—*certainly* believed in God, and the message of their music is that God is with us in our suffering. This is the core of my own belief as well: *God is with us in our suffering*—not to make it go away, not to muffle it, not to cover it up. God suffers with us.

The Cross, for me, is the symbol of suffering—not of exoneration. I used to be really angry that the Christian symbol most commonly seen is the cross, and not the empty tomb. But as I age and see more suffering—encounter more death, poverty, and emotional drought—I have to say that the cross is my sign of hope, that "All is not lost, because Christ was here before, he knows this pain, and is here with me now." Lord have mercy. Christ have mercy. Lord have mercy.

# Blues Kyrie

**Stephen Rush**

# Blues Gloria

Stephen Rush

Fast Boogie

# Blues Credo

**Stephen Rush**

Slow Blues, straight eighths

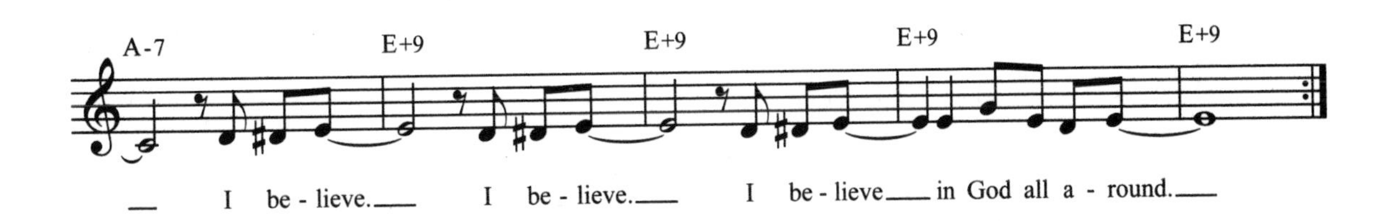


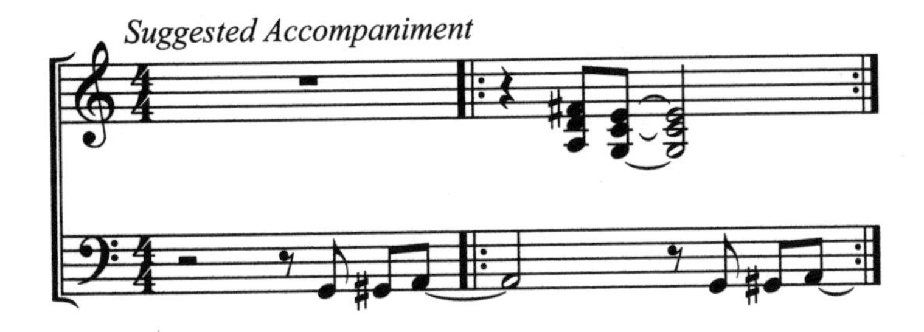


*Performance Directions:*

Start slow and funky with the suggested accompaniment. Repeat as needed. End on A7.

# Blues Sanctus

Stephen Rush

# Blues Agnus Dei

Stephen Rush

# Glossary

**Advent** In the liturgical calendar, an anticipatory season including the four Sundays preceding Christmas. From the Latin word for "coming."

**Agogo Bells** Two cone-shaped metal bells of different pitches attached to the ends of a U-shaped metal rod. Used in African and Latin music.

**Ayler, Albert** (1936–1970) Albert Ayler was a profoundly underappreciated Free Jazz composer and saxophonist whose spiritual interests found expression in his music, on such albums as *Spirits* (Debut, 1964), *Witches and Devils* (Black Lion, 1964), *Prophecy* (ESP/Base, 1964), *Ghosts* (Debut, 1964), and *Spirits Rejoice* (ESP, 1965).

**Bell, John** (b. 1949) Influential writer and composer of hymns and a member of both the Wild Goose Resource Group, which has published numerous books of church music and worship resources, and the Iona Community, an ecumenical Christian community of men and women in Iona, Scotland.

**Bhajan** A Hindu religious song of praise.

**Blues** An American musical form, influenced by field hollers and Negro Spirituals, developed in the 1920s by such artists as Robert Johnson, Son House, Leadbelly, and Ma Rainey.

***Book of Common Prayer*** The primary book of worship in the Episcopal Church. Many other churches, often called "liturgical churches," use textual guides for worship such as the Evangelical Lutheran Church's *Evangelical Lutheran Worship*, the United Methodist Church's *United Methodist Book of Worship*, or the Roman Catholic *Missale Romanum*. Of course, not all churches employ such written resources.

**Cage, John** (1912–1992) Twentieth-century composer who infused his compositions with a combination of Zen Buddhism, chance procedures, and experimental electronics. His controversial composition *4'33"* invites the audience to listen to silence, and the sounds contained therein, for the duration of the composition.

**Canterbury House** A frequently used name for campus ministry in the Episcopal Church. In this book, "Canterbury House" refers to the Episcopal Campus Ministry at the University of Michigan. Episcopal campus ministry was established on the University of Michigan campus in 1887. Canterbury House has long been a leader in its field, and in the late 1960s and early '70s, it achieved national prominence with its coffee-house ministry. Chaplains Dan Burke and Martin Bell, together with student manager Ed Reynolds, created an innovative ministry of music, conversation, and worship. Musicians such as Joni Mitchell, Richie Havens, Odetta, Tom Rush, Gordon Lightfoot, the Byrds, and Janis Joplin, among many others, performed there. Canterbury House continues to be a leader in liturgical innovation and music. Its concert series continues to feature prophetic music including such artists as Pauline Oliveros, Steve Swell, Oliver Lake, and Peter Kowald.

**Chant** An ancient monastic method of singing, usually on a single line or melody. Chant is an aid to memorization of liturgical or scriptural texts, assists in hearing in acoustically difficult space, and enables a community to breathe together, enhancing corporate prayer.

**Chart** A style of notation commonly used in Jazz that contains the tune, suggestions for chords based on a historical understanding of the composition, and guides for form or soloing. A chart contains all the harmonic and melodic information for improvisation, as well as the "head" or precomposed material for the composition (very similar in function to the Baroque figured bass). The chart also either implies or indicates the rhythmic feel of the composition. Much of this information is informed more by tradition than notation, however.

**Coleman, Ornette** (b. 1930) Influential Jazz composer, performer, and pioneer of Free Jazz. Ornette Coleman coined the term "Harmolodics," and won the Pulitzer Prize for Music Composition in 2006 for his album *Sound Grammar* (Phrase Text Incorporated, 2006).

**Davis, Miles** (1926–1991) Trumpeter, bandleader, and composer—one of the most influential musicians of the twentieth century. He was instrumental in the development of Bebop, Cool Jazz, Modal Jazz, and Jazz Fusion. As a band leader, he influenced and developed the careers of many major performers including Sonny Rollins, Thelonius Monk, Charles Mingus, and John Coltrane.

**Djembe** A hand drum shaped like a goblet with a skin head. It originated in West Africa. In Mali the word "dje" means "gather" and "be" means "everybody."

**Dumbek** A goblet or chalice shaped hand drum with a thin resonant head that creates a crisp sound. It is played with a lighter touch and different strokes than the African djembe. Middle Eastern.

**Gospel singing** Deeply rooted in African singing, a very physical style, in three or four parts, often in a call-and-response style, frequently employing a "three-against-two" time feel, a broad dynamic range, and harmonic variety.

**Groove** The term for pulse, implying that there is an associative or collective mood. "In the groove" connotes the idea that the musicians are connected in terms of pulse and aesthetic. "Groovin'" is also a slang term that means "being together," or being "in sync," and initially had a sexual connotation. Other terms that have evolved similarly include "rockin'," "rollin'," and the word "Jazz" itself. "Jazzin' around" meant "fooling around."

**Hagiography** The biography of a saint. From the Greek *hagios*: holy.

**Harmolodics** The term coined by Ornette Coleman describes his theory of Jazz music, particularly associated with "Free Jazz," (named after his seminal album) which allows the musicians to explore all of the (ultimately unlimited) tonal areas, rhythmic structures, and melodic possibilities implied in a composition or musical performance, in an act of collective as well as solo improvisation.

**Head** In a Jazz performance or chart, the main melody or theme.

**Holy Eucharist, Rite II** One of a number of services set forth in the *Book of Common Prayer.* A communion service with several options for music, prayers, readings, and responses—a flexible outline for worship in the Episcopal Church. Differs from "Rite I" in the use of more contemporary and gender-inclusive language.

**Holy Week** The week of liturgical celebrations commemorating the events of Christ's Passion, beginning with the triumphal entry into Jerusalem (Palm Sunday) and continuing through the Last Supper (Maundy Thursday), the Crucifixion (Good Friday), and the Resurrection (The Great Vigil of Easter and Easter Sunday).

**Homiletics** The art and study of preaching, including exegesis of scriptural material, sermon writing, and delivery.

**Improvisation** Technically defined as inventing, composing, or reciting "without preparation" (*American Heritage Dictionary*). In practice, good improvisation in music, worship, or preaching requires proficiency, literacy in the medium, a thorough understanding of material, thoughtfulness, awareness, and much practice. Armed with these, an improviser is prepared to offer deep collaboration and communication with other improvisers and with an audience/congregation.

**Jazz** A form of music developed primarily in the United States beginning in the late nineteenth and early twentieth centuries from diverse sources including African, African-American, Caribbean, and Latin music; characterized by syncopated rhythm resulting in a forward-moving "swing" feel and considerable reliance on solo and collective improvisation and virtuoso performance.

**Jazz Mass** The worship service most frequently conducted at Canterbury House, the Episcopal Campus Ministry at the University of Michigan. Called a "Mass" because it includes communion, and a "Jazz Mass" for good alliteration, it is a church service in which all elements of the service are open to improvisation. We call our service at Canterbury House the "Jazz Mass," not because all of the music is Jazz, for a typical service will also include folk, rock, blues, Taizé music, or even traditional hymns. It's called a Jazz Mass because the entire service is open to spontaneity and improvisation. The Jazz Mass is a principle of worship rather than a style of music.

**Jazz Preaching** Employed in the Jazz Mass, a style of preaching without notes, on a specific theme in response to specific scripture readings and contextual/congregational/pastoral issues. Extemporaneous preaching that requires careful preparation while allowing for the inspiration of the moment and the response of the congregation.

**Kirk, Rahsaan Roland** (1936–1977) Jazz performer and composer, a gifted player of wind instruments including the tenor sax and flute, but also an inventor and modifier of instruments for his own creative purposes. Blind from an early age due to poor medical treatment, Kirk was an innovator and experimentalist, known among other things for playing up to three of his instruments at a time and for perfecting the technique of "circular breathing" that allowed him to hold notes or play rapid sequences nearly endlessly.

**Lent** In the liturgical calendar, a penitential season of forty days (exclusive of Sundays) preceding Easter, beginning with Ash Wednesday.

**Lesser Feasts and Fasts** Liturgical commemorations of the lives of saints and martyrs, called "lesser" feasts and fasts to distinguish them from major liturgical observations such as Christmas (a major feast) or Good Friday (a major fast). Commemorations of the lives of the saints, ancient and modern, are organized in many churches and denominations according to a calendar of observances. In the Episcopal Church, the selected dates, brief biographies of the saints, and scripture lessons and prayers associated with them are contained in a book entitled *The Lesser Feasts and Fasts,* published by Church Publishing and updated from time to time.

**Liturgical Calendar** The liturgical year also known as the "Christian Year" that determines when feasts, fasts, and commemorations are to be observed and sets forth a cycle of scripture readings associated with each observance. The liturgical year is generally seasonal, with both fixed observances such as Christmas, and "moveable feasts" such as Easter. Commemorations of saints are assigned to specific days, usually the date of their death (entrance into glory) if known.

**Liturgy** "A prescribed form or set of forms for public Christian ceremonies; ritual. From Greek *leitourgia,* public service: *leit-,* people (variant of *laos*) + *ergon,* work" (*American Heritage Dictionary*). More informally, the structure or form of any worship service. Some churches and denominations have a written or prescribed liturgy, especially the Roman Catholic and Orthodox Churches and several Protestant denominations such as the Episcopal, Methodist, and various Lutheran and Presbyterian Churches. These are often referred to as "liturgical" churches. "Nonliturgical" churches and congregations also generally have some structure to their worship services that is recognizable to regular worshipers.

**Marley, Bob** (1945–1981) Jamaican singer, songwriter, guitarist, and performer of Ska and Reggae music. A political activist. His songs speak particularly of justice and liberation.

**Mingus, Charles** (1922–1979) Influential Jazz bassist, composer, bandleader, and social justice activist, Mingus was a demanding and often temperamental musician. Nevertheless, he worked with and was profoundly respected by such Jazz luminaries as Charlie Parker, Max Roach, and Dizzy Gillespie. Many avant-garde Jazz performers got their start playing with Mingus.

**Ordinary Time** In the liturgical calendar, the seasons lasting from Epiphany (January 6) until Ash Wednesday, and from Pentecost until the First Sunday of Advent.

**Pentecost** In the liturgical calendar, the Sunday following the seventh Sunday of Easter, commemorating the descent of the Holy Spirit upon the disciples of Jesus after his resurrection and ascension.

**Pointing** Any of several methods for marking a text, particularly the text of a psalm, for the benefit of a singer or cantor, to indicate where changes in note or tone are required. Separations and elisions are marked in this way. A "pointed" text might look like this:

Alleluia, · alle · luia.
Alle · luia, · alle · luia.
Christ our Passover has been · **sacri** · **ficed for** · us,
Therefore · let us · keep the · feast.

**Psalm Tones** From the earliest times of the church, worshiping communities have recited, chanted, or sung psalms together. The earliest examples of Western music notation are chant tones for psalms. Psalm tones have developed from one-line melodies that may be disarmingly simple or maddeningly complex to multiple harmonic compositions evolving eventually to hymns. Often in contemporary practice, psalm tones consist of an antiphon—a repeated phrase or verse intended for singing by the choir or congregation—and verses for a soloist whose singing is directed by "pointing" or textual indications that match the text of the psalm to a brief (four- or eight-measure) melody. Examples of psalm tones in the Roman Catholic tradition are found in the *Liber Usualis* (No. 801; Great Falls, MT: St. Bonaventure Publications, 1997), 112–117.

**Pub Singing** Strongly rhythmic music employing the high male or "tenor" voice, often composed in or for taverns on themes of work, fellowship, women, and drinking. Thought to be the inspiration for many popular Continental and British Protestant hymns written during the sixteenth through the nineteenth centuries, though this idea is controversial as applied to specific composers such as Martin Luther or the Wesley brothers. As a singing style, it requires energy, volume, strong rhythm, and unison breathing.

**Reciting Tone** In psalm tone chanting, the note or notes upon which the cantor or soloist sings the text of the psalm. Changes are indicated in the text by "pointing" (see above)—a method of marking the text that may be as simple or as elaborate as needed for performance.

**Revised Common Lectionary** A lectionary or cycle of scripture readings assembled by collaboration among the North American Consultation on Common Texts (CCT) and the International English Language Liturgical Consultation (ELLC), now widely used in English-speaking "liturgical" churches.

**Riff** In Jazz, a short phrase, especially one repeated in or used as a basis for improvisation.

**Sanctoral Cycle** A cycle of liturgical observances, including appropriate scripture readings, based on commemorations of saints, as opposed to liturgical seasons of the year such as Advent or Lent. The feast or commemoration of a saint is traditionally observed on the date that the saint entered into glory, as opposed to a birthdate.

**Sharrock, Sonny** (1940–1994) Jazz composer and guitarist, much influenced by Miles Davis, John Coltrane, and Herbie Mann. His playing was characterized by saxophone like melody lines. Indeed, he had hoped to be a horn player but was prevented by asthma. Influential recordings include *Ask the Ages* (Axiom) and *Black Woman* (Vortex).

**Silence** The first or original or fundamental "sound" to be employed in worship. Silence is an active principle that does not mean, only, the absence of noise. It is a space in which we are able to listen, and an act of stillness by which we invite the presence of the Holy Spirit. The voice of God is heard in the quiet (1 Kings 19:11–13). Also the title of a book by composer John Cage.

**Singing** An innate capacity of all human beings, employing breath, movement, and vocalization in prayer and praise. At Canterbury House we may, at any point in the service, use one of at least four types of singing, all meant to help us worship in a more cohesive and meaningful way: Taizé singing or traditional chant; pub-style or Southern Harmony singing; African-American or "Gospel" singing; and traditional hymn singing in four parts.

**Southern Harmony** A style of hymn singing that developed in the southern United States in the eighteenth and nineteenth centuries, collected and popularized by William Walker in *The Southern Harmony and Musical Companion,* and his brother-in-law Benjamin Franklin White in *The Sacred Harp.* The music is characterized by "shape-notes," which is a method of notation that assists untrained singers in learning to sing in four-part harmony. Shape-note singers are encouraged to sing with energy and in a plain tone employing little or no vibrato. Characterized by open fifth harmonies.

**Sun Ra** (1914–1993) Jazz composer, multiple keyboardist, and band leader whose musings on race and alienation led to the adoption of an elaborately developed "space-alien" persona. He was a virtuoso performer in many styles of Jazz, including Stride Piano, Post-Bop, and Free Jazz.

**Swing** Traditionally thought of as the syncopated feel of Jazz. More importantly, the emotional or physical response to music, especially Jazz music well played. Also, a specific style of Jazz music that was popular in the 1930s and '40s, characterized by a strong rhythm section (acoustic bass and drums) and performed by such musicians as Louis Armstrong, Duke Ellington, and Benny Goodman. Swing is, in fact, difficult to define. Louis Armstrong, when asked, "What is swing?" replied, "If you have to ask . . . ."

**Taizé** An ecumenical monastic community located in Taizé, Saône-et-Loire, Burgundy, France. Founded in 1940 by Brother Roger Schutz and comprised of more than a hundred men from many nations, the community emphasizes prayer and Christian meditation, and welcomes thousands of visitors annually from around the world.

**Taizé Chant** Simple, repetitive music for worship and prayer, using lines from psalms or other scripture, repeated or sung in canon. Much of the music of the Taizé Community has been written by Jacques Berthier, a Parisian composer and organist at St-Ignace, the Jesuit church in Paris.

**Traditional Hymn Singing** Four-part singing with its origins in European and Scandinavian harmonic styles. Perhaps the most familiar type of singing heard in churches in the United States in the twentieth century. This music particularly lends itself to *a cappella* singing. Melodies tend to emphasize the text.

**Traditional Jazz** Roughly speaking, Jazz music from the Dixieland Era of the 1920s to late Bebop in the '50s, or Sydney Bechét through Charlie Parker.

# Selected Bibliography

Bell, John, and Graham Maule. *Enemy of Apathy*. Rev. ed. Chicago: GIA Publications, Inc., 1990.

Bell, John, and Graham Maule. *Heaven Shall Not Wait*. Rev. ed. Chicago: GIA Publications, Inc., 1989.

Bell, John, and Graham Maule. *Love from Below*. Chicago: GIA Publications, Inc., 1989.

Berthier, Jacques. *Music from Taizé: Vol I*. Chicago: GIA Publications, Inc., 1981.

Berthier, Jacques. *Music from Taizé: Vol II*. Chicago: GIA Publications, Inc., 1984.

Buechner, Frederick. *The Sacred Journey*. San Francisco: Harper & Row, 1982.

Buechner, Frederick. *Secrets in the Dark: A Life in Sermons*. San Francisco: HarperSanFrancisco, 2006.

Buttrick, David. *Homiletic Moves and Structures*. Minneapolis: Augsburg Fortress Publishers, 1987.

Nisenson, Eric. *Ascension: John Coltrane and His Quest*. New York: St. Martin's Press, 1993.

Dillard, Annie. *Pilgrim at Tinker Creek*. New York: Harper Perennial Modern Classics, 2007.

Eckhart, Meister. *The Complete Mystical Works of Meister Eckhart*. New York: Herder and Herder, 2007.

Fox, Matthew. *On Becoming a Musical Mystical Bear: Spirituality American Style*. Mahwah: Paulist Press, 1972.

Fox, Matthew. *Passion for Creation: The Earth-honoring Spirituality of Meister Eckhart*. Rochester: Inner Traditions, 2000.

Harris, Michael W. *The Rise of Gospel Blues: The Music of Thomas Andrew Dorsey in the Urban Church*. New York: Oxford University Press, 1991.

Grew, Eva Mary, and Sydney Grew. *Bach*. New York: Collier Books, 1966.

Kavanagh, Aiden. *Elements of Rite: A Handbook of Liturgical Style*. New York: Pueblo Publishing Company, 1982.

Keating, Thomas. *Intimacy with God*. New York: Crossroad Classic, 1996.

Küng, Hans. *Mozart: Traces of Transcendence*. Trans. John Bowden. Grand Rapids: Wm. B. Eerdmans Publishing Company, 1993.

Küng, Hans. *Art and the Question of Meaning*. New York: Crossroad Publishing Corp., 1981.

L'Engle, Madeleine. *Walking on Water: Reflections on Faith and Art*. Wheaton. IL: Harold Shaw Publishers, 1980.

Lamott, Anne. *Traveling Mercies: Some Thoughts on Faith*. New York: Anchor Books, 1999.

Le Clerq, Jean. *Love of Learning and Desire for God: A Study of Monastic Culture*. New York: Fordham University Press, 1982.

Merton, Thomas. *Contemplative Prayer.* London: Darton, Longman & Todd Ltd., 2005.
Messiaen, Olivier. *Music and Color: Conversations with Claude Samuel.* Trans. E. Thomas Glasow. Portland, OR: Amadeus Press, 1994.
Nisenson, Eric. *Ascension: John Coltrane and His Quest.* New York: St. Martin's Press, 1993.
Norris, Kathleen. *The Cloister Walk.* New York: Riverhead Books, 1996.
Nouwen, Henri J.M. *Return of the Prodigal Son.* London: Darton, Longman & Todd Ltd., 1992.
Otto, Rudolph. *The Idea of the Holy.* Trans. John W. Harvey. Oxford: Oxford University Press, 1958.
Postema, Don. *Space for God: The Study and Practice of Prayer and Spirituality.* Grand Rapids, MI: Faith Alive Christian Resources, 1997.
Ra, Sun. *The Wisdom of Sun Ra: Sun Ra's Polemical Broadsheets and Streetcorner Leaflets.* Ed. Anthony Elms and John Corbett. Chicago: Whitewalls, 2006.
Reilly, Patricia Lynn. *A God Who Looks Like Me: Discovering a Woman-Affirming Spirituality.* New York: Ballantine Books, 1995.
Saliers, Don E. *Worship as Theology.* Nashville: Abingdon Press, 2006.
Saliers, Don E., and Emily Saliers. *A Song to Sing, A Life to Live: Reflections on Music as Spiritual Practice.* San Francisco: Jossey-Bass, 2006.
Samuel, Claude. *Conversations with Oliver Messiaen.* London: Stainer and Bell Ltd., 1976.
Schweitzer, Albert. *J. S. Bach.* Trans. Ernest Newman. Mineola: Dover Publications, 1966.
*Songs of Zion.* Nashville: Abingdon Press, 1991.
*Taizé 2002–2003.* Taizé-Communauté, France: Ateliers et Presses de Taizé, 2002.
Taylor, Barbara Brown. *The Preaching Life.* Boston: Cowley Publications, 1993.
Teresa of Avila. *Interior Castle.* Trans. E. Allison Peers. New York: Image, 1972.
Terkel, Studs. *And They All Sang: Adventures of an Eclectic Disc Jockey.* New York: New Press, 2006.
Tutu, Desmond. *The Rainbow People of God.* New York: Doubleday, 1994.
Underhill, Evelyn. *Practical Mysticism: A Little Book for Normal People.* London: Hesperides Press, 2006.
Walker, William. *The Southern Harmony and Musical Companion.* Lexington: The University Press of Kentucky, 1987.
Warren, Gwendolin Sims. *Ev'ry Time I Feel the Spirit.* New York: Henry Holt and Company, LLC, 1997.
Weiderkehr, Macrina. *A Tree Full of Angels: Seeing the Holy in the Ordinary.* San Francisco: HarperSanFrancisco, 1990.
Work, John W. *American Negro Songs.* Mineola, NY: Dover Publications, 1998.

# Index